GW00792970

GCSE

English

HOMEWORK BOOK

Ian Barr
David Bazen

Letts

EDUCATIONAL

Every effort has been made to trace copyright holders and to obtain their permission for the use of copyright material. The author and publishers will gladly receive information enabling them to rectify any error or omission in subsequent editions.

First published 1996

Letts Educational
Aldine House
Aldine Place
London W12 8AW
0181 740 2266

Text: © Ian Barr and David Bazen 1996

Design and illustrations © BPP (Letts Educational) Ltd 1996

Design and page layout: Ken Vail Graphic Design

British Library Cataloguing-in-Publication Data

A CIP record for this book is available from the British Library

ISBN 1 85758 411 2

Printed and bound in Great Britain by Ashford Colour Press

Letts Educational is the trading name of BPP (Letts Educational) Ltd

CONTENTS

ACKNOWLEDGEMENTS

p2 from *A Question of Courage* by Marjorie Darke, Copyright © Marjorie Darke 1975, reproduced by permission of the author c/o Rogers, Coleridge & White Limited, 20 Powis Mews, London W11 1JN; p6 'Scott Who Challenged the Tobacco Giants', by Jacqui Marson, reprinted with permission from the June 1994 *Reader's Digest*, Copyright © The Reader's Digest Association Limited; p9 '12 killed while fighting fire in the Rockies', from Reuters, published in *The New Straits Times*, 8 July 1994, reprinted by permission of the New Straits Times Sdn Berhad, Kuala Lumpur and Reuters; p11 'The Hero', by Siegfried Sassoon, reprinted by permission of George Sassoon; p11 'The Tale of Custard the Dragon', by Ogden Nash, reprinted with permission; p13 from *Seize the Moment*, by Helen Sharman and Christopher Priest, published by Victor Gollancz, reprinted with permission; p15 excerpt from *For the Children*, reprinted with the permission of Madeline Cartwright; p20 from *Pole to Pole*, by Michael Palin, reprinted by permission of BBC Worldwide Limited; p21 from *The AA New Book of the Road 1986/87*, Copyright © The Reader's Digest Association Limited, reprinted with permission; p24 from *TravelBound European Tours 1995*; p26 from *A Fall of Moondust*, by Arthur C Clarke, published by Victor Gollancz, reprinted by permission of David Higham Associates; p30 from *A Sound of Thunder*, by Ray Bradbury, reprinted by permission of Abner Stein; p33 'Coming to England', from *Selected Poems*, by Zulfikar Ghose, published by Oxford University Press, Karachi; p35 'What's on the Menu', from *Classical and Modern Greece*, by Anthony Selwyn, published by Chancerel and Schools Abroad; p37 from *After the First Death*, by Robert Cormier, published by Victor Gollancz, p39 'Icarus Allsorts', by Roger McGough, from *Penguin Modern Poets 10*, published by Penguin Books Limited, reprinted by permission of Peters Fraser & Dunlop Group; p40 'No More Hiroshimas', by James Kirkup, originally published in *Refusal to Conform*, (Oxford University Press, 1963), reprinted in 1995 in *No More Hiroshimas*, (Cloud Editions, Newcastle upon Tyne), reprinted by permission of James Kirkup; p42 'Tugs Rescue Beached Ferry', by Christian Wolmar and Ian Mackinnon, from *The Independent*, 21 September 1995, reprinted by permission of The Independent Newspaper Publishing Plc.; p43 'Ferry "Safest Place" for 172 Passengers', by Christian Wolmar, from *The Independent*, 21 September 1995, reprinted by permission of The Independent Newspaper Publishing Plc.; p46 from 'Rescue', by William M. Hendryx, from *Family Circle*, 4 April 1995, reprinted by permission of William M. Hendryx; p47 from *Journey's End*, by RC Sherriff, Copyright © RC Sherriff, reproduced by permission of Curtis Brown Group Limited, London; p49 'Putting back together the lives of damaged children', by Susan Elkin from *The Times*, p53 from *Return with Honour*, by Scott O'Grady, published by Bloomsbury Publishing Plc in London in 1995, reprinted with permission; p55 'Song of the Battery Hen', by Edwin Brock, reprinted by permission of Edwin Brock; p56 from *Lord of the Flies*, by William Golding, published by Faber and Faber Limited, reprinted by permission of Faber and Faber Limited; p57 'Down on the funny farm', by Laura Cunningham, from *The New York Times Magazine*, 12 May 1991, Copyright © The New York Times Company, reprinted with permission; p59 'Lessons on the Mountains', by Peter Steinhart', from *Audubon Magazine*, reprinted by permission of Audubon and Peter Steinhart; p60 from *1984*, by George Orwell, Copyright © The estate of the late Sonia Brownell Orwell and Martin Secker and Warburgh Limited, reprinted with permission; p62 from 'Russia's Lake Baikal', by Don Belt, from *National Geographic*, June 1992, reprinted by permission of the National Geographic Society; p63 'Secrets of A-Grade Pupils', by Edwin Kiester and Sally Valentine Kiester, from *Reader's Digest*, November 1994, Copyright © The Reader's Digest Association Limited, reprinted by permission; p66 from 'Flying on a wing and a prayer, Voyager heads for a last rendezvous', by James R Chiles, from *Smithsonian Magazine*, September 1988, reprinted with permission; p69 from *Watership Down*, by Richard Adams; p71 from *Let Sleeping Vets Lie*, by James Herriot, published by Michael Joseph, reprinted by permission of David Higham Associates; p72 'The Carpernter', by Clifford Dyment; p73 from *Appointments Magazine*, 7 November 1995, Copyright © Oxford and County Newspapers; p75 'Fishing for Gold in Ghana', by Clive Beddall, from *The Grocer*, 4 November 1995, Copyright © William Reed Publishing Limited, reprinted

with permission; p78 from *Cannery Row*, by John Steinbeck, published by William Heinemann, reprinted with permission; p80 from 'Just the Job', Employment Department Group; p83 from 'Boozer's Labourer', by Bill Naughton from *The Bees Have Stopped Working and Other Stories*, Copyright © Bill Naughton; p88 from *Roll of Thunder, Hear My Cry*, by Mildred Taylor, published by Victor Gollancz, reprinted with permission; p90 from 'Life Drawing', by Bernard MacLaverty; p92 'Schools return to Classical Mode', by Fran Abrams, from *The Independent* on Sunday, 5 September 1995, reprinted by permission of the Independent Newspaper Plc.; p94 'Dress Sense', by Gary Shawford; p95 from 'Ha'penny', from *Debbie Go Home*, by Alan Paton, published by Jonathan Cape, reprinted with permission; p100 from *Stephen Hawking: A Life in Science*, by Michael White and John Gribbin, published by Viking, reprinted with permission; p104 from 'Winter Nights Appeal', published by Shelter, reprinted by permission of Shelter; p106 from 'The National Trust Lake District Appeal', Copyright © National Trust, reprinted with permission; p108 from *Urban Development and Planning*, by John Hancock, published by Blackwell Publishers; p109 from *Touch and Go*, by Elizabeth Berridge, published by Transworld Books, reprinted by permission of David Higham Associates; p112 'London's Crossroads', by Richard Evans, published in *Geographical Magazine*, September 1992, reprinted with permission; p113 'Slough', from *Collected Poems*, by John Betjeman, published by John Murray Limited, reprinted with permission; p114 from *The AA Book of the British Countryside*, Copyright © Reader's Digest Association Limited, reprinted with permission; p119 'Napoleon's Sacred Gate', from *France Magazine*, Summer 1992, reprinted by permission of France Magazine; p122 'The Man by the Fountain', by George Hebbelinck; p124 from 'Badger on the Barge', from *Badger on the Barge and Other Stories*, by Janni Hawker; p129 'No Game for the Playground', from The Sunday Times: p131 'Rising Five', from *Collected Poems*, by Norman Nicholson, published by Faber and Faber Limited, reprinted by permission of David Higham Associates; p133 'My Daughter, My Friend', by Patricia Lorenz, from *Working Mother*, New York, March 1993; p135 'Protest of a Sixth Former', by Robert Hayes; p136 'Mother and Son', by R S Thomas, from *R S Thomas Collected Poems 1945-1990*, published by J M Dent, reprinted by permission of The Orion Publishing Group; p136 'The Young Ones', from *Collected Poems*, by Elizabeth Jennings, published by Carcanet, reprinted by permission of David Higham Associates; p137 'The Boys', from *Poems 1953-1983*, by Anthony Thwaite, published by Secker and Warburg; p138 from *David and Broccoli* (play), by John Mortimer, reprinted by permission of the Peters Fraser & Dunlop Group Limited; p140 from *Cider With Rosie*, by Laurie Lee, published by Chatto & Windus, reprinted with permission; p141 from *Of Mice and Men*, by John Steinbeck, published by William Heinemann, reprinted by permission; p143 from *Thomas*, by Shelley Mydans; p145 from *Murder in the Cathedral*, by T S Eliot, reprinted by permission of Faber and Faber Limited; p147 from *Cromwell: Our Chief of Men*, by Antonia Fraser; p149 '50th anniversary of the liberation of Auschwitz', by Neal Ascherson, from *The Independent* on Sunday, 22 January 1995, reprinted by permission of the Independent Newspaper Publishing Plc.; p153 'Fire – ways to save your family', by Deborah Sawyer; p155 'Death of a Teenager', by Ben Pimlot, from Today, 10 November 1986; p157 'A Vicious Sport', by Jeffrey Cundy; p159 from *The Day of the Triffids*, by John Wyndham, published by Michael Joseph; p163 'On a Wing and a Prayer', by Frances Howell, from *The Independent*, 7 October 1995, reprinted by permission of the Independent newspaper Plc.; p165 from Midland Examining Group IGCSE English, May 1992, Paper 0500/2, questions 1 and 2, reprinted by permission of The University of Cambridge Local Examination Syndicate; p167 'Debbie pulls it off', by Jessica Berens, from *The Independent Magazine*, 7 October 1995, reprinted by permission of the Independent Newspaper Plc., p170 from 'Robot AL-76 Goes Astray', by Isaac Asimov, Copyright © Ziff-Davis Publishing Company, from *The Rest of the Robots*, by Isaac Asimov, published by HarperCollins Science Fiction and Fantasy; p172 'Science-Fiction Cradlesong', by C S Lewis, from *Poems*, edited by Walter Hooper, published by Geoffrey Bles, London and Harvest Books, reprinted with permission.

INTRODUCTION

Welcome to your homework book! You will find that this book follows the same 10 themes found in your classbook, with a variety of stimulus material and tasks for you to tackle by yourself.

Each chapter provides approximately 14 hours of homework, which translates into roughly 2 hours of homework per week.

You will find that, sometimes, we have reprinted stimulus material which appears in the classbook. However, the accompanying homework tasks are new and are designed to build on the work you have already carried out in class, by asking you to take your thinking further forward.

The remainder of the stimulus material is completely new and the tasks challenge you to think for yourself. However, you will find that we include tips and advice to help you on your way. Plus, there is a detailed glossary at the back of the book, which contains useful terms, as well as the basic parts of speech.

Each homework has an indication of the time needed to complete it. Yet, please note that the times stated are intended to be guidelines only – you may find that you work faster than we have indicated; or you might want to. take more time than we are suggesting. Please also note that one stimulus material may be used for more than one homework session.

COURAGE

In your classbook we introduced the chapter on 'Courage' by saying that courage could be shown in a great variety of ways.

Through your homeworks we shall continue to explore, with a variety of stimulus material and tasks, just how this is so.

Votes for Women

(1 hour 30 minutes)

You have already read the extract which is printed below and have used it in class as the basis for some discussion and writing. First, read the extract again.

A Question of Courage

'I met someone,' Louise replied to her unformed question. 'Mary Grant. She came up from London to speak at one of our drawing-room meetings. It was incredible listening to her. She has been in Holloway prison four times and she described the way she was forcibly fed. Oh – it is monstrous – disgusting! I don't know how she could have borne it, she is so frail and delicate, like a tiny bird. But she's got the courage of a lion.'

Emily shivered, recognising the undercurrent of violence in Louise's voice again.

'Those prison doctors are brutes. Some of the things Mary said made me want to vomit …'

Emily was afraid Louise was going to describe the scenes in detail and hastily interrupted. 'She must be brave.'

'She is … but there are many others and they're all prepared to go back again and again even though it means going through the whole ghastly business once more.' Louise sounded almost as if she were enjoying the horror.

'Would you do it? Go on hunger strike, I mean?' asked Emily.

Louise did not answer straight away and when she did, sounded uncertain.

'I believe I could. Thinking about it now, in the open air, it would be easy to say "Of course". But it's when you are there, shut away inside the prison that counts. It will all be different then.'

Will be? She made it sound as if this was waiting for them just round the corner, an inevitable happening. 'You really mean that,' Emily said slowly. The implications were enormous. 'Are you going to keep on doing things like tonight?'

'This is just the beginning. You'll see!'

'Mary Grant must have been a real soul-mover,' Emily said with conviction.

'She is. Hearing her tipped the scales.'

So there *was* something else. Before she could probe further Louise touched her arm.

'There's a cart track here. If we go up it there are two gates, one on each side. They lead on to the golf course. It spreads out either side. Used to be farm land, you see. The farmhouse is still there just at the top of this track.'

'Does anyone live there?'

'Oh yes. The farmer has land the other side of the course.'

Then there were people near by; dogs perhaps. Emily tied up the remains of her courage. She'd come this far. It was no use getting cold feet now. Cold feet? Hers were freezing! 'Let's get a move on, before we turn into snowmen. You go first and tell me what to do.' It occurred to her that she had no idea what a green was, had never seen a golf course. All she knew of golf were some strange pictures she had seen in a magazine.

They left the track, edging through the swing gate into rough grass. The ground was hard and lumpy beneath their feet. The full moonlight revealed the land falling away into a shallow valley, to rise against a horizon that was broken by the dark bunching of trees and bushes.

'Down here,' Louise whispered.

Rime flicked from long grass blades as they

tramped downhill to a flat, closely-mown lawn which had a flag on a pole sticking out of the ground. So *that* was the purpose of the flags she had stitched. Eighteen! They'd have to work fast or it would be daylight before they finished.

'Here!' Louise handed her a pair of scissors. 'Cut off the old flags and tie on one of ours. I'll start painting.'

Emily moved towards the flag. Never in her life had she done anything remotely outside the law. 'Keep your nose clean,' Dad always said. 'Steer clear of them bobbies. They'll as soon nick you as look' – and here she was about to destroy something belonging to someone else … deliberately! She glanced at Louise and saw she had already finished the first long white stroke of her V. Emily tightened her hold on the flag bunting, closed the scissors and hacked. Then crouching down, she untied her bundle, selected a new flag and tied it to the pole with the four stout tapes May had sewn on. Louise had painted VOTES FOR W …. The letters gleamed clearly in the moonlight. They would be seen for miles, Emily felt sure, if anyone was looking.

'There!' Louise finished the N with a flourish. 'Mind where you walk.'

Emily took her bundle and picked her way over the whitewash. Now she was a *law-breaker* … a *criminal*. She'd burned her boats … cut her flag! There was something oddly exciting about demonstrating her decision. The martyr part was there in the background, an unsolved dilemma, but it was too distant to worry about. What was happening now reminded her of Vic's Penny Dreadfuls. All wild adventure. Blood and thunder … only it was quiet as anything except for the rustle made by the two of them walking.

The next green was farther down the slope over to their left. Emily pushed through clumps of scutch grass.

'There's a great pit of sand here,' she said.

'Bunker,' Louise corrected. 'A sort of trap to catch the golf balls.'

Emily attached her second flag, puzzling over the odd hazards of this strange game. 'What made you pick on a golf course?'

'Private property. Owned by wealthy men, like my father. They don't like their property damaged. It's sacred. They will take a lot of notice when it's spoiled, much more than listening to reasonable argument.' There was a hardness to Louise's voice.

Her father? Was that the other reason … the deeper one? 'Your father will be furious.'

Louise did not answer directly, but muttered threats under her breath, one to each brushstroke. Emily caught broken phrases.

'… Being pig-headed … can't stop me … won't give in … it's my life … I'm not his property …'.

So it was a twofold thing after all. One blow for Women's Rights, the other directed at her father! Which mattered most? Emily felt let down, as if this personal feud had tarnished her golden image of Louise. But perhaps the two things were connected anyway. Fathers were men and both were trouble! If anger at that final row in the kitchen had pushed her into coming, then Louise had just as much right to be forced on by her emotions. You could love and detest people at the same time, be driven to all sorts of rash acts, but it didn't mean those acts weren't *right*.

'Why did you ask *me* to come? There's all them ladies at the drawing-room meetings like Una and Maude Holiday … or there's Vera.'

'Ladies!' The amount of scorn Louise put into the word was remarkable. 'Meek creatures. They wouldn't say boo to a goose, let alone approve. As for Vera … I don't know; there's something sort of *closed*. I'd never be certain.'

'But me … why me?' Emily insisted.

'Because you are a fighter, like me. Nerve, courage, call it what you like. You are reliable. Besides, I like you.' She paused in mid-stroke. Emily thought she was smiling. Whitewash, dripping off her brush, made a thin white line down her skirt. 'Oh, now look what I've gone and done!'

'Here, mop it up with the matching bit on this flag.'

Emily was all concern in the middle of her joy. Another link had been forged between them. Louise's pedestal, in shrinking a little, had brought friendship closer.

An owl hooted with startling clarity. Farther off came an answering call and a great white bird sailed out from a clump of skeleton trees.

'It'll be witches on broomsticks next,' Emily said shakily.

'If they do I shall rapidly paint VOTES FOR WOMEN on our remaining flags and persuade the old dears to tie them on their broom handles. It'd be the best bit of advertising the Cause has ever had. Just think of the newspaper headlines – SUFFRAGETTES HARNESS THE SUPERNATURAL … CAN PARLIAMENT WITHSTAND THIS ATTACK?'

The idea wasn't really funny, but they found themselves giggling on the way to the next green and the next. Emily fumbled with the tapes, all thumbs, pulling hard, tearing the stitching. 'Oh, blast it!'

'Tell you what, we could change over next time if you like,' Louise offered.

'All right.'

The walking was rough. They crossed a small brook by way of a flat wooden bridge, the noise of their footsteps shatteringly loud. Over a ridge into a second valley and back again. Surely someone must hear? But it seemed they had the night to themselves.

'We have to cross the farm track to the other part of the course now,' Louise said.

They could see the farmhouse black and silver against a quiet sky. Nine greens done, another nine and they would be finished.

And then the dog barked. Not a single enquiring sound, but on and on with the rattle of his chain as he ran backwards and forwards. He knew they were there.

'It's all right, he's tied up,' Louise whispered.

'But we ain't finished.'

'We've done enough. Come on!'

They were coming out of the valley with the gate in sight when the farmhouse door banged. A man's voice called out:

'All right, Tiger. Down boy!' Metal chinked on stone.

'The dog's free,' Louise hissed. 'Run!' She spurted forward, Emily close on her heels. Suddenly Emily saw Louise spread her arms, body twisting, but there was no time to take evasive action. As Louise sprawled full length on the turf, Emily tripped helplessly over her legs. The remaining whitewash splashed from the can over them both. Louise curled up, clutching her ankle. Boots crunched over the stony track. The barking closed in.

'Go, can't you … run!' Louise was almost sobbing with pain and frustration.

Emily said nothing, but moved up close to her friend, crouching as if to shield her from attack. The dog was on them now with growls and panting breath. Too terrified to move, they waited for him to charge, but he stood, hackles raised, daring them to try.

'Sit, Tiger! And you … don't try anything or I'll pepper you good and proper!' The voice changed from threat to astonishment. 'Well I'll be danged … a couple of gels!'

But still they didn't move. Looking up, they found themselves staring into the menacing barrels of a shotgun.

MARJORIE DARKE

In the next chapter of the book Louise and Emily are in court. They are found guilty and fined. Imagine you are a reporter for a newspaper and your editor has sent you to the court to report the 'crime'.

TASKS

1 Write two short articles from different points of view.

   a Write an article for readers who will think that Emily and Louise deserve everything they get.

   b Write an article for a newspaper produced by the 'Women's Suffrage Movement'.

Think carefully before you start about what will be the right style to write in. Clearly you will need a different style of writing for each article because the newspapers will have different readerships and purposes.

Human Rights

(1 hour)

Today, in many countries, thousands of brave men and women are enduring imprisonment and torture in their struggle to achieve the liberty we already have. What follows is the story of one of them, Liu Gang, a Chinese scientist.

The Scientist

Liu Gang and Zhang Dong Feng were fleeing to save Liu's life – and their life together. It was June 18, 1989. China had just put a bloody stop to the seven-week, student-led protest in Tiananmen Square. Liu Gang, a protest organiser, was now third on China's most-wanted list.

Liu had not been one of the protest's media superstars. A short, stocky man, he was neither charismatic nor eloquent. But the government knew the crucial role he had played. So now Liu and Zhang, his shy and pretty girlfriend, were bound for Qinghai Province near Tibet.

They stopped in Baoding. Liu could not risk seeking lodging, but he would not let Zhang stay with him on the park bench where he was planning to spend the night. Therefore, she was not with him when the guard came. Zhang saw his arrest on television. She was destined for sorrow. He was destined for prison and torture.

Liu Gang, the son of a policeman, was born in Changchun in the northern province of Jilin. A talented science student, Liu was one of the few admitted to China's prestigious University of Science and Technology. There he studied under the renowned physicist and famed advocate of democracy Fang Lizhi. Physics, in Fang's hands, was never *just* physics. It was also free speech and free thinking. No student listened more avidly than Liu Gang.

In 1985, Liu put up a poster about corruption in the Chinese government. Undercover agents videotaped him. Two years later, he nominated Fang's wife to run for regional People's Representative in the upcoming nationwide elections, against a Communist Party candidate. Enraged, the authorities accused Liu of stealing a bicycle two years earlier and warned they could prosecute him.

'Do what you want' he replied 'I will never kneel down to beg.'

After he graduated in 1987, Liu won a coveted government job, but within a few months he left. He wanted to live 'on my own efforts and accomplishments', he told a friend. Once again, Liu – supported by Zhang – threw himself into pro-democracy activism.

In the spring of 1989, Liu became deeply involved in the historic Tiananman Square protest – organising and cajoling, sleeping in a different bed each night, struggling to avert tragedy. He left Beijing to rest and to plan where he and associates could go underground in case of a crackdown. While he was away, martial law was declared.

Liu was by now a wanted man. He returned to Beijing. Then, with Zhang, he boarded the train to Baoding – and his arrest.

Liu was convicted of conspiring to subvert the government and sentenced to six years in prison. There he has acquired the nickname 'Iron Man' for his refusal to bow to corrupt authority.

He has been beaten, shocked with a 12 000-volt cattle prod and held in a damp, cold room for seven months at a stretch. In two years he was allowed to bathe five times. He has been fed as little as nine ounces of food a day for months at a time. From the dirt and damp, psoriasis covers his head and mars his face. Although he is not yet 35, his hair has turned white and is falling out.

Zhang vowed to stay faithful. For months she visited him in prison and brought him food. Then the authorities ordered her to take a job in Sichuan Province, more than a thousand miles away. Now Liu is alone.

In a statement smuggled from his prison cell in January last year, Liu declared: 'Handcuffs and shackles won't frighten me. Neither cattle prod nor electric whip will silence me. Regardless, I shall use all peaceful means to overcome tyranny'.

He pleads for the struggle for freedom not to stop. 'There are still people in this dark corner of the earth deprived, repressed and enslaved' he writes 'Please persist and march on'.

TASKS

2 Using the information in the article, write a brief character study of Liu Gang.

3 Having read the story you decide that you want to try to help Liu Gang by writing a letter to the Chinese Embassy. Draft your letter. Remember that your letter is probably going to be received by someone who just doesn't want to know, and you must therefore be as persuasive as you possibly can.

Scot who Challenged the Tobacco Giants

(1 hour)

Here is a passage which you have already read and studied in class. Read the passage again.

Scot who Challenged the Tobacco Giants

When Alfred McTear learned he had lung cancer, he made a hero's vow: to spend his dying days bringing to justice the industry he held responsible

Net curtains twitched in Cherrywood Drive in the little Scottish town of Beith, near Glasgow, as the cul-de-sac began to fill up with gleaming Mercedes and BMWs. Well-groomed men in expensive overcoats picked their way up the garden path to number 20. Inside they squashed themselves on to a three-piece suite or perched on kitchen chairs, files resting on a fold-down dining-table.

They had come to take part in a rare legal event – a court hearing held in a private house. Because the key witness was too ill to travel, the judge, court clerk, lawyers and company executives had left behind the pomp of the Edinburgh court-house to hear Alfred McTear's evidence, under oath, in his own front room.

Everyone knew Alfred had only a short time to live as he walked slowly into the makeshift court that morning of March 16, 1993, and lowered himself carefully into an armchair. Each breath was drawn in pain, rasping up from cancer-ridden lungs; his best suit hung in folds off his emaciated body; the bones of his face were visible through papery skin. Yet his eyes shone with vitality and determination. 'Alfred showed fantastic guts, energy and enthusiasm,' recalls solicitor John Carruthers. 'He was even cracking jokes.'

Giving court evidence had been a looming hurdle since Alfred, a 48-year-old retired telephone engineer, volunteered to sue the Bristol based Imperial Tobacco company on behalf of the anti-smoking lobby. His case, that Imperial Tobacco was selling a dangerous product which caused his lung cancer, would be the first of its kind to go to court in Britain.

If successful, the case would mean tobacco companies could be held liable for the effects of their product, which kills an estimated 110,000 people every year in the UK alone. Such a legal ruling would open the floodgates to claims against tobacco companies, weakening their business and perhaps saving thousands of lives.

Margaret McTear, married to Alfred for 28 years, was apprehensive about the onslaught of attention.

A shy, self-contained woman with greying hair and baby-soft skin, she didn't know how to answer journalists' insistent questions. What she did know was that she would continue the battle after his death.

Because she was going to give evidence later in the case, Margaret was not allowed to hear her husband's testimony, and she waited anxiously in the kitchen. 'Freddie was so weak he could hardly speak,' she recalls.

'The reporters kept asking questions – before the hearing, in the break, at lunchtime – when he should have been resting. I could see he was getting exhausted.'

Sure enough, by lunchtime on Wednesday, the second day of the hearing, Margaret had to call the doctor, who declared that Alfred was not strong enough to continue his evidence that day.

On Thursday and Friday morning the expensive cars once more rolled up to 20 Cherrywood Drive. But Alfred's GP, the stern, no-nonsense Dr Sheila McCarroll, said he was again too ill to continue. He died on the following Tuesday.

Ten months earlier, Alfred had gone to see Dr McCarroll at her surgery. He had been so off-colour for about a month that he had finally given up cigarettes, after almost 30 years of smoking between 20 and 60 a day. A bronchoscope examination confirmed a cancerous tumour on Alfred's lung. The optimism of the man who woke the family every morning singing Scottish folk songs in the bathroom was suddenly extinguished. 'He became quite down,' recalls Margaret. 'I couldn't mention the subject to him because I couldn't believe it was happening myself.'

A few weeks later, Alfred read a short article in the Scottish *Daily Record* reporting a partial victory for the family of Rose Cipollone, who was suing several US tobacco manufacturers for causing her death. The US Supreme Court ruled that government health warnings on cigarette packets did not automatically protect the company against such legal claims. Even though the Cipollone family could not afford to continue the case, it was a breakthrough for the anti-smoking lobby.

Reading on, Alfred saw that the charity Action on Smoking and Health (ASH) in Scotland was seeking anyone who thought they might have a strong case against a tobacco manufacturer.

Next morning he rang ASH and volunteered himself. Says Alison Hillhouse, director of ASH Scotland, 'I got a stream of calls, but Alfred was the person who stood out. He made a deep impression on me.'

Ross Harper & Murphy, a large firm of Glasgow solicitors who had offered their services for free, agreed with her. 'I felt that here was a genuine, caring man who wanted to send a warning about smoking before he died,' says solicitor John Carruthers.

While there has been talk of damages of up to £500,000, Alfred dismissed suggestions that he was in it for financial gain. 'I'm doing this because I believe smoking is evil and I'd like to put a stop to it once and for all. A lot of people think of me as fighting a losing battle, but some

day the common man must win.'

As the self-appointed small man in a classic David-and-Goliath battle, he captivated the media. And he handled them with masterly assurance. At a press conference to announce the legal action, a journalist shouted, 'How does it feel to be dying of lung cancer, Alfred?' McTear paused, then said softly in his strong Glaswegian accent: 'I am a dying man. I haven't got a future. But that's why I'm doing this. So that other people might have.'

The room went silent, ASH's Alison Hillhouse was moved to tears. 'His sincerity touched everyone. It was extraordinary to see the effect he had on those case-hardened hacks.'

But it takes more than a sympathetic personality to win a complex legal case. Solicitors John Carruthers and Cameron Fife believe that Alfred's smoking history provides winning legal arguments.

First there is the timing. Alfred started smoking in 1964, long before the Government put health warnings on packets, and when smoking was openly advertised as desirable and glamorous. As Alfred said, everyone smoked, from cinema matinée idols to sports stars. 'I just went along with the crowd. I hadn't the slightest idea it was bad for your health.'

But at least some of the tobacco companies knew. As far back as the 1940s they had commissioned their own research in the US into the effects of tobacco smoke. The Cipollone evidence included a 1946 letter from a company chemist of the Lorillard Tobacco Company to the manufacturing committee. It analysed a media report about animal experiments that had revealed a cancer-causing chemical 'presumed to be a combustion product of burning tobacco'. Internal memos from the mid-1950s and early 1960s, generated by Lorillard and some other tobacco companies, also confirm their awareness of the growing evidence of a link between smoking and cancer. But none of these companies released findings of their own investigations to the public.

Though Imperial Tobacco deny that the link between smoking and lung cancer has been conclusively proved, they maintain that by the time Alfred started smoking, doctors had already publicised the dangers. However, in Britain health warnings did not appear on cigarette packets until 1971.

Once Alfred realised how dangerous his habit was, he tried repeatedly to give up, but by then he was strongly addicted to nicotine. Although he sought help from Dr McCarroll and another GP in the same practice, every attempt failed. 'Whenever he gave up for a few days', recalls Margaret, 'he was like a bear with a sore head.'

Nicotine is a powerfully addictive substance. A 1988 report by the US Surgeon General concludes that the chemical processes that determine tobacco addiction are similar to those that mark addiction to drugs such as heroin and cocaine. Says Cameron Fyfe: 'Alfred became addicted to a dangerous substance before the manufacturers were willing to tell him how potentially damaging it was.'

The second strong legal argument, say his lawyers, is Alfred's brand loyalty to John Player's cigarettes, manufactured by Imperial Tobacco. According to medical evidence 90 per cent of lung cancer cases are caused by smoking. On that basis, his lawyers claim Imperial Tobacco's product almost certainly caused the lung cancer which killed him. Says Cameron Fyfe, 'Numerous expert medical witnesses will testify that in this case smoking was the cause beyond all reasonable doubt.'

The firm is so confident of success that when its legal-aid application was turned down last year, it decided to finance the case itself.

Alfred both inspired, and was buoyed up by, this optimism. He campaigned on behalf of ASH, he wrote to people in the news who had cancer, or who had lost loved ones through the disease. And along one side of his bedroom he created a morbid yet fascinating 'wall of death', covering it with newspaper cuttings about cigarettes, lung cancer and death.

Margaret knew this calm exterior masked a devastated man who discovered by chance that he had only months left. 'None of the doctors had ever given him a time limit,' explains Margaret. 'Then in November we saw a copy of a solicitor's letter, saying that Freddie was not expected to see another summer. It was like receiving his death sentence through the post.'

In February, Alfred and Margaret went away to Malta. It was unseasonably cold but, despite the chill wind and rain and his own increasing frailty, he was determined to make the most of his final holiday. 'You see things you think you'll never see again,' he explained, 'so everything has an added urgency.'

Two weeks back from Malta, he went to see his specialist, Anna Gregor, at Edinburgh's Western General Hospital. She showed him his X-ray. One lung was completely filled with tumour, making him breathless and compressing his windpipe. 'I'm sorry, Alfred,' Anna had to tell him, 'we can help control the pain but we have nothing to shrink the tumour, stop it growing or make it go away.'

By now Alfred was often in such excruciating pain that 11 different drugs scarcely contained it. Conversation tired him within minutes, and he would slump back on his pillows, sweat trickling down his ashen forehead. Margaret nursed him patiently, and his solicitors worked desperately to organise a court hearing in the McTears' home.

Cameron Fyfe was only too aware of the delaying tactics used by tobacco companies in the US. Lawyers there have engineered to keep cases like Alfred's going through various courts for years, wearing the plaintiff down financially until he drops the case.

The US tobacco companies have also employed researchers and lawyers to muckrake for something damaging, like a venereal disease or family suicide, that will intimidate the plaintiff into giving up. In 40 years of lawsuits, the US tobacco industry has never paid out a cent in damages or settlement for smoking-related claims.

However, Scottish law allows only two appeals, one to the Inner House of the Court of Session, and finally to the House of Lords. And, says Cameron Fyfe: 'Anything about Alfred's family or marriage would be ruled irrelevant.'

In any case, Alfred was a devoted family man. Back in the 1960s when their three children were small, he worked nights and looked after them during the day while Margaret was out at her job as a coupon checker for Littlewoods Pools. He changed nappies, read stories, helped with home-work, baked bread, did the washing and ironing.

The hardest part of accepting his imminent death was the prospect of leaving his adored grandchildren, four-year-old Joe, Cheryl and Gemma, both two, and baby Graeme, who came to the house every day. 'It really hurts me to think I'll never see them grow up, because I love them so deeply.'

After the supreme effort of giving his evidence, Alfred spent his final days drifting in and out of consciousness. Holding his hand not long before he died, Margaret broke down for the first time. 'He saw me crying and said, "Has my time come?" I said, "No". Now I wonder if I let him down. He wanted to talk to me about death all the time, but I couldn't face it.'

Today it is left to Margaret to carry on the battle. This 49-year-old widow, still working as a coupon checker, is an unlikely champion of the anti-smoking cause. But she has blossomed under the responsibility. She now answers reporters' questions with measured confidence and is passionately articulate in her condemnation of the tobacco industry. She patiently awaits the date of the final hearing, which will take place later this year or in early 1995.

The eyes of the western world will be on its outcome. Alfred's solicitors already have 30 similar cases on their books, and London solicitors Leigh, Day another 300. Meanwhile, Cameron Fyfe is confident that Alfred gave sufficient evidence before he died, and Margaret is determined to see the legal action through to the final appeal. It is what Alfred wanted.

'People still don't realise the damage that smoking does,' she says. 'I feel that if one person stops smoking because of this publicity, then my husband's death was not in vain. This became his purpose. I hope it will become his great achievement.'

JACQUI MARSON

TASK

4 Imagine you were the journalist who, at the press conference, called out the question, 'How does it feel to be dying of lung cancer, Alfred?' Write the article which you submitted to your editor later that same day.

The question you called out was unfeeling and thoughtless. Are you really like that? Or are you going to try to make amends in your article? Think carefully about the effect you want your article to have.

12 killed while fighting fire in the Rockies
(2 hours)

Printed below is a brief report of a forest fire which occurred in the Rocky Mountains in Colorado. It describes the enormous courage of a number of fire–fighters and the circumstances in which they die.

12 killed while fighting fire in the Rockies

GLENWOOD SPRINGS (Colorado), Thurs. – At least 12 fire-fighters died when they were overrun by a fast-moving Rocky Mountain forest fire whipped up by high winds, officials

The tragedy, thought to be one of America's worst wild fire disasters, happened when a blaze on the heavily forested Storm King Mountain near the tourist resort of Glenwood Springs suddenly raged out of control.

Glenwood Springs Police Chief Richard Hollar, who had earlier said 13 fire-fighters died in the blaze, revised the death toll down to 12 early today, saying the revision was due to a miscommunication.

He said two fire-fighters were still missing.

A spokesman for the Bureau of Land Management, a federal agency which had fire-fighters combating the blaze, said 38 fire-fighters had escaped from the inferno.

Three fire-fighters were treated for burns or smoke inhalation, officials said.

They said no effort had yet been made to retrieve the bodies. A helicopter would go out at daylight to look for the missing fire-fighters, they added.

Colorado Governor Roy Romer rushed to the scene last night and Interior Secretary Bruce Babbitt was expected to arrive today, the Bureau of Land Management spokesman said the area is about

190km west of Denver.

'Everybody is trained very thoroughly not to have this happen, safety is the first and foremost objective on every incident ... but life has its risks and those risks overcame it tonight,' Romer told reporters.

The Bureau of Land Management spokesman said fire-fighters had been getting the upper hand over the fire when winds suddenly picked up to speeds of 65kph yesterday afternoon.

A local television reporter said the fire-fighters were climbing up a ridge to get away from the fire below them when they were met by fire coming up the other side of the ridge. They became trapped between two walls of flame.

The fire-fighters each carried small fireproof tents that can be quickly thrown over them if they were unable to escape the flame's onslaught, but some witnesses doubted the fire-fighters would have had time to use them.

The blaze, which had been contained to just 20 hectares yesterday, swelled to 810 hect-ares by nightfall and was threat-ening homes and businesses in Glenwood Springs, a town of 6,000 people famous for its natural hot springs.

The fire, which was started by lightning last week, was reported to be moving at up to 30 metres a minute.

Seventy-five people were evacuated from their homes in the town last night, the Bureau of Land Management said.

TASKS

5   Imagine that you are the local television reporter who has been sent to get the story. You interview the Police Chief, the Governor of Colorado and one of the fire-fighters. Write the interviews. (Think of the different roles of the people you are interviewing and try to vary the tone of each interview in keeping with how you imagine each person to react.)

6   Imagine that a natural catastrophe, a fire, a flood, an earthquake, happens near your home. Write an article for your local newspaper, writing as realistically as possible. Refer in your article to several local residents who have shown immense bravery.

Wider reading

(any length of time)

Here are some suggestions on the theme of 'courage' for you to do some reading of your own. Find at least one of the books in your school or your local library and read it.

- *A Question of Courage* — Marjorie Darke
- *As I Walked Out One Midsummer Morning* — Laurie Lee
- *Walkabout* — James Vance Marshall
- *I Know Why the Caged Bird Sings* — Maya Angelou
- *Let the Circle be Unbroken* — Mildred Taylor
- *Z for Zachariah* — Robert O'Brien
- *1984* — George Orwell
- *Jane Eyre* — Charlotte Brontë
- *Oliver Twist* — Charles Dickens
- *The Diary of Anne Frank* — Anne Frank
- *Kidnapped* — Robert Louis Stevenson

The Hero

(1 hour)

You have read the poem *The Hero* by Seigfried Sassoon in class, and looked at the themes and images used within the poem. We have reprinted the poem here, as a stimulus for some personal writing.

The Hero

'Jack fell as he'd have wished,' the Mother said,
And folded up the letter that she'd read.
'The Colonel writes so nicely.' Something broke
In the tired voice that quavered to a choke.
She half looked up. 'We mothers are so proud
Of our dead soldiers.' Then her face was bowed.
Quietly the Brother Officer went out.
He'd told the poor old dear some gallant lies
That she would nourish all her days, no doubt.
For while he coughed and mumbled, her weak eyes
Had shone with gentle triumph, brimmed with joy,
Because he'd been so brave, her glorious boy.

He thought how 'Jack', cold-footed, useless swine,
Had panicked down the trench that night the mine
Went up at Wicked Corner; how he'd tried
To get sent home, and how, at last, he died,
Blown to small bits. And no one seemed to care
Except that lonely woman with white hair.

SIEGFRIED SASSOON

TASK

7 Write your own story entitled:
'Cowardice in the face of the enemy'
(You are free to interpret the title in any way you like – it certainly needn't be a war story unless you want it to be.)

The Tale of Custard the Dragon

(1 hour)

Ogden Nash is a well-known writer of amusing poems. The poem which is printed overleaf tells the story of a rather cowardly dragon who, just for one moment, behaved as dragons should, showing courage and fierceness.

The Tale of Custard the Dragon

Belinda lived in a little white house,
With a little black kitten and a little gray mouse,
And a little yellow dog and a little red wagon,
And a realio, trulio little pet dragon.

Now the name of the little black kitten was Ink,
And the little grey mouse, she called her Blink,
And the little yellow dog was as sharp as Mustard,
But the dragon was a coward. and she called him Custard.

Custard the dragon had big sharp teeth,
And spikes on top of him and scales underneath,
Mouth like a fireplace, chimney for a nose,
And realio, trulio daggers on his toes.

Belinda was as brave as a barrel full of bears,
And Ink and Blink chased lions down the stairs,
Mustard was as brave as a tiger in a rage,
But Custard cried for a nice safe cage.

Belinda tickled him, she tickled him unmercifuly,
Ink, Blink and Mustard they rudely called him Percival,
They all sat laughing in the little red wagon
At the realio, trulio cowardly dragon.

Belinda giggled till she shook the house,
And Blink said Weeck! which is giggling for a mouse,
Ink and Mustard rudely asked his age,
When Custard cried for a nice safe cage.

Suddenly, suddenly they heard a nasty sound,
And Mustard growled and they all looked around.
Meowch! cried Ink, and Ooh! cried Belinda,
For there was a pirate climbing in the winda.

Pistol in his left hand, pistol in his right,
And he held in his teeth a cutlass bright,
His beard was black, one leg was wood;
It was clear that the pirate meant no good.

Belinda paled, and she cried Help! Help!
But Mustard fled with a terrified yelp,
Ink trickled down to the bottom of the household,
And little mouse Blink strategically mouseholed.

But up jumped Custard, snorting like an engine,
Clashed his tail like irons in a dungeon,
With a clatter and a clank and a jangling squirm
He went at the pirate like a robin at a worm.

The pirate gaped at Belinda's dragon,
And gulped some grog from his pocket flagon,
He fired two bullets, but they didn't hit,
And Custard gobbled him, every bit.

Belinda embraced him, Mustard licked him,
No one mourned for his pirate victim.
Ink and Blink in glee did gyrate
Around the dragon that ate the pyrate.

Belinda still lives in her little white house,
With her little black kitten and little grey mouse,
And her little yellow dog and her little red wagon,
And her realio, trulio little pet dragon.

Belinda is as brave as a barrel full of bears,
And Ink and Blink chase lions down the stairs,
Mustard is as brave as a tiger in a rage,
But Custard keeps crying for a nice safe cage.

OGDEN NASH

TASK

8 Part of the humour of this poem is created by its subject matter; part of the humour is created by the rhythm and form of the poem. It is written in simple 'sing-song' quatraines each of which consists of two couplets.

Spend an hour writing a poem of your own, in the same form and style, telling a little story where someone surprisingly acts in a very courageous way (for instance the class swot who saves the school bully when his canoe sinks on a school outward bound holiday!).

Woman in Space

(1 hour)

You have already read the story of Helen Sharman in class. We have printed it again so that you can remind yourself of it. Read the story again.

Seize the Moment

MAY 18, 1991. My training as Britain's first astronaut was over, Now, in the warm midmorning at Baikonur Cosmodrome, deep in the south of the then Soviet Union, I was about to be launched into space with two soviet cosmonauts – but not before a traditional ceremony.

Ungainly in our stiff, padded spacesuits we walked out on to the parade-ground, where three white squares were painted to show us where to stand. It was here that Yuri Gagarin received his official send-off before his momentous launch in 1961, when he became the first man in space. Russians cherish his memory; they love their hero. So, like all Soviet cosmonauts since, we followed the ritual set for Gagarin.

Flight engineer Sergei Krikalev and I stood on either side of our commander, Anatoly ('Tolya') Artsebarski. Tolya saluted the Soviet general in charge of the ceremony and announced: 'We are ready to fly the Soyuz TM–12 mission.'

The general saluted back. 'I give you permission to fly. I wish you a successful flight and a safe return.'

A great cheer went up from the hundreds of onlookers as we turned to board the long blue and silver bus waiting to take us to the launch site. My father and mother, sister Andrea and brother Richard had flown from Sheffield to see the launch, and Mum managed to push through the crowd to the bus door. We stole a quick hug.

Then, preceded and followed by police cars, their lights flashing, the bus headed into Kazakhstan's desolate scrubland beyond the main cosmodrome complex. The atmosphere on board was cheerful: we had astronauts from earlier missions for company. Alexei Leonov, the first man to walk in space, stood beside my seat, grinning mischievously.

'Ilenechka,' he said using the Russian diminutive of my name, 'on the space station it's traditional for everyone to eat a dinner together. The two guys already on Mir won't have had a meal with a lady for six months. I thought you might like to dress for dinner, so I bought you something.' He produced from his jacket pocket a pink chiffon jumpsuit, with elasticised bits to go round my knees and a wonderfully frilly front and billowing sleeves. 'Just for fun!' he said. I was delighted. I undid the zips of my spacesuit and pushed the garment inside the chest piece before Tolya and Sergei could see it.

The mood on the bus now suddenly became serious. Ahead lay the launch pad. Nothing in training can prepare you for the prospect of your own rocket, the actual one that will blast you into the sky. There was ours: grey, solid and dauntingly huge. I stared at it in awe. Close to the top they had painted the Soviet flag and, for the first time in manned space travel, the Union Jack.

As Tolya, Sergei and I stood in the cage lift that took us up to the spacecraft part of the rocket, white vapour rolled down over us, condensed out of the atmosphere against the bitterly cold fuel tanks.

The crew area consisted of the orbital capsule – an elongated sphere the size of a tiny boxroom, which was our living quarters – and below it the command capsule (also used for re-entry), where the main controls were located. Both capsules were slightly larger than eight feet in diameter. I hauled myself into the orbital capsule head first and went feet first down into the command capsule. It was so crammed with equipment we had to ease ourselves into the seats, bumping elbows. As soon as Tolya and Sergei weren't looking I slipped the chiffon jumpsuit out of my chest piece and quickly pushed it into the space beneath my chair.

With a clang the orbital capsule hatch was closed by a technician on the launch-gantry platform outside. We glanced at each other, the same feeling sweeping across us. No more lectures, no more salutes and smiles. This was it. We were sealed away from the world, isolated, the rocket swaying perceptibly in the wind.

I thought of the tension my family on the spectators' platform little more than a mile away, would be experiencing; the wait for ignition seemed interminable. I thought of the similarities between me and the US astronaut Christa McAuliffe, who died in the Shuttle Challenger launch explosion. We were both civilian women. She, like me, had sat high inside a space vehicle, waiting for the torch to be lit beneath her. I thought, too, of the unimaginable energy pent up in this rocket's tanks. It couldn't happen twice, could it?

In our earphones, a voice from the bunker said, 'Five minutes to go.' 'Two minutes.' Then, 'One minute.' Deep below, there came a rumbling as the rocket engines ignited. Two seconds, three – the rumbling grew louder. The four arms of the launch-gantry swung away. I could feel vibration and knew we must be in that momentary limbo where the rocket seems to balance precariously on its thrust, surely destined to topple.

But as the engines continued to roar, we could feel the pressure of g-forces growing steadily. After 40 seconds the bunker confirmed a successful launch. At 115 seconds came a bump and a loud bang; the escape rocket, designed to snatch us clear and parachute us to safety if the launch had failed, was jettisoned. We were 28.5 miles from the ground. Three seconds later, there was another big jolt and a bang from below as the first-stage booster rockets separated from us.

We passed the 31–mile mark. Now we were using the second-stage engine. Golden sunlight streamed in through the window beside me.

The second stage separated after 288 seconds; then the third stage fired ferociously. At 530 seconds the third stage cut out and was jettisoned. One moment we were being pressed hard into our seats, thrilled with the sensation of tremendous acceleration, the next we were not. Quite involuntarily, all of us exclaimed, 'Uhh!'

I looked out of the window again. We were already over the Pacific! Just nine minutes ago I had been bound to the Earth's surface. Now I could see the curvature of the Earth and speckly white clouds. I was weightless. I was in space. Dreams sometimes do come true.

HELEN SHARMAN
CHRISTOPHER PRIEST

TASK

9 Near the beginning of the extract, in the sixth paragraph, Helen mentions her mother. Imagine that you are Helen Sharman's mother. Write your thoughts and feelings as you stand there watching.

You will want to use facts from the passage in your article, however, you should also consider the whole range of feelings which a mother would naturally have for her child.

For the Children

(3 hours)

At the beginning of the classbook chapter on courage we talked of people who show courage in their everyday lives. We are going to end this homework chapter by using three extracts from a long article which is about a headmistress who showed considerable courage in establishing her role in her school.

When Madeline Cartwright became head of Blaine Primary School in North Philadelphia, Pennsylvania, she found a filthy building infested with vermin, a teaching staff that had all but given up, and children who came to school thinking not about the three Rs, but about surviving one more day in a world of pain and violence.

For the Children

I decided to hold my first parents' meeting. When I told the staff, most of them scoffed. 'They're not going to come, Madeline. Never have. Never will.'

My first step was to get the children excited about the meeting. I called an assembly and told them: 'Your mother has to know Mrs Cartwright. It's important. Every day between now and the meeting, I want you to go home and tell your mother that it is coming up. And tell her something about me too. If you can't think of anything I did or said that day, tell her what I was wearing. Say "Mrs Cartwright had on a green dress today".'

The next morning I was sitting in my office, with the door wide open. I could see children passing by, stopping and peering in to see the colour of my dress.

'What does she have on? What colour is it?'

'Blue! It's blue!'

The week of the meeting , I drove slowly up and down the streets, sounding the horn and yelling at the children out on the kerbs 'Go get your mother! Get your father!'

As the kids brought out their astonished parents, I said, 'We're having the meeting on Thursday night, and you've gotta come.'

I saw adults waiting for a bus and pulled over to tell them about the meeting. I made them promise they would be there too.

When Thursday came, I was on tenterhooks. Early in the day, I asked the administrative assistant to put out folding chairs in the auditorium as extra seats. At 4pm I noticed that nothing was done. I tracked him down. 'Where are the chairs?' I asked.

'Mrs Cartwright,' he said, 'I hate to burst your bubble, but you don't need any chairs. Those parents aren't coming.'

I was furious. 'No matter what,' I said, 'I want you to *act* like you believe in this and any other programme we launch here. If you don't think you belong in that role, then pretend you do until the time comes you can transfer out. Now put out the chairs as I asked you, please.'

The chairs went up. At 6pm people started arriving. Soon parents were pouring through the doors as if they were coming to a free pop concert. I stood shaking hands with them, and by 7pm the auditorium was so packed people were spilling into the corridor. I went to the front of the room and faced them with a huge grin.

'I am so happy to be here with you,' I began. 'I knew you were going to come so we could show our children that we are together.' After introducing all the teachers, I began my speech.

'I am here to make this school serve the children. They are going to enjoy coming here everyday, and they are going to learn.'

I told the audience about my childhood, about being the thirteenth of 13 children, about sleeping on the floor. I told them how once, when we didn't have any shoes, my mother brought home a bag of cast-off women's high heels. My daddy took the shoes to the back of our house, dumped them by a tree stump, and chopped the high heels off every one of them. Then he handed them out to us kids, boys and girls alike, and we all wore them to school the next day.

The assembly laughed so loud at this story I had to stop for a minute. I told them, 'I'm going to make sure your children get the best education we can deliver. They are going to get a fair chance to succeed. For one thing, there will be no suspensions unless your child presents a clear danger to other children or the staff. And I have yet to meet an 11- or 12-year-old child that I can't handle.'

The audience cheered. There had been plenty of suspensions at Blaine before I arrived. Discipline was strict – too strict. The children were tense, apprehensive, afraid of making a wrong move. It is hard for children to absorb lessons when they're wound up like that. Besides, suspension simply didn't work; it meant only that the child was on the streets, and not at school learning.

'But your children have got to treat us with respect,' I went on. 'Our teachers must feel good about themselves. You parents here tonight, see how nice these teachers look? Give them a cheer.'

By this time the teachers were laughing and clapping along with the parents.

'I want to be successful,' I said. 'If your children learn, that's going to help. If your children don't, ladies and gentlemen, I will not be keeping this job and I *need* this job. I love children, but I need my salary too. The Cadillac parked outside belongs to me. But I can't pay for it without you. Will you help me pay for that car?'

The room burst into an ovation. 'Are you telling me that I will be able to keep it?'

The cheers and applause got even louder. And they meant it.

TASK

10 Against the background of failure Madeline Cartwright showed great courage in demanding the cooperation of parents. Imagine you were one of the parents waiting for the bus. Write your own account of what you thought of Madeline Cartwright from the moment when she stopped her car and called out to you.

My primary concern when I first came to Blaine was: how can we ensure that the children here reach their maximum potential? Going into their homes, and seeing some of the horror they lived with, allowed me to identify needs that had to be met before learning could take place.

I told my teachers we might not know what kind of life our youngsters had before they stepped into our school each morning, but we did know what was happening to them here. The least we can do, I said, is let the boys and girls know that their school is a place where they can smile and be happy and safe.

I'll never forget the morning I came to school and found seven-year-old Tyrone waiting outside the front doors. Tyrone was the youngest of three children who lived with a mentally handicapped mother. All too often, his family's food and money were exhausted before the next social security payment came.

That morning Tyrone's brown eyes were wet with tears. He was cradling an arm that was covered with raw third-degree burns. Hurrying him inside, I asked what had happened, while Liz McCain tried to find his mother so I could take them to the hospital.

Tyrone explained that the night before he had been helping his mother pour hot fat from a frying pan into a glass jar. He was steadying the jar when it burst, spilling the scalding oil on to his arm.

There was no telephone in the building to call for help, no transport to the hospital. But there was the school. That's how little Tyrone made it through the long night with his arm burned to the bone; knowing that when morning came, it would bring school and help of this teachers.

Making sure the school always served as a safe haven for children like Tyrone was one thing I talked about to my staff. Another was self-esteem. You may correct the children, I told them, or discipline them within the guidelines of school policy. But you may never demean them or put them down or criticise too much.

It was important to me to nurture self-respect. I went round the school daily touching children, giving them pats, squeezes and hugs. For some of the children, the only touching they experienced daily was being pushed, shoved or hit. I let them all know that there would be absolutely no hitting on school property. I would be the only person allowed to dole out corporal punishment, an option I chose only very rarely.

I also came to realise that, even in primary school, appearance greatly affects the way a child feels about himself. So I told my staff we would do all we could to help. Between 8am and 4pm, I said, our children were going to be well groomed and hold their heads high.

Many of the children had nobody at home who could buy them new clothes, or even wash the ones they already had. Some of our kids slept in the same clothes in which they came to school. Some had no running water, and launderettes were expensive for a mother living on the dole.

I began bringing children home with me. I'd put them in the bath, toss in some soap and tell them to play for a while. Then I'd put their clothes in the washer. I also took children to my home who did not need grooming, to avoid any stigma that might attach to the visits. The children clamoured to come with me. I usually had no trouble getting permission from parents.

But the relatively few children I was able to help this way were not enough to make a real difference. What we needed was our own washing-machine and drier at the school. So we set about buying them.

The parents came to my assistance by running a raffle. The project provided 600 dollars (£280), and our washing programme was under way.

While we were raising money, we also began collecting clothing. Now, when children needed laundry done, they could change clothes as they arrived in the morning. We had set up a private area, using portable blackboards. If the children were dirty, they could scrub themselves at the sink in the nurse's office.

Clean and changed, they put their dirty clothes in a bag, left it on a table and went to class. When they came back in the afternoon, their clothes were fresh and folded. Almost everyone pitched in. Nobody *had* to. But there were enough people – a classroom assistant, a teacher, a parent, me – who did get involved to take care of what needed to be done.

We offered other services as well. A neighbourhood teenager who had helped with our summer clean-up began coming regularly to cut the children's hair. Some older girls volunteered to do our little girls' hair.

There were critics who questioned what we were doing. They said we were not social services, that school could not be all things to all children and was never intended to be.

My answer was simple. We speak of how we want to help children, but then allow ourselves to get tangled up in bureaucratic nonsense, and help never actually reaches those who need it. If a child is hungry, someone must feed him. If he's dirty, someone must wash him. If the child has no clean clothes, get him clean clothes.

Do whatever it takes. It's as simple as that. 'And it can make all the difference in the world for the child.

TASK

11 When you have read the passage carefully answer the questions below.
   a Briefly describe Tyrone's home background.
   b What does Madeline Cartwright mean when she says her teachers may never demean the children?
   c Why did Madeline Cartwright take the better off children to her home as well as the very poor ones?
   d As various 'services' were offered at the school so critics questioned what was being done. Why was the school criticised?
   e In answer to her critics Madeline Cartwright talks of getting 'tangled up in bureaucratic nonsense'. What does she mean by this?

Sara Brooks was one of the able white teachers who stayed at Blaine year after year and helped keep our turnover rate below the unreal levels that afflict many inner-city schools.

A petite, soft-spoken woman, Sara had every single minute planned. While her class stood in the queue for lunch, she tested then on spelling words. When the children went to have photos taken, I watched Sara stand by her pupils holding up maths flashcards.

Sara Brooks believed that every child could get top marks. She even believed it in the case of a six-year-old boy named Larry.

Our experience with him reminded me that sometimes the best thing I could do as head was to make sure foolish bureaucratic rules didn't get in the way of my teachers.

Three weeks after my first autumn term began, a district supervisor came to Blaine to check on our remedial-teaching pupils. Larry was one of those on her list. But according to the teacher, he had not reported to school yet that year.

I phoned Larry's home. His mother arrived at school in a matter of minutes, very upset. She knew her son was coming to school every day, because she walked him here herself. She demanded to know where he was – that instant.

Liz McCain, my community co-ordinator, happened on us at that moment. 'Oh, you're talking about Larry. He's in Room 202,' she said, leading us to Sara Brooks' classroom.

I'd been in Sara's room several times that year, and had seen her bending over this particular boy, poking and prodding him to 'Do! Do! Do!' At other times, I noticed her walking with him down the corridor, urging him to straighten up and walk erect.

I didn't know what his name was. I didn't

know he had had a heart operation as a baby and several operations after that, and that his mother considered him as fragile as a china doll. I didn't know he was classified as trainable mentally retarded (TMR) or that he was supposed to be in the remedial class down the corridor. Remedial children were assigned from the district office. Since Larry's records hadn't arrived, I had simply sent him to Sara's room at the beginning of the year.

Sara didn't know any of this either. She could see only that Larry was different, walking as if his limbs were welded together, his body curled up like an arthritic old man. She just assumed he was another six-year-old falling short of his potential.

No one had ever tried to get him to stand straight. No one had ever made him sit at his desk, prised his fingers open, put a pencil in there and showed him how to write. No one had imagined he could do these things. But Sara could not imagine that he could *not*.

Now, three weeks into the year this little boy was sitting up at his desk, writing his name. His mother said she knew he had been going to class and doing well, because he was coming home every night and showing her what he was learning.

The woman from the district office was a by-the-book supervisor. As far as she was concerned, this situation was outrageous. The boy did not belong in this room. He had tested TMR, and that's what he was: TMR.

'Look at the boy,' I told her. 'Sara has him sitting and walking straight. He is holding his pencil and writing. He could do none of this when school opened just three weeks ago. This boy is not TMR.'

'Mrs Cartwright,' the supervisor said, 'I know what the laws are. You cannot just move these kids round at your whim.'

'Very well,' I responded. 'Would you please put Larry on the list to be re-evaluated?'

'I can do that,' she said. 'But he'll have to wait his turn like everyone else.' Then she took him by the hand and led him to Room 207, the TMR class.

As soon as the woman left, I walked straight back upstairs, got Larry out of that classroom, and returned him to Sara's room.

Sara grabbed Larry and hugged him. Then she hugged his mother and me. Tears streaked all our faces.

Larry stayed in Sara's room until January, when he was re-evaluated and upgraded to EMR – educable mentally retarded. He went on through the next five years at Blaine and became one of our most popular pupils. When break dancing became a fad, Larry went on stage and brought the house down with his performance. This little boy, whose body Sara coaxed open like a flower, was spinning around the stage like a cyclone.

All I could think of was people telling us what can't be done with our children.

MADELINE CARTWRIGHT

TASKS

12 In this third extract Madeline Cartwright again talks of bureaucratic rules getting in the way of her teachers and she shows courage in ignoring that bureaucracy. In your own words tell Larry's story.

13 Now look back at the three extracts and write a character study of Madeline Cartwright, explaining why we can certainly use the word 'courageous' to describe her.

TRAVEL AND ADVENTURE

I n this homework chapter we are going to continue exploring the adventures which people have had and have written about on their travels and we are going to ask you to carry on using your imagination.

Pole to Pole

(1 hour)

In class you have already read an extract from Michael Palin's book *Pole to Pole*. Below we have printed another extract which takes the story of the journey a little further.

Day 57 Luxor

An early start to catch the sunrise over the ruins of the Temple of Karnak. The name is taken from the town of Carnac in Brittany and is a reminder that it was the French who, in 1798, rediscovered this temple under 30 feet of sand. We have a local Egyptologist with us who has obtained permission for us to climb up onto one of the pylons – the massive 150-foot high towers that flank the entrance to the temple. This involves a scramble up a narrow passage-way enclosed between the tomb of Seti II and the pylon wall. We must have disturbed a colony of bats, for the dark tunnel is suddenly filled with flapping creatures trying to find a way out. My hat is knocked off as they brush my face. At the top, the view is splendid but the sunrise isn't and the crew return to our boat for breakfast. I decide to stay in the temple and enjoy some pre-tourist solitude.

The buildings and the monuments here are as impressive as any man-made thing I have seen in the world. They were created to extol the power and strength of the Pharaohs and the Gods whose likenesses they were, and it is impossible to walk amongst the columns and beside the obelisks and not feel the presence of this power. In the Hypostyle Hall, where 134 columns rise in a symbolic forest, 60 feet high, from bases whose circumference could be contained within a ring of 12 people with outstretched arms, I feel a sense of awe and wonder unlike any I've experienced before, compounded by the awareness that similar feelings must have been experienced here over thousands of years.

I'm brought back down to earth as the first wave of tourists appears, adjusting cameras, complaining about meals the night before and arguing over who has the air tickets. Then I catch sight of Tadorus, who I must remember to call Peter, like a white wraith among the massive pillars, stick at the back of his head. If you need a lost sense of wonder restored then Peter is the man. Despite his 80-odd years spent in and around these buildings with scholars and archaeologists, he still finds some things unexplainable. A statue of Rameses II, 97 feet high and made from a single piece of granite, weighs 1,000 tons. Cranes nowadays can only lift 200 tons, yet this massive statue was brought to Luxor from Aswan overland, 3,000 years ago. Peter strikes a theatrical pose, 'How, Tadorus, they say?' He pauses and his big round sad eyes blink slowly, 'My answer, magic.'

The temple of Abu Simbel, further south, was, he tells me, aligned by the ancient Egyptians so that the sun shone onto the face of Rameses twice a year – once on his birthday and once on his coronation day. When Abu Simbel was re-sited in a 40-million-dollar operation to save it from the rising waters of Lake Nasser, all the calculations of the world's experts could not enable the sun to shine on Rameses' face more than once a year.

Peter shakes his head sorrowfully, 'Nothing better,' he sighs, 'Nothing better.'

Here is surely a man born 3,000 years too late. I'm sad to say goodbye to him.

MICHAEL PALIN

TASK

1   You have now read quite a lot about the Egyptian city of Luxor. One of the tasks in your classbook made it clear that Michael Palin was not writing a guidebook.

Use all of the information you now have and in no more than 20 lines write an entry on Luxor for a guidebook.

Life on the Canal!

(1 hour per task)

As well as working with narrative accounts it is important to use material which is written for other purposes.

Printed below are several pages from *The Reader's Digest AA New Book of the Road*. They contain a great deal of information. The first thing you should do is read through the information fairly quickly to form a general impression of what it is about.

We are going to use this information as the basis for a series of homeworks. You will need to re-visit sections of the material as you approach each task.

Inland Waterways

Exploring Britain's quiet backwaters

Britain's inland waterway system blossomed with the Industrial Revolution. In the late 18th century when roads were still poor, 6,000 miles of navigable rivers and canals became vital arteries between bustling mill and factory towns and the seaports. More canals continued to be opened well into the 19th century, but they were already doomed by the railways, and by 1830 they were declining rapidly.

Now life is returning to these old canals, but the colourful commercial narrow boats and barges have mostly given way to the hired motor-launch, the canoe and the sailing dinghy.

On the towpaths once trodden by towing horses, walkers seek the countryside while anglers sit under green umbrellas. The 3,000 miles of open canals form Britain's newest pleasure ground.

The attraction of the canals for many people is their loneliness. They seem to follow their own secret routes through the countryside, usually far from the noise of road and rail routes, penetrating right into the unspoilt green heart of the land.

Each canal has its own character whose subtle differences cannot be seen from a distance but only close at hand along the bank. There are towns and villages which owe their existence to them, because they grew up at junctions and wharves. The villages often consist of a warehouse, inn, shop and group of cottages, dating from the early days when the boatmen and bargees lived ashore.

The effect of the railways can still be noticed by the canals. Rail competition forced canal owners to cut their prices, which in turn forced the boatmen to give up their cottages and take their families on their barges for a life afloat. Inns sprang up along the canals for the boat crews and these are still there today.

Exploring by boat is only one way of enjoying the canals, with their villages, humpbacked bridges, aqueducts and secretive tunnels.

Walking and hiking on the towpaths is

growing more popular as even minor roads become more crowded with traffic. Every year stretches of towpath are being repaired and opened to the public. On some urban sections there is no right of way, but those on foot are welcome in the rural areas – at their own risk. Walkers are advised to wear stout boots because hedges are often overgrown and banks are eroded by the wash from boats.

Wildlife is abundant along the waterways. The more remote rivers and canals, particularly in the Fens, support many species of birds and wild plants. Some stretches are now designated as Nature Reserves, and conservation associations and local authorities have formed nature trails beside waterways.

For the motorist taking a canal holiday, parking arrangements can usually be made at the yard at which the boat is hired.

Details of alternative routes when canal repairs necessitate diversions can be obtained from the British Waterways Board.

How to start planning a holiday afloat

When planning a holiday afloat calculate how far you can travel in the time available on your chosen stretch of waterway. The speed limit on canals is 4 mph and 6 mph on rivers. The time taken to get through a lock varies, but ten minutes is average. In practice, 6 or 7 hours cruising a day is comfortable, and one would expect to cover 12 –15 miles and 6 locks in this time. Make allowance for river currents, summer peak traffic and unforeseen delays such as weed clogging the propeller. Canal boats from 2 to 12 berths may be hired, and often there is room for a makeshift bunk, so a couple with one child would be comfortable in a 2-berth cruiser.

To obtain a list of hire firms telephone or write to the Inland Waterways Association, 114 Regent's Park Road, London NW1 8UQ.

Britain's canals cross under roads, and often run close to them before meandering into the countryside. Those planning a holiday cruise can choose a circular route to avoid having to return along the same stretch of waterway. Britain's canals were either 'narrow' or 'broad' because they were constructed by different engineers to serve the needs of local industry, and so no standard system was adopted. The determining factor is the width and length of the locks.

Maximum boat sizes are – Narrow canal: length 70 ft, beam, or width, 6 ft 10 in. Broad canal: length: 55–70 ft (depending on the particular canal), beam 14 ft. Fens: length 45 ft, beam 10 ft 6in. Rivers: 55–174 ft, beam 10–19 ft.

Guide to terms used by the watermen

Balance beam Large timber running horizontally from a lock gate. It is used as a lever for opening and closing the gate.

Bridge hole The arch under a canal bridge.

Butty An unpowered narrow boat towed behind a motor boat.

Cut A canal, so called because it is an artificial cut of land.

Draw To open a sluice or paddle of a lock.

Gates The moveable watertight gates at each end of the lock. The gate where the water level is highest is known as the *top gate*; and where the water is at the lower level, the *bottom gate*.

Keb Long rake kept at locksides for removing debris from the lock.

Lengthman A man employed by a navigation authority to maintain a section of the water-way, especially the water levels.

Narrow beam A canal on which the locks do not exceed a width of 7 ft 6 in.

Narrow boat A boat designed for narrow canals. Generally 70 ft long with a 7 ft beam.

Paddle The sluice for filling or emptying a lock of water. In the North of England a paddle is called a clough (pronounced 'clow'). In Ireland it is a 'rack'.

Pound The stretch of water between two canal locks.

Side pond A small reservoir re-using water to refill a lock rather than letting it run away.

Sill The masonry beneath a lock gate, sometimes projecting several feet from the gate.

Stop gates Wood or metal gates, similar to a lock gate, used to retain a section of a canal during repairs. Also known as planks.

Summit The highest stretch of water on a canal – often fed by a reservoir.

Wheeler or **Lock wheeler** A person – at one time a cyclist – who travels ahead of the boat to set the locks in readiness.

Winding hole A wide place on the waterway for turning boats. So called as the wind was used to assist in turning.

Windlass The L-shaped crank or handle used for winding the paddles up and down, usually detachable, but sometimes fixed.

How to get through a canal lock

The busiest part of canal cruising is going through locks. They are easy to negotiate if the correct sequence of opening and closing the gates and raising and lowering the water level is followed, as shown below. Every time a lock is used water is drained down the canal, so it is important not to waste water by

A lock is a chamber in which a boat can be floated from one level to another. The gates, which are of elm or oak, always point uphill so that water pressure forces push them together.

Operating a lock

1 If the lock is empty when your boat is going uphill, fill the lock by opening the ground paddles which let water in through the culverts. If there are gate paddles only, raise them slowly. When the lock is full, open the top gates and enter.

2 Close the paddles and gates. Open the bottom paddles so that the lock empties. Keep your boat clear of the sill underneath the top gates. Do not secure the boat to bollards or it will be left suspended as the water falls. Get one of the crew to hold a mooring line from the side of the lock.

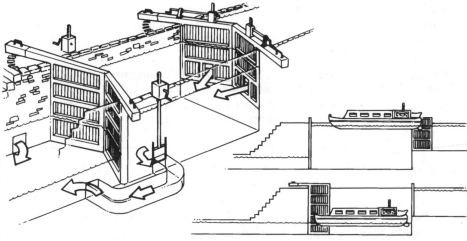

3 When the boat has floated down and the lock is 'empty', open the bottom gates and leave the lock. Unless there is a vessel approaching or waiting to enter the lock to go uphill, close the bottom paddles and gates so that a following boat can repeat your manoeuvre. Close all gates at the top lock of a flight and the last lock before a long pound – a stretch of canal.

4 Close the gates by hand and wind down the paddles. Never slam the gates or drop the paddles suddenly; this may cause damage or injury. If a lock is closed or 'against' you on arrival do not empty or fill it if a boat is approaching from the opposite direction. A similar sequence is used for going uphill through a lock.

The waterway code and canal language

One of the pleasures of inland cruising is the freedom to go where you choose, but there are several important 'rules of the road' which must be observed. When meeting another craft pass on the right, except where it would be dangerous. For example, a laden working boat may need the deeper water on the outside of a bend, which will mean your passing on the left. The oncoming vessel will signal two horn blasts for you to do this. Overtake if possible on a straight stretch. Working boats or barges always have priority over pleasure craft; otherwise, priority at locks is on a 'first come, first served'

basis, except where the water level in the lock is in favour of a craft seen approaching.

Speed limits are laid down by each waterway authority. Never allow the wash waves to break on the banks. Slow down on bends, and when approaching or passing moored craft, other craft under way, anglers, bridges and tunnels.

The boat should be equipped with a white headlamp for tunnels and night cruising on canals. Full navigational lighting is obligatory on rivers and estuaries. Mooring is possible on most straight stretches but do not moor on bends or near locks and bridges.

TASKS

2 You decide that you are going to take your family on a canal holiday. You hold a family conference to outline your plans and to discuss the idea.

Write several pages of the discussion as a play script. Use the information you have. You may introduce a member of the family who thinks it is a bad idea and who needs to be persuaded.

3 You are on your holiday and you have arrived at the first lock. (Look again at the diagrams and instructions in the material.) You have read the instructions but are rather nervous. The rest of the family are there to help (or hinder). Write the story of what happens as you manoeuvre your way through the lock.

4 You have read the waterway code and are very careful to make sure that you try to do things properly. One day on your holiday you come across some other holiday-makers who don't seem to care about other canal-users. You know that a very heavily laden barge is behind you on the canal. Describe what happens.

5 Your holiday is over and you have had an absolutely great time. You are so enthusiastic that you want to encourage others to go on canal holidays. You have phoned your local newspaper and they have suggested that you write an article for the travel section of the newspaper. Write the article.

Take a School Trip to Adventure

(2 hours)

Printed below is an extract from a travel brochure which is advertising school trips to Poland. Read the information carefully.

POLAND

*T*ravelBound aims to be always at the forefront of school travel, allowing you to experience the changing face of Eastern Europe. This is ever evident in Poland whose recent political history has witnessed the rise to power of the Solidarity Movement, from its origins in the Gdansk shipyard to the establishment of the first non-communist government in Eastern Europe since the Second World War.

A visit to Poland provides an insight into modern history and history in the making. Poland also enjoys a rich cultural heritage, evident in the great cities of Warsaw and Craców included in our itinerary.

Poland has endured a chequered past as it has struggled through the centuries against invasions to maintain its nationhood. The Polish people have undergone much hardship and yet they remain resilient, generous, friendly and welcoming.

A visit to Poland is a rich and enjoyable educational experience.

◆ **Day 1**: School to Poznan, overnight by coach

Your coach collects you from school to connect with an afternoon sailing to the Continent. Continue through the night.

◆ **Day 2**: Arrive Poznan

Arrive in Poznan for lunch (first included meal). Here you will meet your Polish escort who will remain with you during your stay in Poland.

In the afternoon you will be taken on a walking tour of the city to see the Gothic Cathedral, Renaissance town hall and beautifully restored merchants' houses.

◆ **Day 3**: Poznan to Warsaw via Zelazowa Wola

Depart Poznan after breakfast, taking a packed lunch. Continue to Zelazowa Wola, birthplace of Chopin. Chopin's house, set in lovely gardens, has been beautifully restored and is now a museum. Concerts are held here in the summer months.

Evening dinner and overnight in Warsaw.

◆ **Day 4**: Full Day in Warsaw

Capital of Poland for the last 400 years, this city has endured a beleaguered past. Of most interest perhaps is the role that Warsaw has played in modern history. Hitler ordered the complete annihilation of the city following the uprising of 1944. Two thirds of the population perished and the city was almost rased to the ground. After the war, within ten years, much of the city had been reconstructed. Today Warsaw retains its historical heritage due to this remarkable achievement.

At the centre of the old town is the Royal Castle, more recently restored in the 1970s through private donations from Poles all over the world. See also St John's Cathedral and the lively and colourful old town square. There are many other remarkable buildings and museums including the Warsaw Historical Museum which gives an insight into the courage and determination of the Polish people, in particular in World War II.

The Royal Way is the most elegant street in the city which leads past the beautiful Lazienki Park and Palace.

The Ghetto, where thousands of Jews were imprisoned during the war, has now been redeveloped but there are memorials to their suffering.

The Communist past has, of course, left its cultural mark on the city, particularly in its post-war architecture.

Evening disco with Polish youth.

◆ **Day 5**: Craców via Czestochowa and Auschwitz

Depart after breakfast with packed lunch. Visit Czestochowa, the most important place of pilgrimage in Poland. Within the impressive walls of the 600 year old monastery of Jasna Gora, in a Gothic chapel, is the painting of the Black Madonna. The painting is traditionally believed to have been the work of St Luke and is said to have miraculous properties.

The monastery also has a Knights' Hall, Treasury and Arsenal devoted to the military history of the fortress.

Continue to Auschwitz. A place to reflect on the harrowing horrors of war. Auschwitz was the largest Nazi concentration camp of World War II. Four million people of 28 different nationalities, including 2.5 million Jews died here. Much of the camp remains as the Museum of Martyrdom. There is a film showing the horrific scenes discovered by the Allies when they liberated the camp. Children under 13 are **NOT** allowed to visit Auschwitz.

Arrive in Craców for evening dinner and overnight accommodation.

◆ **Day 6**: Craców

Listed by UNESCO as one of the world's twelve most historic sites, Craców is a beautiful city with a tremendous architectural and cultural heritage. Former Polish capital and residence of the Kings of Poland for 500 years, the city mercifully survived widespread structural damage in World War II.

This old university city is still a lively cultural centre attracting many visitors all year round.

The old town has a wealth of Gothic, Renaissance and Baroque architecture. At its heart is the largest market square of medieval Europe, surrounded by splendid buildings.

The square contains the Cloth Hall, rebuilt during the Renaissance, and now a covered market, and the Art Gallery. On nearby Wawel Hill is the Royal Castle, former seat of the Polish monarchy and government and the magnificent cathedral.

Beyond the Wawel Hill is the 'Kazimierz', the Jewish quarter.

Craców had one of the largest Jewish communities in Europe until the mass extermination in the gas chambers of Auschwitz in World War II.

Craców's most famous sons include Nicolaus Copernicus and of course Pope John Paul II, who was formerly Archbishop of Craców.

◆ **Day 7**: Craców to Berlin

Depart after breakfast taking a packed lunch and drive to Berlin to arrive for evening dinner and overnight accommodation.

◆ **Day 8**: Day at leisure in Berlin before evening departure

Due to EC drivers' hours regulations your coach will not be available to you. Berlin does have an excellent public transport system.

See the Reichstag, the former Parliament building. Walk through the Brandenburg Gate, down Unter den Linden, with its magnificent buildings.

Visit to Pergamon Museum with its treasures of the classical world.

Departure after evening dinner (last meal) and continue by overnight coach.

◆ **Day 9**: Arrive at school

Cross the Channel in the morning and continue by coach to your school.

TASKS

6 Imagine that you are a teacher and have decided that you would like to take a party of tenth-year students to Poland. You have obtained the headteacher's permission to go ahead and are now preparing to advertise the visit.

Write the preliminary letter to parents and students telling them about the visit and the sorts of things which you are likely to do. Remember that you need to sound very enthusiastic as you are hoping that enough people will respond positively so that the visit can go ahead.

One piece of information which you will need to use in addition to that in the extract is that the cost of the visit will be £250.

7 Later on, having had a successful response, you hold a meeting to answer any questions which parents or students might have. Write about the meeting. You can either write it as a playscript with parents and students asking questions and you answering them, or you can write it as a report of the meeting for the headteacher.

The sorts of questions you are likely to be asked will include questions about the food (some students will imagine that the food will be absolutely horrible), about sleeping arrangements, about whether or not the students will have to wear school uniform (a fate worse than death!) and parents will want to know about safety. It is your job to reassure.

A Fall of Moondust

(1 hour + reading time)

The next two items in this homework chapter are going to take us to the different world of science fiction, which might well be a type of literature which you read for your own pleasure.

Printed opposite is the first chapter of *A Fall of Moondust* by Arthur C Clarke. It is about a journey on the moon.

A Fall of Moondust

To be the skipper of the only boat on the Moon was a distinction that Pat Harris enjoyed. As the passengers filed aboard *Selene*, jockeying for window seats, he wondered what sort of trip it would be this time. In the rear-view mirror he could see Miss Wilkins, very smart in her blue Lunar Tourist Commission uniform, putting on her usual welcome act. He always tried to think of her as 'Miss Wilkins', not Sue, when they were on duty together; it helped to keep his mind on business. But what she thought of him, he had never really discovered.

There were no familiar faces; this was a new bunch, eager for their first cruise. Most of the passengers were typical tourists – elderly people, visiting a world that had been the very symbol of inaccessibility when they were young. There were only four or five passengers on the low side of thirty, and they were probably technical personnel on vacation from one of the lunar bases. It was a fairly good working rule, Pat had discovered, that all the old people came from Earth, while the youngsters were residents of the Moon.

But to all of them the Sea of Thirst was a novelty. Beyond *Selene*'s observation windows its grey, dusty surface marched onwards unbroken until it reached the stars. Above it hung the waning crescent Earth, poised for ever in the sky from which it had not moved in a billion years. The brilliant, blue-green light of the mother world flooded this strange land with a cold radiance – and cold it was indeed, perhaps three hundred below zero on the exposed surface.

No one could have told, merely by looking at it, whether the Sea was liquid or solid. It was completely flat and featureless, quite free from the myriad cracks and fissures that scarred all the rest of this barren world. Not a single hillock, boulder or pebble broke its monotonous uniformity. No sea on Earth – no mill-pond, even – was ever as calm as this.

It was a sea of dust, not of water, and therefore it was alien to all the experience of men – therefore, also, it fascinated and attracted them. Fine as talcum powder, drier in this vacuum than the parched sands of the Sahara, it flowed as easily and effortlessly as any liquid. A heavy object dropped into it would disappear instantly, without a splash, leaving no scar to mark its passage. Nothing could move upon its treacherous surface except the small, two-man dust-skis – and *Selene* herself, an improbable combination of sledge and bus, not unlike the Sno-cats that had opened up the Antarctic a lifetime ago.

Selene's official designation was Dust-cruiser, Mark I, though to the best of Pat's knowledge a Mark 2 did not exist even on the drawing-board. She was called 'ship', 'boat' or 'moon-bus' according to taste; Pat preferred 'boat', for it prevented confusion. When he used that word, no one would mistake him for the skipper of a space-ship – and space-ship captains were, of course, two a penny.

'Welcome aboard *Selene*,' said Miss Wilkins, when everyone had settled down. 'Captain Harris and I are pleased to have you with us. Our trip will last four hours, and our first objective will be Crater Lake, a hundred kilometres east of here in the Mountains of Inaccessibility —.'

Pat scarcely heard the familiar introductions; he was busy with his countdown. *Selene* was virtually a grounded space-ship; she had to be, since she was travelling in a vacuum, and must protect her frail cargo from the hostile world beyond her walls. Though she never left the surface of the Moon, and was propelled by electric motors instead of rockets, she carried all the basic equipment of a full-fledged ship of space – and all of it had to be checked before departure.

Oxygen – OK. Power – OK. Radio – OK. ('Hello, Rainbow Base, *Selene* testing. Are you receiving my beacon?') Inertial navigator – zeroed. Airlock Safety – On. Cabin Leak detector – OK. Internal lights – OK. Gangway – disconnected. And so on for more than 50 items, every one of which would automatically call attention to itself in case of trouble. But Pat Harris, like all spacemen hankering after old age, never relied on autowarnings if he could carry out the check himself.

At last he was ready. The almost silent motors started to spin, but the blades were still feathered and *Selene* barely quivered at her moorings. Then he eased the port fan into fine pitch, and she began to curve slowly to the right. When she was clear of the embarkation building, he straightened her out and pushed the throttle forward.

She handled very well, when one considered the complete novelty of her design. There were no millennia of trial and error here, stretching back to the first Neolithic man who ever launched a log out into a stream. *Selene* was the very first of her line, created in the brains of a few engineers who had sat down at a table and asked themselves: 'How do we build a vehicle that will skim over a sea of dust?'

Some of them, harking back to Ole Man River, had wanted to make her a stern-wheeler, but the more efficient submerged fans had carried the day. As they drilled through the dust, driving her before them, they produced a wake like that of high-speed mole, but it vanished within seconds, leaving the Sea unmarked by any sign of the boat's passage.

Now the squat pressure-domes of Port Roris were dropping swiftly below the skyline. In less than ten minutes they had vanished from sight: *Selene* was utterly alone. She was at the centre of something for which the languages of mankind have no name.

As Pat switched off the motors and the boat coasted to rest, he waited for the silence to grow around him. It was always the same; it took a little while for the passengers to realise the strangeness of what lay outside. They had crossed space and seen stars all about them; they had looked up – or down – at the dazzling face of Earth, but this was different. It was neither land nor sea, neither air nor space, but a little of each.

Before the silence grew oppressive – if he left it too long, someone would get scared – Pat rose to his feet and faced his passengers.

'Good evening, ladies and gentlemen,' he began. 'I hope Miss Wilkins has been making you comfortable. We've stopped here because this is a good place to introduce you to the Sea – to give you the feel of it, as it were.'

He pointed to the windows, and the ghostly greyness that lay beyond.

'Just how far away,' he asked quietly, 'do you imagine our horizon is? Or to put it in another way, how big would a man appear to you, if he

was standing out there where the stars seem to meet the ground?'

It was a question that no one could possibly answer, from the evidence of sight alone. Logic said 'The Moon's a small world – the horizon *must* be very close.' But the senses gave a wholly different verdict; this land, they reported, is absolutely flat, and stretches to infinity. It divides the Universe in twain; for ever and ever, it rolls onwards beneath the stars …

The illusion remained, even when one knew its cause. The eye has no way of judging distances, when there is nothing for it to focus upon. vision slipped and skidded helplessly on this featureless ocean of dust. There was not even – as there must always be on Earth – the softening haze of the atmosphere to give some hint of nearness or farness. The stars were unwinking needle points of light, clear down to that indeterminate horizon.

'Believe it or not,' continued Pat, 'you can see just three kilometres – or two miles, for those of you who haven't been able to go metric yet. I know it looks a couple of lightyears out to the horizon, but you could walk it in 20 minutes, if you could walk on this stuff at all.'

He moved back to his seat, and started the motors once more.

'Nothing much to see for the next 60 kilometres,' he called over his shoulders, 'so we'll get a move on.'

Selene surged forward. For the first time there was a real sensation of speed. The boat's wake became longer and more disturbed as the spinning fans bit fiercely into the dust. Now the dust itself was being tossed up on either side in great ghostly plumes; from a distance, *Selene* would have looked like a snow-plough driving its way across a winter landscape, beneath a frosty moon. But those grey, slowly-collapsing parabolas were not snow, and the lamp that lit their trajectory was the planet Earth.

The passengers relaxed, enjoying the smooth, almost silent ride. Every one of them had travelled hundreds of times faster than this, on the journey to the Moon – but in space one was never conscious of speed, and this swift glide across the dust was far more exciting. When Harris swung *Selene* into a tight turn, so that she orbited in a circle, the boat almost overtook the falling veils of powder her fans had hurled into the sky. It seemed altogether wrong that this impalpable dust should rise and fall in such clean-cut curves, utterly unaffected by air resistance. On Earth it would have drifted for hours – perhaps for days.

As soon as the boat had straightened out on a steady course and there was nothing to look at except the empty plain, the passengers began to read the literature thoughtfully provided for them. Each had been given a folder of photographs, maps, souvenirs ('This is to certify that Mr/Mrs/Miss ... has sailed the Seas of the Moon, aboard Dust-cruiser *Selene*') and informative text. They had only to read this to discover all that they wanted to know about the Sea of Thirst, and perhaps a little more.

Most of the Moon, they read, was covered by a thin layer of dust, usually no more than a few millimetres deep. Some of this was debris from the stars – the remains of meteorites that had fallen upon the Moon's unprotected face for at least five billion years. Some had flaked from the lunar rocks as they expanded and contracted in the fierce temperature extremes between day and night. Whatever its source, it was so finely divided that it would flow like a liquid, even under this feeble gravity.

Over the ages, it had drifted down from the mountains into the lowlands, to form pools and lakes. The first explorers had expected this, and had usually been prepared for it. But the Sea of Thirst was a surprise; no one had anticipated finding a dust-bowl more than 100 kilometres across.

As the lunar 'seas' went, it was very small; indeed, the astronomers had never officially recognised its title, pointing out that it was only a small portion of the Sinus Roris – the Bay of Dew. And how, they protested, could part of a Bay be an entire Sea? But the name, invented by a copy-writer of the Lunar Tourist Commission, had stuck despite their objections. It was at least as appropriate as the names of the other so-called Seas – Sea of Clouds, Sea of Rains, Sea of Tranquillity. Not to mention Sea of Nectar ...

The brochure also contained some reassuring information, designed to quell the fears of the most nervous traveller, and to prove that the Tourist Commission had thought of everything. 'All possible precautions have been taken for your safety,' it stated. '*Selene* carries an oxygen reserve sufficient to last for more than a week, and all essential equipment is duplicated. An automatic radio beacon signals your position at regular intervals, and in the extremely improbable event of a complete power failure, a Dust-ski from Port Roris would tow you home with little delay. Above all, there is no need to worry about rough weather. No matter how bad a sailor you may be, you can't get sea-sick on the Moon. There are never any storms on the Sea of Thirst; it is always a flat calm.'

Those last comforting words had been written in all good faith, for who could have imagined that they would soon be proved untrue?

As *Selene* raced silently through the earthlit night, the Moon went about its business. There was a great deal of business now, after the aeons of sleep. More had happened here in the last 50 years than in the five billions before that, and much was to happen soon.

In the first city that Man had ever built outside his native world, Chief Administrator Olsen was taking a stroll through the park. He was very proud of the park, as were all the 25,000 inhabitants of Port Clavius. It was small, of course – though not as small as was implied by that miserable TV commentator who'd called it 'a window-box with delusions of grandeur'. and certainly there were no parks, gardens, or anything else on Earth where you could find sunflowers ten metres high.

Far overhead, wispy cirrus clouds were sailing by – or so it seemed. They were, of course, only images projected on the inside of the dome, but the illusion was so perfect that it sometimes made the C. A. homesick. Homesick? He corrected himself; *this* was home.

Yet in his heart of hearts, he knew it was not true. To his children it would be, but not to him. He had been born in Stockholm, Earth; they had been born in Port Clavius. They were citizens of the Moon; he was tied to Earth with bonds that might weaken with the years, but would never break.

Less than a kilometre away, just outside the main dome, the head of the Lunar Tourist

Commission inspected the latest returns, and permitted himself a mild feeling of satisfaction. The improvement over the last season had been maintained; not that there *were* seasons on the Moon, but it was noticeable that more tourists came when it was winter in Earth's northern hemisphere.

How could he keep it up? That was always the problem, for tourists wanted variety and you couldn't give them the same thing over and over again. The novel scenery, the low gravity, the view of Earth, the mysteries of Farside, the spectacular heavens, the pioneer settlements (where tourists were not always welcomed, anyway) – after you'd listed those, what else did the Moon have to offer? What a pity there were no native Selenites with quaint customs and quainter physiques at which visitors could click their cameras. Alas, the largest life-form ever discovered on the Moon needed a microscope to show it – and its ancestors had come to her on Lunik 2, only a decade ahead of Man himself.

Commissioner Davis rifled mentally through the items that had arrived by the last telefax, wondering if there was anything here that would help him. There was, of course, the usual request from a TV company he'd heard of, anxious to make yet another documentary on the Moon – if all expenses were paid. The answer to that one would be 'No'; if he accepted all these kind offers, his department would soon be broke.

Then there was a chatty letter from his opposite number in the Greater New Orleans Tourist Commission, Inc., suggesting an exchange of personnel. It was hard to see how that would help the Moon, or New Orleans either, but it would cost nothing and might produce some goodwill. And – this was more interesting – there was a request from the water-ski-ing champion of Australia, asking if anyone had ever tried to ski on the Sea of Thirst.

Yes – there was definitely an idea here; he was surprised that someone had not tried it already. Perhaps they had, behind *Selene* or one of the small dust-skis. It was certainly worth a test; he was always on the look-out for new forms of lunar recreation, and the Sea of Thirst was one of his pet projects.

It was a project which, within a very few hours, was going to turn into a nightmare.

ARTHUR C CLARKE

TASK

8 When you have read the chapter, answer the following questions.

a How do Pat Harris and Miss Wilkins seek to make the trip exciting for the passengers without frightening them?

b Using information from the chapter, write a brief introductory character study of Pat Harris.

c What does Arthur C Clarke tell us about moondust in this chapter?

d You are a passenger on *Selene*. Write about your first impressions.

Now borrow a copy of *A Fall of Moondust* from your school or local library and read it.

A Sound of Thunder

(1 hour 30 minutes)

We have already looked at one piece of science fiction writing; now we are going to examine another. What is printed opposite is part of a story by Ray Bradbury called *A Sound of Thunder*. Read the extract.

A Sound of Thunder

The sign on the wall seemed to quiver under a film of sliding warm water. Eckels felt his eyelids blink over his stare, and the sign burned in this momentary darkness:

TIME SAFARI, INC.
SAFARIS TO ANY YEAR IN THE PAST.
YOU NAME THE ANIMAL.
WE TAKE YOU THERE.
YOU SHOOT IT.

A warm phlegm gathered in Eckels's throat; he swallowed and pushed.

The muscles around his mouth formed a smile as he put his hand slowly out upon the air, and in that hand waved a cheque for ten thousand dollars to the man behind the desk.

'Does this safari guarantee I come back alive?'

'We guarantee nothing,' said the official, 'except the dinosaurs.' He turned. 'This is Mr Travis, your Safari Guide in the Past. He'll tell you what and where to shoot. If he says no shooting, no shooting. If you disobey instructions, there's a stiff penalty of another ten thousand dollars, plus possible government action, on your return.'

Eckels glanced across the vast office at a mass and tangle, a snaking and humming of wires and steel boxes, at an aurora that flickered now orange, now silver, now blue. There was a sound like a gigantic bonfire burning all of Time, all the years and all the parchment calendars, all the hours piled high and set aflame.

A touch of the hand and this burning would, on the instant, beautifully reverse itself. Eckels remembered the wording in the advertisements to the letter. Out of chars and ashes, out of dust and coals, like golden salamanders, the old years, the green years, might leap; roses sweeten the air, white hair turn Irish-black, wrinkles vanish; all, everything fly back to seed, flee death, rush down to their beginnings, suns rise in western skies and set in glorious easts, moons eat themselves opposite to the custom, all and everything cupping one in another like Chinese boxes, rabbits in hats, all and everything returning to the fresh death, the seed death, the green death, to the time before the beginning. A touch of a hand might do it, the merest touch of a hand.

'Hell and damn,' Eckels breathed, the light of the Machine on his thin face. 'A real Time Machine.' He shook his head. 'Makes you think. If the election had gone badly yesterday, I might be here now running away from the results. Thank God Keith won. He'll make a fine President of the United States.'

'Yes,' said the man behind the desk. 'We're lucky. If Deutscher had gotten in, we'd have the worst kind of dictatorship. There's an anti-everything man for you, a militarist, anti-Christ, anti-human, anti-intellectual. People called us up, you know, joking but not joking. Said if Deutscher became President they wanted to go live in 1492. Of course it's not our business to conduct Escapes, but to form Safaris. Anyway, Keith's President now. All you got to worry about is –'

'Shooting my dinosaur,' Eckels finished it for him.

'A *Tyrannosaurus rex*. The Thunder Lizard, the damnedest monster in history. Sign this release. Anything happens to you, we're not responsible. Those dinosaurs are hungry.'

Eckels flushed angrily. 'Trying to scare me!'

'Frankly, yes. We don't want anyone going who'll panic at the first shot. Six Safari leaders were killed last year, and a dozen hunters. We're here to give you the damnedest thrill a *real* hunter ever asked for. Travelling you back sixty million years to bag the biggest damned game in all Time. Your personal cheque's still there. Tear it up.'

Mr Eckels looked at the cheque for a long time. His fingers twitched.

'Good luck,' said the man behind the desk. 'Mr Travis, he's all yours.'

They moved silently across the room, taking their guns with them, toward the machine; toward the silver metal and the roaring light.

✳ ✳ ✳

First a day and then a night and then a day and then a night, then it was day-night-day-night-day. A week, a month, a year, a decade! A.D. 2055, A.D. 2019. 1999! 1957! Gone! The Machine roared.

They put on their oxygen helmets and tested

the intercoms.

Eckels swayed on the padded seat, his face pale, his jaw stiff. He felt the trembling in his arms and he looked down and found his hands tight on the new rifle. There were four other men in the Machine. Travis, the Safari Leader, his assistant, Lesperance, and two other hunters, Billings and Kramer. They sat looking at each other, and the years blazed around them.

'Can these guns get a dinosaur cold?' Eckels felt his mouth saying.

'If you hit them right,' said Travis on the helmet radio. 'Some dinosaurs have two brains, one in the head, another far down the spinal column. We stay away from those. That's stretching luck. Put your first two shots into the eyes, if you can, blind them, and go back into the brain.'

The Machine howled. Time was a film run backward. Suns fled and ten million moons fled after them. 'Good God,' said Eckels. 'Every hunter that ever lived would envy us today. This makes Africa seem like Illinois.'

The sun stopped in the sky.

The fog that had enveloped the Machine blew away and they were in an old time, a very old time indeed, three hunters and two Safari Heads with their blue metal guns across their knees.

'Christ isn't born yet,' said Travis. 'Moses has not gone to the mountain to talk with God. The Pyramids are still in the earth, waiting to be cut out and put up. *Remember* that, Alexander, Caesar, Napoleon, Hitler – none of them exists.'

The men nodded.

'That' – Mr Travis pointed – 'is the jungle of sixty million, two thousand and fifty-five years before President Keith.'

He indicated a metal path that struck off into green wilderness, over steaming swamp, among giant ferns and palms.

'And that,' he said, 'is the Path, laid by Time Safari for your use. It floats six inches above the earth. Doesn't touch so much as one grass blade, flower, or tree. It's an antigravity metal. Its purpose is to keep you from touching this world of the past in any way. Stay on the Path. Don't go off it. I repeat. *Don't go off.* For *any* reason! If you fall off, there's a penalty. And don't shoot any animal we don't OK.'

'Why?' asked Eckels.

They sat in the ancient wilderness. Far birds' cries blew on a wind, and the smell of tar and an old salt sea, moist grasses, and flowers the colour of blood.

'We don't want to change the Future. We don't belong here in the Past. The government doesn't *like* us here. We have to pay big graft to keep our franchise. A Time Machine is damn finicky business. Not knowing it, we might kill an important animal, a small bird, a roach, a flower even, thus destroying an important link in a growing species.'

'That's not clear,' said Eckels.

'All right,' Travis continued, 'say we accidentally kill one mouse here. That means all the future families of this one particular mouse are distorted, right?'

'Right.'

'And all the families of the families of that one mouse! With a stamp of your foot, you annihilate first one, then a dozen, then a thousand, a million, a *billion* possible mice!'

'So they're dead,' said Eckels. 'So what?'

'So what?' Travis snorted quietly. 'Well, what about the foxes that'll need those mice to survive? For want of ten mice, a fox dies. For want of ten foxes, a lion starves. For want of a lion, all manner of insects, vultures, infinite billions of life forms are thrown into chaos and destruction. Eventually it all boils down to this: fifty-nine million years later, a cave-man, one of a dozen on the *entire* world, goes hunting wild boar or sabre-toothed tiger for food. But you, friend, have *stepped* on all the tigers in that region. By stepping on *one* single mouse. So the cave-man starves. And the cave-man, please note, is not just *any* expendable man, no! He is an *entire future nation*. From his loins would have sprung ten sons. From *their* loins one hundred sons, and thus onward to a civilisation. Destroy this one man, and you destroy a race, a people, an entire history of life. It is comparable to slaying some of Adam's grandchildren. The stomp of your foot, on one mouse, could start an earthquake, the effects of which could shake our Earth and destinies, down through Time, to their very foundations. With the death of that one cave-man, a billion others yet unborn are throttled in the womb. Perhaps Rome never rises on its seven hills. Perhaps Europe is forever a dark forest, and only Asia waxes healthy and teeming. Step on a mouse and you crush the Pyramids. Step on a mouse and you leave your print, like a Grand Canyon, across Eternity. Queen Elizabeth might never be born, Washington might not cross the Delaware, there might never be a United States at all. So be careful. Stay on the Path. *Never* step off!'

RAY BRADBURY

TASKS

9 The adventure which is written about here centres around the idea of being able to go back in time. It is, however, made clear that there is a danger; if one of the adventurers makes a mistake then the future might be changed disastrously.

Explain in your own words the idea which Travis explains to Eckels.

10 Later in the story Eckels steps off the path. What do you think happens? Continue the story from the point where Eckels steps off the path.

Send a Postcard

(1 hour)

In the classbook chapter on *Travel and Adventure* we presented you with a variety of photographs to use as a stimulus for your own writing.

TASK

11 Find a postcard or a photograph from a magazine or a photograph of your own to use as the basis for a piece of your own writing.

You might choose to write:
- a story;
- a description;
- a poem;
- a short play;
- an article.
– the choice is yours.

Coming to England

(1 hour)

In the poem which is printed on the next page Zulfikar Ghose describes how when he was young he travelled with his family from one place to another, finally ending up in England.

Coming to England

My father moved house the day I was born
(Mother must've been swift as a kangaroo)
Like a bird that has gathered stalks of corn
For its nest and found its time to migrate.
I arrived early and father was late
And mother was busy as a sparrow.

Two years passed and I hadn't said a word
When cart-wheels creaked outside the door.
Out came the beds, the pots and pans, and, Lord!
We were moving house again. We ran out,
In seven years, of houses in Sialkot.
Now it was autumn, the rains had stopped, so

We did the next best thing and followed the birds
A thousand miles south to Bombay. The sea
Was warm, the hills were green, and our cupboards
Were full of meat and milk. So, shrewd as a mouse,
Father bought land and planned to build a house.
Four acres it was with a mango-tree.
The world war ended, the price of land rose,
But down went father's Import & Export,
And down went, too, 'The Plans of Mr Ghose'.
The sea was blue, the horizons were pale,
Father stroked his paunch that bulged like a whale's.
Trains end in Bombay, Bombay is a port:

We thought of Brazil, we thought of Uganda,
But England, O England, it had to be.
Mother dragged me along as a child her panda,
We took the next ship to Tilbury Docks.
It was spring in London, I saw flocks
Of birds alight upon tree after tree.

ZULFIKAR GHOSE

TASK

12 Write in detail about this poem.

You should make sure that you mention the following in your writing:
- what the poem is about;
- what form the poem takes (what it looks like on the page and how easy it is to read);
- the poet's use of language and how effective you think it is;
- what you think of the poem.

What's on the Menu?

(1 hour)

In the classbook chapter on this theme we used a meal in France as the basis for some work. Printed below is a section from a guidebook to Greece which tells you something about Greek food.

What's on the Menu?

Moussaka, taramosalata and kebabs are Greek dishes often included in modern cookery books. Greece lies on the edge of the Middle East and 400 years of Turkish rule have left their mark in the kitchen. Many recipes which the Greeks have come to think of as their own were in fact introduced by the Turks.

Eating in Greece is usually a family affair, with everyone from granny to the latest addition to the family present. The mild climate makes it possible to eat outside for much of the year.

For breakfast there is coffee for adults and hot goat's milk for children, bread with jam or honey and sometimes cake. In many villages a goat is kept specially to provide milk for the children.

A mid-morning snack of bread, tomato and cheese is followed by a light lunch at about 2 pm. The evening meal, served as late as 10 pm, has a wider variety of dishes.

Greek main meals start with an appetiser, like *dolmades* (vine leaves stuffed with mince and rice), *taramosalata* (fish roe paste), *oktapodhi* (octopus) or *kalamarakia* (squid), *tzatziki* (yogurt and cucumber) or olives. The main course may be a Greek speciality (*moussaka*), meat (steak, chicken or lamb), seafood (squid fried in batter) or fish. In many restaurants you are invited into the kitchen to choose your own fish. Greeks are prepared to pay well for good fresh fish and expect the best. *Greek* or *country salad* is served as a side dish. It includes onion, tomatoes, olives and *feta*, a strong-smelling, soft goat's milk cheese, and has an olive oil and lemon dressing.

Potatoes and vegetables are served separately.

No Greek could possibly eat a meal without bread, which is delicious, hot from the baker's oven.

Desserts may be pastries, flavoured with almonds and oozing honey – triangular-shaped *bakhlava* or *kataïfi* (rolls of shredded pastry). The fresh fruit – oranges, grapes, figs, melons, peaches and apricots – has the juicy sweetness of fruit ripened in the sun.

Drinking is an important part of a meal. People often take a glass of *ouzo* as an appetiser. It is a strong aniseed-based aperitif distilled from crushed grape stems. During the meal wine or beer is served. There are many wines in Greece, one of the specialities being *retsina*, which is strongly flavoured with pine resin. Demestika or Santa Laura are well known unresinated (*aretsinoto*) red and white table wines which visitors may find more to their taste than *retsina*. Greek beer is light and pleasant, and soft drinks are easily available. If these do not appeal, try the pure water, of which the Greeks are very proud.

To round off a meal coffee is served, usually accompanied by a glass of water. The coffee comes in tiny cups and is very black. It is another inheritance from the Turks, but the Greeks do not appreciate reminders of centuries of occupation. So do not call it Turkish coffee by mistake!

ANTONY SELWYN

TASK

13 You are travelling in Greece and you have been invited for a meal by a Greek family you have met. They are determined that you will have a typically Greek meal and you are very doubtful of some of the dishes which arrive.

Write about the meal using information from the passage you have read. You may write either a piece of continuous prose or a play script.

Write Your Own Adventure Story

(1 hour)

TASK

14 You have read quite a lot of stimulus material in this chapter which might have given you some ideas for your own writing. You might be naturally adventurous and spend at least part of your life dreaming of some great adventure. You might have been lucky enough to have had a great adventure. Someone you know, an elderly relative for instance, might have told you about a terrific adventure which they had.

Put your ideas together and write an adventure story for 11-year-olds. Make sure that the style of the writing is suitable for your target audience.

Write An Essay On Your Own

(2 hours)

Write an essay or a composition using one of the following titles. There is no right or wrong approach to the titles but you should plan your writing carefully and you may well improve your work by writing a first and second draft. (Remember your teacher might read your first draft and give you some tips on how to improve it, but someone at home could also help you by reading it and saying constructively what they think of it.)

- 'Survival of the fittest!'
- A Survival Kit.
- Against the odds.
- No-one thought they could possibly survive …
- A Survival Plan.

After the First Death

(1 hour)

You will find printed below the extract from *After the First Death* which you have already encountered in your classbook. Read it again to remind yourself of it.

After the First Death

Okay. She wasn't panicky. She listened to the boy, telling herself to be sharp, alert, on her toes, cheerleading herself onward. She knew the boy's name was Miro and the man was Artkin. She'd heard them exchanging names a few moments ago, and somehow the realisation that they had names restored a sense of normality to the situation, reduced the degree of terror that had engulfed her during the bus ride to the bridge. Miro, Artkin was much better then the boy, the man, rendering them human. And yet what this boy named Miro was telling her now was inhuman, a horror story. The child was dead.

'Murdered,' she said, the word leaping to her lips, an alien word she had never uttered before in its real meaning.

'Not murder, miss,' the boy said. 'It was an accident. We were told the drugs were safe, but this boy died.'

'Does this mean the other kids are in danger, too?'

'No. We have checked them all – you can see for yourself – and they are normal. Perhaps this boy had a weak heart. Or he was allergic to the drugs.' He pronounced 'allergic' as three separate words.

Kate turned to look at the children. They were still subdued, although some yawned and stirred restlessly in their seats.

'We want you to help us with the children,' the boy said. 'Take care of them. See to their needs. This will convince you that we mean them no harm.'

'How long are we going to be here?' she asked. She nodded towards the man, who was going from seat to seat, touching the children, their foreheads, their cheeks, speaking to them gently and soothingly. 'He said it would be all over when we reached the bridge.'

Miro thought fast. 'We have had a change of plans. Because of the death of the boy. We will be here a bit longer.'

'How long?' she asked, pressing on, sensing a sudden uncertainty in the boy.

He shrugged. 'No one knows, really. A few

hours ...'

At that moment, a noise at the door claimed her attention. The big lumbering man who had forced open the door with a crowbar was back at the door again. He shattered the windows in the door with a rock.

'What's he doing?' she asked.

The man broke the glass with a glowering intensity, looking neither at the girl nor the Miro.

'He is breaking the glass to put a lock on the door so that it cannot be opened with the handle there,' Miro said.

Her glance went automatically to the emergency door on the left halfway down the bus. The boy did not miss the direction her eyes had taken. He did not smile; he seemed incapable of smiling. But his eyes brightened. 'The emergency door will be locked with a clamp,' he said. 'And the windows – we will seal the windows shut. It is useless to think of escaping.'

She felt mildly claustrophobic and also transparent, as if the boy could see right into her mind. Turning away, she saw the man standing now at the set where the dead boy lay. She wondered which child was dead and yet, in a way, she didn't want to know. An anonymous death didn't seem so terrible. She didn't really know any of the children, anyway, although their faces were familiar from the few times she'd substituted for her uncle. She'd heard them call each other by name – Tommy, Karen, Monique. But she couldn't place names with faces.

'May I see the child?' she asked. And realised she didn't really want to see the child. Not a dead child. But she felt it was her responsibility to see him, to corroborate the fact of his death.

Miro paused.

'What is your name?' he asked.

'Kate. Kate Forrester.'

'My name is Miro,' he said. He realised that this was perhaps the first time he had ever introduced himself to anyone. Usually, he was anonymous. Or Atkin would say 'The boy's name is Miro' when they encountered strangers.

Kate pretended that she hadn't learned his name earlier. 'And your friend's name?' she asked.

'Artkin,' he said.

The huge man outside the bus was now testing the lock. Kate didn't care to know his name. His name would only establish his existence in her life, and he was so ugly and menacing that she didn't want to acknowledge him at all. She glanced at the van and saw the black fellow at the wheel, staring into space, as if in a dream world of his own, not really here in the van, on the bridge.

'Please,' Kate said. 'May I see the child?'

Miro shrugged. 'We are going to be together for a while on this bus. You should call me Miro and I should call you Kate.' Miro found the words difficult to say, particularly to a girl and an American girl at that. But Artkin had told him to win her confidence.

The girl didn't answer. Miro, flustered, turned away and then beckoned her to follow him. He led her to the centre of the bus. 'She wants to see him,' he told Artkin.

Kate drew a deep breath and looked down. The child lay still, as if asleep. His pallor had a bluish tint. Miro also looked, seeing the child from the girl's viewpoint, wondering what she thought. Had she ever seen a dead person before? Probably not; not in her well-scrubbed American world. The girl shuddered slightly. 'Come,' Miro said. She looked grateful as she turned away from the child. At least she had not fainted. Her flesh was pale, however, and this somehow made her blond hair more pronounced, more radiant. He realised that American boys would consider her beautiful.

Artkin accompanied them to the front of the bus.

'What happens now?' Kate asked. Would she ever forget that blue child on the bus seat?

'As far as your part is concerned, miss,' Artkin said, 'it will consist mostly of waiting. For a few hours. We have sent messages and are waiting for a reply. Meanwhile, you will care for the children. They will be awakening soon. I want you to reassure them. Most of all, keep them in control, keep them quiet.'

ROBERT CORMIER

TASK

1 Write a story of your own entitled 'The Hijacking'. As well as telling a good exciting story concerned with the survival of the people involved, concentrate on making the reader feel sympathy either for the hostages or for the hijackers.

Poetry

(2 hours)

Printed below are two poems which look at the issue of nuclear warfare and man's survival from different points of view.

Icarus Allsorts

'A meteorite is reported to have landed in New England. No damage is said ...'

*A littlebit of heaven fell
From out the sky one day
It landed in the ocean
Not so very far away
The General at the radar screen
Rubbed his hands with glee
And grinning pressed the button
That started World War Three.*

*From every corner of the earth
Bombs began to fly
There were even missile jams
No traffic light in the sky
In the time it takes to blow your nose
The people fell, the mushrooms rose*

*'House!' cried the fatlady
As the bingohall moved to various parts
of the town*

*'Raus!' cried the German butcher
as his shop came tumbling down*

*Philip was in the countinghouse
Counting out his money
The Queen was in the parlour
Eating bread and honey
When through the window*

*Flew a bomb
And made them go all funny
(By the way if you're wondering
What happened to the maid
Well in this particular raid
She lost more than her nose
In fact she came to a close
Or so the story goes.)*

*In the time it takes to draw a breath
Or eat a toadstool, instant death.*

*The rich
Huddled outside the doors of their fallout
shelters
Like drunken carolsingers
The poor
Clutching shattered televisions
And last week's editions of TV Times
(but the very last)*

*Civil defence volunteers
With their tin hats in one hand
And their heads in the other
CND supporters
Their ban the bomb mojos beginning to rust
Have scrawled 'I told you so' in the dust.*

A littlebit of heaven fell
From out the sky one day
It landed in Vermont
North-Eastern USA.
The general at the radar screen
He should have got the sack

But that wouldn't bring
Three thousand million, seven hundred and
    sixty-eight people back,
Would it?

ROGER McGOUGH

No More Hiroshimas

At the station exit, my bundle in hand,
Early the winter afternoon's wet snow
Falls thinly round me, out of a crudded sun.
I had forgotten to remember where I was.
Looking about, I see it might be anywhere –
A station, a town like any other in Japan,
Ramshackle, muddy, noisy, drab; a cheerfully
Shallow permanence: peeling concrete, litter, 'Atomic
Lotion, for hair fall-out', a flimsy department-store;
Racks and towers of neon, flashy over tiled and tilted waves
Of little roofs, shacks cascading lemons and persimmons,
Oranges and dark-red apples, shanties awash with rainbows
Of squid and octopus, shellfish, slabs of tuna, oysters, ice,
Ablaze with fans of soiled nude-picture books
Thumbed abstractedly by schoolboys, with second-hand looks.

The river remains unchanged, sad, refusing rehabilitation.
In this long, wide, empty official boulevard
The new trees are still small, the office blocks
Basely functional, the bridge a slick abstraction.
But the river remains unchanged, sad, refusing rehabilitation.

In the city centre, far from the station's lively squalor,
A kind of life goes on, in cinemas and hi-fi coffee bars,
In the shuffling racket of pin-table palaces and parlours,
The souvenir-shops piled with junk, kimonoed kewpie-dolls,
Models of the bombed Industry Promotion Hall, memorial ruin
Tricked out with glitter-frost and artificial pearls.

Set in an awful emptiness, the modern tourist hotel is trimmed
With jaded Christmas frippery, flatulent balloons; in the hall,
A giant dingy iced cake in the shape of a Cinderella coach.
The contemporary stairs are treacherous, the corridors
Deserted, my room an overheated morgue, the bar in darkness.
Punctually, the electric chimes ring out across the tidy waste
Their doleful public hymn – the tune unrecognisable, evangelist.

Here atomic peace is geared to meet the tourist trade.
Let it remain like this, for all the world to see,
Without nobility or loveliness, and dogged with shame
That is beyond all hope of indignation. Anger, too, is dead.
And why should memorials of what was far
From pleasant have the grace that helps us to forget?

In the dying afternoon, I wander dying round the Park of Peace.
It is right, this squat, dead place, with its left-over air
Of an abandoned International Trade and Tourist Fair.
The stunted trees are wrapped in straw against the cold.
The gardeners are old, old women in blue bloomers, white aprons,
Survivors weeding the dead brown lawns around the Children's Monument.

A hideous pile, the Atomic Bomb Explosion Centre, freezing cold,
'Includes the Peace Tower, a museum containing
Atomic-melted slates and bricks, photos showing
What the Atomic Desert looked like, and other
Relics of the catastrophe'.

The other relics:
The ones that made me weep;
The bits of burnt clothing,
The stopped watches, the torn shirts.
The twisted buttons,
The stained and tattered vests and drawers,
The ripped kimonos and charred boots,
The white blouse polka-dotted with atomic rain, indelible,
The cotton summer pants the blasted boys crawled home in, to bleed
And slowly die.

Remember only these.
They are the memorials we need.

JAMES KIRKUP

TASKS

2 First of all read the two poems and write briefly about each one of them, explaining what you think they are saying.

3 *No More Hiroshimas* describes an area by focusing on details for us to picture. Pick what for you are the three best brief descriptions. Write them down and say why you think they are particularly effective.

4 *Icarus Allsorts* uses humour to get its message across. Pick out three of the humorous ideas. Write them down and say if you find the humour effective. You might like to try to explain the title.

5 In each case the poet is concerned about the survival of the world. Which of them do you consider more successful in getting his message across? Give reasons for your opinion.

Tugs Rescue Beached Ferry

(2 hours)

Printed below is a front-page story and an inside-page analysis of the same story from *The Independent* on Thursday 21 September 1995. They tell the story of a cross–channel ferry which became lodged on the beach at Calais, having gone off course. Perhaps the most important thing about the story is that everything turned out well and everyone survived.

Cause of accident a mystery after 250 spend 23 hours on stranded vessel

Tugs Rescue Beached Ferry

NEARLY 250 passengers and crew arrived safely in Calais last night after spending 23 hours stranded on a beached ferry just outside the entrance to port.

The 18,500-ton *Stena Challenger* was floated at the second attempt at high tide when an ocean-going tug turned the ship's stern into the wind and towed her off the beach.

An attempt 12 hours earlier to shift the ferry failed as the vessel was buffeted by huge waves which proved too strong for a smaller tug to pull the four-year-old ship off the gently-sloping sands.

There were few clues on the cause of the accident. Earlier reports that an engine failure had caused the incident were discounted by Stena, leaving two possible explanations – a steering failure or a navigational error by the captain.

Senior ferry company executives, aware of the public relations implications in view of growing popularity of the Channel Tunnel, spent the day

Ian MacKinnon in Calais
Christian Wolmar
in London

frantically trying to ensure the comfort of the passengers. They were in no danger although some grew angry at their enforced stay on the ship which was tantalisingly close to the beach.

A helicopter dropped blankets, mattresses and pillows on to the ship in case the passengers and crew had to spend a second night aboard. Several dozen mobile phones were also sent aboard to allow them to contact relatives.

Even though there were no casualties, the incident has reawakened the controversy over the safety of roll-on, roll-off ferries which have been involved in a series of disasters in recent years. The International Maritime Organisation is due to report in November on safety improvements which it will recommend as a result of the *Estonia* disaster in the Baltic last year in which 900 people died.

Last night, an unlikely carnival atmosphere enveloped the beach near Calais as hundreds of locals turned out to watch the rescue operation. Parents and children clambered over sand dunes on to the beach to get the best view of the bizarre spectacle of the giant ferry stuck in the sand yards from where they stood.

The ship was finally freed by one large tug, with five smaller vessels standing by, at high tide at 9pm local time, ending an ordeal which began at 10.30 on Tuesday night.

The 160-metre long ferry, which can carry up to 500 passengers, had left Dover in heavy seas little more than an hour earlier with her crew of 73 and 172 travellers.

The ship, with a British captain in charge, should have entered the French port along a dredged channel which can be as little as 12 metres deep at low tide.

But for some reason which may only be explained once the Department of Transport and French maritime authorities have carried out their own mandatory investigations, the *Challenger* was beached in the fierce north-easterly winds. Because of the ferocity of the waves which battered the port side of the ship, washing over the superstructure, it was decided that the safest option was to leave the passengers on board while rescue attempts were plotted.

Ballast tanks were filled to ensure that the vessel's flat-bottomed hull remained firmly on the beach.

As daylight broke over the scene yesterday morning, it was an eerie sight with the huge ship sitting almost high and dry with the lights on, but no passengers visible.

The first attempt to pull the ship off came at about 7.30 am, during high tide, after a helicopter dropped lines to the ship and then to five tugs which had been positioned nearby.

However, with the severity of the conditions, only one of the towing lines was attached by the time the tide was at its highest and, even with the ship's engines on full power, it was only possible to free the stern, pulling the vessel around to sit at 90 degrees to the beach.

With that failure Stena declared the vessel 'open salvage' to encourage suitable equipped tugs to come to the area quickly to facilitate the rescue at a cost which will be fixed later by an independent arbitrator.

In the afternoon, each passenger – there was only one child aboard – was interviewed by the crew to determine how much they had been inconvenienced and discover how much compensation would be appropriate, as well as seeing if they had any other special dietary or medical needs.

Apart from the food and bedding which was sent aboard, new videos were also dropped to supplement the efforts of the entertainer already on the ship for the crossing.

Gareth Cooper, Stena's managing director, said that the company was doing everything in its power to make the passengers' ordeal as bearable as possible.

Ferry 'Safest Place' for 172 Passssengers

THE 172 passengers aboard the stricken *Stena Challenger* were not evacuated from the ferry while it was beached because of the dangers involved in such procedures.

There are three ways of getting people off the ship, but Jim Hannah, a Stena spokesman, admitted that all three 'posed perils' for the passengers.

'There was a risk of personal injury', he said.

Although the ferry is fitted with lifeboats which can be

Christian Wolmar
Transport correspondent

lowered from their davits, this would have been a very perilous operation because of the strong waves running onto the beach where the ship was grounded. Mr Hannah said: 'It is much easier to evacuate in the middle of the Channel in a relatively predictable sea.'

The second method involves the use of large chutes on which people, wearing life-

jackets, slide into the sea and are then picked up by boats or inflatables. This has obvious dangers as well as resulting in those rescued getting very wet.

Alternatively, the passengers could have been winched off by helicopter. This too, has obvious risks and would also have been very lengthy since the passengers would have had to be taken off one by one.

Shipping experts agreed with the ferry captain's

decision to leave the passengers on the ship. Richard Clayton, news editor of *Fair Play,* a magazine for the shipping industry, said: 'The big danger with these "ro-ro" ferries is when they get holed. They get water on the car deck and capsize quickly. But in this case, there was no damage and the passengers were not at risk, so the captain was right to leave them there. The safest place is the ship.'

In a report published earlier this summer, the all-party Commons committee on transport expressed concerns about the lack of practice for evacuation procedures.

The committee found that the biggest test had involved a ship loaded with 500 passengers because the ferry companies said that any tests with larger numbers would be too dangerous. The committee recommended that a test evacuation with 1000 passengers should be carried out by coastguards.

Paul Flynn MP, a member of the committee, said yesterday: 'We felt that the procedures were a joke. Apparently when the marine chute was tested with service personnel, many refused to use it because it was so frightening.' He said that while the ferries claimed that the ships could be evacuated

in half an hour, this seemed to assume perfect weather conditions.

Mr Flynn said: 'We felt they could barely muster the passengers together in half an hour, let alone get them off the ship. The ships have been turned into floating super-markets and are a maze with lots of different decks.

'It is no good evacuation procedures being designed for use in calm conditions or in the open sea.

'That's not when accidents happen. They are much more likely to occur near the coast and in bad weather, and procedures must be able to be used in those circumstances' he said.

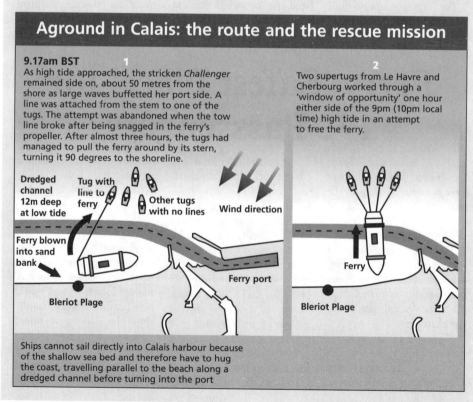

Aground in Calais: the route and the rescue mission

9.17am BST 1

As high tide approached, the stricken *Challenger* remained side on, about 50 metres from the shore as large waves buffetted her port side. A line was attached from the stem to one of the tugs. The attempt was abandoned when the tow line broke after being snagged in the ferry's propeller. After almost three hours, the tugs had managed to pull the ferry around by its stern, turning it 90 degrees to the shoreline.

Dredged channel 12m deep at low tide

Tug with line to ferry

Other tugs with no lines

Wind direction

Ferry blown into sand bank

Ferry port

Bleriot Plage

2

Two supertugs from Le Havre and Cherbourg worked through a 'window of opportunity' one hour either side of the 9pm (10pm local time) high tide in an attempt to free the ferry.

Ferry

Bleriot Plage

Ships cannot sail directly into Calais harbour because of the shallow sea bed and therefore have to hug the coast, travelling parallel to the beach along a dredged channel before turning into the port

Damaging Blow in Battle for Channel Trade

Eurotunnel could benefit from ferry accident, says **Christian Wolmar**

YESTERDAY'S grounding of a cross-Channel ship could not have come at a worst time for the ferry industry.

The ferry companies are locked in a fierce war with the Channel tunnel which has just come into full operation and is battling for market share. Far from reducing their number of ships, the ferry companies have increased them in a seemingly suicidal contest that seems bound to result in massive losses for all concerned.

Already faced with this unexpectedly sharp competition, Eurotunnel, which owns and operates the tunnel, is teetering on the brink of bankruptcy, having stopped interest payments to its banks last week.

Safety considerations have been a key factor in many people's choice of travel arrangements, and the ferry companies are still suffering from the effect of disasters such as the *Herald of Free Enterprise* in 1987 and the *Estonia* last year. Most recently, the inadequacy of safety and evacuation procedures was highlighted when the catamaran *St Malo* ran aground in Jersey and 58 people were injured while being evacuated.

The repercussions of the *Estonia* in which 900 people died almost exactly a year ago after the bow doors were stoved in by heavy seas, are still being felt. The International Maritime Organisation is due to report in November on the safety of roll-on-roll-off ferries and is likely to recommend the fitting of lateral bulkheads to prevent water swilling through-out the car deck, which caused vessels to capsize rapidly.

The industry, having long resisted their introduction of bulkheads – even after the *Herald* disaster when the ship capsized in a matter of minutes resulting in 193 deaths – now accepts they are inevitable and, despite earlier protests, say that they will not slow down operation.

The IMO report may also recommend the addition of spontoons to the outside of ships – a kind of metal balloon intended to make them more stable.

Currently, ferries have several years to comply with the 'Safety of Lives at Sea' 90 regulations, drawn up in the wake of the *Herald* disaster and which specify that ships must be able to remain up-right for 45 minutes after a collision. Most ferries now comply with the rules, which are bound to be updated by the new IMO report.

Eurotunnel has long complained that over-stringent safety requirements has led to massive extra costs, deterring people from travelling on what is inherently a safer form of transport. Eurotunnel also complains that while it has had to produce a 'safety case' detailing procedures in every imaginable emergency, the ferry companies do not have to do so.

TASKS

6   First of all look carefully at the ways in which the articles are written. Look at the vocabulary which is used. Look at what is quoted. Do you think it is a fair report or do you think any of the writers are trying to persuade you to a particular point of view? Explain what you think.

7   Imagine that you were one of the passengers on the ferry. Use the information in the articles and write your story.

8   One of the articles is headed 'Damaging blow in battle for Channel trade'. You are the public relations officer for Stena Sealink. You are being interviewed on the television news. Write the interview, both the questions asked by the interviewer and your replies. (Remember you must use the facts accurately but you do not want passengers to swap to using the Channel Tunnel.)

Balloon Going Down!

(1 hour)

Mike, John and Debra are having a quiet early morning ride in a hot air balloon when everything begins to go wrong. The problem is the weather which deteriorates. For a time it looks as though they are not going to survive. The miracle is that they do.

Printed below is an extract from an account of their experience.

Rescue

'The weather's getting too tricky,' said Mike. 'We're going to have to take her down.' It was just past 8 am. He began a gradual, controlled descent by allowing the heated air in the balloon to cool. Then he pointed into the distance. 'See that big field just past the motorway?' he said. 'We'll set down there.'

Debra peered towards the road and the field. What she saw made her gasp. 'Mike,' she said nervously, 'You *do* see those power lines? We're getting pretty close!'

'Yes, I have the lines,' Mike replied calmly. He'd noted the wires before selecting the landing site. Towering at 100 feet, the lines ran parallel to the motorway. To touch down immediately after passing over them, he'd have to cut it a little close. But the weather was worsening, and good landing sites were scarce. At their current descent angle the gondola should clear the top wire by at least 20 feet. Mike radioed his landing plans to Nancy in the chase van.

Just then another down draught shook the balloon. The electricity cables were now less than 100 yards ahead. Mike powered the double-burner back-up system in an attempt to rise over the wires, but the balloon was in the grip of the down draught. The high-voltage lines were now 50 yards away, with only 10 seconds to impact. Then 25 yards, 5 seconds.

'We're heading straight into the high-voltage lines!' John yelled into his microphone. 'Dear God, please let the end come quickly!'

In a blur of motion, Mike shut down the balloon's propane burners and closed the fuel-tank valves, hoping to avert a fire. He knew that while it was rare for anyone to survive a power-line strike, most balloonist were killed by falling to the ground or by the explosion of the balloon's propane canisters. Mike also knew, however, that the top wire is typically an uncharged shield – or

ground – designed to protect the live lines below it from lightning strikes.

They felt a sickening thud and heard a loud scrape. With a hard jolt the bottom half of the gondola snared the uncharged ground wire knocking Debra to the floor.

'Grab that wire and push it down!' Mike yelled to John. Both men leaned dangerously over the basket's edge and pushed down with all their strength on the wire. Mike hoped to free the gondola from the uncharged wire's grasp and allow them to pass above the charged lines. But the basket kept sinking from its own weight. Eight feet below, the next line carried 138,000 volts.

'We're going down!' John announced to his listeners.

Mike again became a whirr of motion. From a side pouch on the gondola he grabbed a coiled length of heavy nylon strapping. To try to keep them from going further down, he looped it over and over the thick ground wire as it continued to slide up the side of the basket and over his head. Then he laced the nylon strapping through the basket rails, under the overhead propane burners, and around the support poles.

Dazed but unhurt by the initial jolt, Debra – still on the floor – wiggled her fingers and toes just to be sure everything was intact. In the next instant a resounding boom and a blinding flash of light swallowed her in glowing orange, red and white. The brilliant light was caused by an arc of electricity that blasted through the gondola as it touched the charged lines.

To Debra it was as if the world was ending. She was certain she was going to die. She thought of Michael, her husband of 17 years, and their son. *At least they'll have each other*, she told herself.

WILLIAM HENDRYX

TASK

9 Answer the following questions to demonstrate that you have read the passage carefully.

a In what two ways might people die if they are in a balloon and hit an electricity cable?

b Explain the following three phrases:
'gradual controlled descent',
'blur of motion',
'whirr of motion'.

c Explain what is often the purpose of the top wire between pylons.

d Give two examples of Mike's quick thinking during this episode.

e Explain in your own words exactly what happened to the balloon during this episode.

The Raid

(1 hour)

You will see that we have reprinted below the extract in your classbook from *Journey's End*. Read it again, to remind yourself of the situation.

Journey's End

OSBORNE: The colonel came here while you were asleep.

TROTTER: Oh?

OSBORNE: We've got to make a raid tomorrow afternoon.

TROTTER: Oh, Lord! What – all of us?

OSBORNE: Two officers and ten men.

TROTTER: Who's got to do it?

OSBORNE: Raleigh and I.

TROTTER: Raleigh!

OSBORNE: Yes.

TROTTER: But 'e's only just come!

OSBORNE: Apparently that's the reason.

TROTTER: And you're going too?

OSBORNE: Yes.

TROTTER: Let's 'ear all about it.

OSBORNE: I know nothing yet. Except that it's got to be done.

TROTTER: What a damn nuisance!

OSBORNE: It is, rather.

TROTTER: I reckon the Boche are all ready waiting for it. Did you 'ear about the raid just south of 'ere the other night?

OSBORNE: Nothing much.

TROTTER: The trench-mortars go and knock an 'ole in the Boche wire to let our fellers through – and in the night the Boche went out and tied bits o' red rag on each side of the 'ole!

OSBORNE: Yes. I heard about that.

TROTTER: And even then our fellers 'ad to make the raid. It was murder. Doesn't this tea taste of onions?

OSBORNE: It does a bit.

TROTTER: Pity Mason don't clean 'is pots better.

MASON *brings some bread on a plate*
This tea tastes of onions.

MASON: I'm sorry, sir. Onions do 'ave such a way of cropping up again.

TROTTER: Yes, but we 'aven't 'ad onions for days!

MASON: I know, sir. That's what makes it so funny.

TROTTER: Well, you better do something about it.

MASON: I'll look into it. sir.
He goes out.

OSBORNE *and* TROTTER *prepare themselves slices of bread and jam.*

TROTTER: Joking apart. It's damn ridiculous making a raid when the Boche are expecting it.

OSBORNE: We're not doing it for fun.

TROTTER: I know.

OSBORNE: You might avoid talking to Raleigh about it.

TROTTER: Why? How do you mean?

OSBORNE: There's no need to tell him it's murder—

TROTTER: Oh, Lord! no. (*He pauses.*) I'm sorry 'e's got to go. 'E's a nice young feller—

OSBORNE *turns to his book. There is silence.*
What are you reading?

OSBORNE (*wearily*): Oh, just a book.

TROTTER: What's the title?

OSBORNE (*showing him the cover*): Ever read it?

TROTTER (*leaning over and reading the cover*): *Alice's Adventures in Wonderland* – why, that's a kid's book!

OSBORNE: Yes.

TROTTER: You aren't *reading* it?

OSBORNE: Yes.

TROTTER: What – a *kid's* book?

OSBORNE: Haven't you read it?

TROTTER (*scornfully*): No!

OSBORNE: You ought to. (*Reads*):
'How doth the little crocodile
Improve his shining tail,
And pour the waters of the Nile
On every golden scale?
'How cheerfully he seems to grin
And neatly spread his claws,
And welcomes little fishes in
With gently smiling jaws!'

TROTTER (*after a moment's thought*): I don't see no point in that.

OSBORNE (*wearily*): Exactly. That's just the point.

TROTTER (*looking curiously at* OSBORNE): You *are* a funny chap!

STANHOPE *returns.*

STANHOPE: The sergeant-major's getting volunteers.

OSBORNE: Good!

TROTTER: Sorry to 'ear about the raid, skipper.

STANHOPE (*shortly*): So am I. What do you make the time?

TROTTER: Just on four.

MASON *brings in more tea.*

STANHOPE (*taking the mug of tea*): Was Hibbert asleep when you came out of there?

TROTTER: No. 'E was just lying on 'is bed, smoking.

STANHOPE (*going to the sleeping dug-out*): Hibbert!

HIBBERT (*coming out*): I'm ready, Stanhope

STANHOPE: Had some tea?

HIBBERT: Yes, thanks.

TROTTER: I reckon Raleigh'll be glad to be relieved. Rotten being on dooty for the first time alone.

OSBORNE: I don't think he minds.

STANHOPE: I shall be up there some time, Uncle.

OSBORNE: I say, why don't you have a rest? – you've been on the go all day.

STANHOPE: There's too much to do. This raid's going to upset the arrangements of the wiring party tonight. Can't have men out there while the toch-emmas are blowing holes in the Boche wire. (*He drinks up his tea.*) Ready, Hibbert? Come on, my lad.

STANHOPE *and* HIBBERT *leave the dug-out together.*

TROTTER *looks after them curiously, and turns to* OSBORNE.

TROTTER: Can't understand that little feller, can you?

OSBORNE: Who?

TROTTER: Why, 'Ibbert. D'you see 'is eyes? All red. 'E told me in there 'e'd got 'ay-fever.

OSBORNE: Rotten thing, hay-fever.

TROTTER: If you ask me, 'e's been crying —

OSBORNE *is writing at the table.*

OSBORNE: Maybe.

TROTTER: Funny little bloke, isn't 'e?

OSBORNE: Yes, I say – d'you mind? I just want to get a letter off.

TROTTER: Oh, sorry. They 'aven't collected the letters yet, then?

OSBORNE: Not yet.

TROTTER: I'll get one off to my old lady. (*He goes towards his dug-out.*) She's wrote and asked if I've got fleas.

OSBORNE: Have you?

TROTTER (*gently rotating his shoulders*): I wish it *was* fleas.

TROTTER *goes into his dug-out;* OSBORNE *continues his letter.*

RALEIGH *comes down the steps from the trench.*

RALEIGH (*excitedly*): I say, Stanhope's told me about the raid.

OSBORNE: Has he?

RALEIGH: Just you and me, isn't it – and ten men?

OSBORNE: Yes, tomorrow. Just before dusk. Under a smoke cloud.

RALEIGH: I say – it's most frightfully exciting!

OSBORNE: We shall know more about it after Stanhope sees the colonel tonight.

RALEIGH: Were you and I picked – specially?

OSBORNE: Yes.

RALEIGH: I say!

THE CURTAIN FALLS

R C SHERRIFF

TASK

10 The raid is happening. Will Raleigh, Osborne and the ten men survive or will they all die? How will they fight to survive?

Use your imagination and write your account of the raid.

Putting Lives Back Together

(1 hour 30 minutes)

Printed below is an article from *The Times*. Read it carefully.

Putting back together the lives of damaged children

Therapy and caring techniques restore an atmosphere of trust

He shouts, swears, attacks people and smashes things. Parentless, almost from birth, he has by ten years old been passed though dozens of 'care placements' – foster homes and the like – and has been excluded from ten schools. Unsurprisingly, he trusts nobody, *Susan Elkin writes.*

Then there is the 14-year-old girl who, as a response to a minor disappointment, recently stripped naked and ran amok, screaming obscenities.

Seventy such damaged children are being looked after and educated by the Caldecott Community, a children's home specialising in therapeutic care, with an excellent on-site school, near Ashford in Kent. It was founded in the East End in 1911 and has an unbroken record of providing a loving

place of safety for acutely deprived children. Today most Community members are victims of abuse – sexual, physical or emotional – and often all three.

Jonathan Stanley, a former social worker and teacher, is Caldecott's assistant director of education. He oversees the teaching of 70 of the most vulnerable and disturbed children in the country, spanning an age range of 4 to 16.

New arrivals, irrespective of age, start in a transitional nurturing class. There is a comfortably furnished 'coming-together' corner for chats, stories and sharing snack food and drink, prepared in the classroom kitchen. There are also a dressing-up area, sand, water and all the things you might look for in a good nursery.

Mr Stanley says: 'None of these children can play when they arrive. We give them opportunities to learn all the things they've missed. We have to compensate for years of deprivation. Most of the children are educationally at least two years behind, so at first we concentrate on their developmental stage rather than their chronological age.'

Beyond the nurturing classes, the school is conventionally divided into junior and secondary phases. The school staff comprises 11 teachers and 14 special support assistants – these latter 'the bedrock of the school', according to Mr Stanley – and no class is larger than eight. The warm, light-bright and well-equipped classrooms are converted from 18th-century stables. Each table has flowers or a plant on it. 'We set great store by environment at Caldecott,' says Mr Stanley.

The aim is to teach the National Curriculum. English classes work on a different Shakespeare play each term: *Hamlet* this term, *Romeo and Juliet* the last. One stable is a fully equipped miniature science lab with eight work stations, where a science teacher, Perminder Bhamra, relishes the challenge of building pupil confidence and working with their anxieties. She is delighted at how well some of them are doing in their regular tests, too. All the children I saw in school were busily working, and cheerful and polite. The atmosphere was quiet and orderly – an astonishing achievement considering that every one of these children has a long history of bad behaviour.

Children are carefully and caringly escorted to and from morning and afternoon school by staff who take a parent-like personal interest. Children live as valued individuals in single-bedroom households of about ten in the Community's main building: a fine house, with parklands and views.

Soon ten of them will move into the purpose-built New House with its beech staircase, conservatory and rural vista. The children have chosen their own furniture, fittings and decorations: every inch a house and about as far from an old-fashioned children's home as you can get.

Out of school, the children are the responsibility of Babs Seymour, the assistant director of therapeutic child care, who manages more than 80 staff. They look after the children day and night 365 days a year. Emma and Daniel, both nine, entertained Babs and me to lunch. On school days there is a whole-Community midday meal served in a former reception room with classical statues in niches and ancestral portraits on the walls. At other times children and staff eat in their households.

Everyone waited quietly for grace to be said. Daniel asked, as courteously as any prep schoolboy: 'Would you pass the salt, please?' When Emma got bored and a bit silly with her cutlery, she was sharply reprimanded by Tony, 'her' adult. Firmly defined discipline is continuously asserted. Establishing clear boundaries is a crucial part of the healing and learning process.

What does it cost and who pays? Between £50,000 and £70,000 a child a year is paid by local education authorities and social services departments. Capital and development costs are met though trusts, legacies and appeals. It seems expensive, but as Michael Jinks, the director, points out: 'It's a timely investment. If these damaged children are left untended, they will wreak havoc in the future and cost the state many millions in prison and other costs.

'About 80 per cent of approved-school pupils quickly found their way to Borstals and prisons. Few Caldecott "graduates" do.'

Now there is scope to spread the Caldecott method further afield. Caldecott College is an exciting new development half a mile down the road. Under Andrew Hardwick's enthusiastic leadership, the Victorian Paddocks building is being tastefully refurbished. It offers multidisciplinary training, accredited by the universities of Kent and Greenwich, for all who work with young people.

Government ministers would be well advised to take a long look at the Caldecott Community, and to discover the effectiveness of some of its working methods before they proceed any further with reinventing the long-discredited approved school.

TASKS

11 Summarise what the article has to say into a piece of your own writing which is about half the length of the original. Remember that you will have to cut out examples and quotations and concentrate on the facts.

12 You are one of the staff who are helping the children to survive. Plan a talk which you will be giving to a group of businessmen and women to try to persuade them to provide additional funds for the centre. Use the information in the article.

Pride and Prejudice

(1 hour)

Printed below you will find the extract from *Pride and Prejudice* which you have already seen in your classbook and used as the basis for some of your writing. Read it through again and then do the accompanying task.

Pride and Prejudice

'Let me be rightly understood. This match, to which you have the presumption to aspire, can never take place. No, never. Mr. Darcy is engaged to my daughter. Now what have you to say?'

'Only this; that if he is so, you can have no reason to suppose he will make an offer to me.'

Lady Catherine hesitated for a moment, and then replied, 'The engagement between them is of a peculiar kind. From their infancy, they have been intended for each other. It was the favourite wish of his mother, as well as of hers. While in their cradles, we planned the union: and now, at the moment when the wishes of both sisters would be accomplished, in their marriage, to be prevented by a young woman of inferior birth, of no importance in the world, and wholly unallied to the family! Do you pay no regard to the wishes of his friends? To his tacit engagement with Miss de Bourgh? Are you lost to every feeling of propriety and delicacy? Have you not heard me say, that from his earliest hours he was destined for his cousin?

'Yes, and I had heard it before. But what is that to me? If there is no other objection to my marrying your nephew, I shall certainly not be kept from it, by knowing that his mother and aunt wished him to marry Miss de Bourgh. You both did as much as you could, in

planning the marriage. Its completion depended on others. If Mr. Darcy is neither by honour nor inclination confined to his cousin, why is not he to make another choice? And if I am that choice, why may not I accept him?'

'Because honour, decorum, prudence, nay, interest, forbid it. Yes, Miss Bennet interest; for do not expect to be noticed by his family or friends, if you wilfully act against the inclinations of all. You will be censured, slighted, and despised, by every one connected with him. Your alliance will be a disgrace; your name will never even be mentioned by any of us.'

'These are heavy misfortunes,' replied Elizabeth. 'But the wife of Mr. Darcy must have such extraordinary sources of happiness necessarily attached to her situation, that she could, upon the whole, have no cause to repine.'

'Obstinate, headstrong girl! I am ashamed of you! Is this your gratitude for my attentions to you last spring? Is nothing due to me on that score?

'Let us sit down. You are to understand, Miss Bennet, that I came here with the determined resolution of carrying my purpose; nor will I be dissuaded from it. I have not been used to submit to any person's whims. I have not been in the habit of brooking disappointment.'

'That will make your ladyship's situation at

present more pitiable; but it will have no effect on me.'

'I will not be interrupted. Here me in silence. My daughter and my nephew are formed for each other. They are descended on the maternal side, from the same noble line; and, on the father's, from respectable, honourable, and ancient, though untitled families. Their fortune on both sides is splendid. They are destined for each other by the voice of every member of their respective houses; and what is to divide them? The upstart pretensions of a young woman without family, connections, or fortune. Is this to be endured! But it must not, shall not be. If you were sensible of your own good, you would not wish to quit the sphere, in which you have been brought up.'

'In marrying your nephew, I should not consider myself as quitting that sphere. He is a gentleman; I am a gentleman's daughter; so far we are equal.'

'True. You are a gentleman's daughter. But who was your mother? Who are your uncles and aunts? Do not imagine me ignorant of their condition.'

'Whatever my connections may be' said Elizabeth, 'if your nephew does not object to them, they can be nothing to you.'

'Tell me once for all, are you engaged to him?'

Though Elizabeth would not, for the mere purpose of obliging Lady Catherine, have answered this question; she could not but say, after a moment's deliberation,

'I am not.'

Lady Catherine seemed pleased.

'And will you promise me, never to enter into such an engagement?'

'I will make no promise of the kind.'

'Miss Bennet I am shocked and astonished. I expected to find a more reasonable young woman. But do not deceive yourself into a belief that I will ever recede. I shall not go away, till you have given me the assurance I require.'

'And I certainly never shall give it. I am not to be intimidated into anything so wholly unreasonable. Your ladyship wants Mr. Darcy to marry your daughter; but would my giving you the wished-for promise, make their marriage at all more probable? Supposing him to be attached to me, would my refusing to accept his hand, make him wish to bestow it on his cousin? Allow me to say, Lady Catherine, that the arguments with which you have supported this extraordinary application, have been as frivolous as the application was ill-judged. You have widely mistaken my character, if you think I can be worked on by such persuasions as these. How far your nephew might approve of your interference in his affairs, I cannot tell; but you have certainly no right to concern yourself in mine. I must beg, therefore, to be importuned no farther on the subject.'

'Not so hasty, if you please. I have by no means done. To all the objections I have already urged, I have still another to add. I am no stranger to the particulars of your youngest sister's infamous elopement. I know it all; that the young man's marrying her, was a patched-up business, at the expense of your father and uncles. And is such a girl to be my nephew's sister? Is her husband, is the son of his late father's steward, to be his brother? Heaven and earth! – of what are you thinking? Are the shades of Pemberley to be thus polluted?'

'You can now have nothing farther to say,' she resentfully answered. 'You have insulted me, in every possible method. I must beg to return to the house.'

And she rose as she spoke. Lady Catherine rose also, and they turned back. Her ladyship was highly incensed.

'You have no regard, then, for the honour and credit of my nephew! Unfeeling, selfish girl! Do you not consider that a connection with you, must disgrace him in the eyes of everybody?'

'Lady Catherine, I have nothing farther to say. You know my sentiments.'

JANE AUSTEN

TASK

13 Imagine that Elizabeth writes a letter to her elder sister, Jane, about this interview. Write the letter expressing feelings and ideas in the way you think Elizabeth would do so.

Return with Honour

(45 minutes)

In the classbook you read about Captain Scott O'Grady, an american pilot who was shot down over Bosnia. Printed below is another extract from his book, *Return with Honour*.

Return with Honour

I wasn't particularly hungry; a stomach shrinks fast when you put nothing in it. But this was my fifth day on the run in Bosnia and I had to keep my strength up. So far all I had eaten was a few leaves. Then, as I lay curled up in the undergrowth, I saw an ant crawl by my head. One of those cartoon light bulbs went on inside.

Most insects are edible. I knew that. In some parts of the world they are seen as tasty treats; high in fat and salt, more protein than beef, chock-full of vitamins. In Africa and Asia, the big beetles are especially popular – they're supposed to have a nutty flavour when roasted.

I had never eaten so much as a termite, but now I was on the prowl. The spiders and bees I'd seen didn't perk my appetite. Had I run into a grasshopper, I'd have peeled off its head and legs and wings, all the hard parts, and mucked it down. But though they raised a racket, the grasshoppers stayed out of eyeshot.

Which left me with the ants. They were a good size, with reddish heads and brown bodies. I watched a group of them munching on a decaying worm: Were they fire ants? Would they sting me? I reached out, let one of them crawl on my mittened hand, then squished it and popped it whole into my mouth.

There are honey ants so sweet that children cry for them, but this guy was sour as lemon. I waited for a minute or two, then crunched him up and swallowed. The chase was on for the rest. Within half an hour I'd caught and thrown down another 15.

To be honest, there isn't much bulk to an ant, and the episode was worth more just in keeping my mind occupied than in nutrition. I can't deny, too, that it was nice to be the hunter for a change.

SCOTT O'GRADY

TASK

14 This extract describes the rather repulsive experience of eating ants.

Imagine yourself in this position and write no more than ten lines in which you describe your thoughts and feelings as you crunch your supper.

The Taming of the Shrew

(1 hour)

Printed below you will find again Kate's last speech from *The Taming of the Shrew*. You have already read it in class and discussed what it means. Read it again to remind yourself.

The Taming of the Shrew

Act 5 Scene 2

KATE:

Fie, fie, unknit that threatening unkind brow
And dart not scornful glances from those eyes
To wound thy lord, thy king, thy governor.
It blots thy beauty as frosts do bite the meads,
Confounds thy fame as whirlwinds shake fair buds,
And in no sense is meet or amiable.
A woman moved is like a fountain troubled,
Muddy, ill-seeming, thick, bereft of beauty,
And while it is so, none so dry or thirsty
Will deign to sip or touch one drop of it.
Thy husband is thy lord, thy life, thy keeper
Thy head, thy sovereign – one that cares for thee,
And for thy maintenance commits his body
To painful labour both by sea and land,
To watch the night in storms, the day in cold,
Whilst thou li'st warm at home, secure and safe;
And craves no other tribute at thy hands
But love, fair looks, and true obedience:
Too little payment for so great a debt.
Such duty as the subject owes the prince,
Even such a woman oweth to her husband,
And when she is froward, peevish, sullen, sour,
And not obedient to his honest will,
What is she but a foul contending rebel
And graceless traitor to her loving lord?
I am ashamed that women are so simple
To offer war where they should kneel for peace,
Or seek for rule, supremacy, and sway,
When they are bound to serve, love, and obey.
Why are our bodies soft and weak and smooth,
Unapt to toil and trouble in the world,
But that our soft conditions and our hearts
Should well agree with our external parts?
Come, come, you froward and unable worms,
My mind hath been as big as one of yours,
My heart as great, my reason haply more,
To bandy word for word and frown for frown.
But now I see our lances are but straws,
Our strength as weak, our weakness past compare,
That seeming to be most which we indeed least are.
Then vail your stomachs, for it is no boot,
And place your hands below your husband's foot,
In token of which duty, if he please,
My hand is ready, may it do him ease.

WILLIAM SHAKESPEARE

TASK

15 Write a story about a modern situation in which a wife sets out to tame her husband.

Song of the Battery Hen

(45 minutes)

In your classbook we printed an article about the tiger, which is an endangered species. The chicken is hardly an endangered species but many people disapprove of the way in which it is treated. These people would argue that chickens don't live but merely survive for a limited time.

Printed below is a poem called *Song of the Battery Hen* by Edwin Brock.

Song of the Battery Hen

We can't grumble about accommodation:
we have a new concrete floor that's
always dry, four walls that are
painted white, and a sheet-iron roof
the rain drums on. A fan blows warm air
beneath our feet to disperse the smell
of chicken-shit and, on dull days,
fluorescent lighting sees us.

You can tell me: if you come by
the North door, I am in the twelfth pen
on the left-hand side of the third row
from the floor; and in that pen
I am usually the middle one of three.
But, even without directions, you'd
discover me. I have the same orange-
red comb, yellow beak and auburn
feathers, but as the door opens and you
hear above the electric fan a kind of
one-word wail, I am the one
who sounds loudest in my head.

Listen. Outside this house there's an
orchard with small moss-green apple
trees; beyond that, two fields of
cabbages; then, on the far side of
the road, a broiler house. Listen:
one cockerel crows out of there, as
tall and proud as the first hour of sun.
Sometimes I stop calling with the others
to listen, and wonder if he hears me.

The next time you come here, look for me.
Notice the way I sound inside my head.
God made us all quite differently,
and blessed us with this expensive home.

EDWIN BROCK

TASK

16 Write about this poem.
- What does it say?
- From what point of view is it written?
- What is the attitude of the poet?
- What can be said about the structure?
- What do you think of the poem?

4

WORLDS APART

Lord of the Flies

(1 hour)

In your classbook we printed two extracts from *Lord of the Flies*. You will find the first extract reprinted below.

Lord of the Flies

Here the beach was interrupted abruptly by the square motif of the landscape; a great platform of pink granite thrust up uncompromisingly through forest and terrace and sand and lagoon to make a raised jetty four feet high. The top of this was covered with a thin layer of soil and coarse grass and shaded with young palm trees. There was not enough soil for them to grow to any height and when they reached perhaps twenty feet they fell and dried, forming a criss-cross pattern of trunks, very convenient to sit on. The palms that still stood made a green roof, covered on the underside with a quivering tangle of reflections from the lagoon. Ralph hauled himself on to this platform, noted the coolness and shade, shut one eye, and decided that the shadows on his body were really green. He picked his way to the seaward edge of the platform and stood looking down into the water. It was clear to the bottom and bright with the efflorescence of tropical weed and coral. A school of tiny, glittering fish flicked hither and thither. Ralph spoke to himself, sounding the bass strings of delight.

'Whizzoh!'

Beyond the platform there was more enchantment. Some act of God – a typhoon perhaps, or the storm that had accompanied his own arrival – had banked sand inside the lagoon so that there was a long, deep pool in the beach with a high ledge of pink granite at the further end. Ralph had been deceived before now by the specious appearance of depth in a beach pool and he approached this one preparing to be disappointed. But the island ran true to form and the incredible pool, which clearly was only invaded by the sea at high tide, was so deep at one end as to be dark green. Ralph inspected the whole thirty yards carefully and then plunged in. The water was warmer than his blood and he might have been swimming in a huge bath.

Piggy appeared again, sat on the rocky ledge, and watched Ralph's green and white body enviously.

'You can't half swim.'

'Piggy.'

Piggy took off his shoes and socks, ranged them carefully on the ledge, and tested the water with one toe.

'It's hot!'

'What did you expect?'

'I didn't expect nothing. My auntie—'

'Sucks to your auntie!'

Ralph did a surface dive and swam under water with his eyes open; the sandy edge of the pool loomed up like a hillside. He turned over, holding his nose, and a golden light danced and shattered just over his face. Piggy was looking determined and began to take off his shorts. Presently he was palely and fatly naked. He tip-toed down the sandy side of the pool, and sat there up to his neck in water smiling proudly at Ralph.

'Aren't you going to swim?'

Piggy shook his head.

'I can't swim. I wasn't allowed. My asthma—'

'Sucks to your ass-mar!'

Piggy bore this with a sort of humble patience.

'You can't half swim well.'

Ralph paddled backwards down the slope, immersed his mouth and blew a jet of water into the air. Then he lifted his chin and spoke.

'I could swim when I was five. Daddy taught me. He's a commander in the Navy. When he gets leave he'll come and rescue us. What's your father?'

Piggy flushed suddenly.

'My dad's dead,' he said quickly, 'and my mum—'

He took off his glasses and looked vainly for something with which to clean them.

'I used to live with my auntie. She kept a sweet-shop. I used to get ever so many sweets. As many as I liked. When'll your dad rescue us?'

'Soon as he can.'

Piggy rose dripping from the water and stood naked, cleaning his glasses with a sock. The only sound that reached them now through the heat of the morning was the long, grinding roar of the breakers on the reef.

'How does he know we're here?'

Ralph lolled in the water. Sleep enveloped him like the swathing mirages that were wresting with the brilliance of the lagoon.

'How does he know we're here?'

Because, thought Ralph, because, because. The roar from the reef became very distant.

'They'd tell him at the airport.'

Piggy shook his head, put on his flashing glasses and looked down at Ralph.

'Not them. Didn't you hear what the pilot said? About the atom bomb? They're all dead.'

Ralph pulled himself out of the water, stood facing Piggy, and considered this unusual problem.

Piggy persisted.

'This is an island, isn't it?'

'I climbed a rock,' said Ralph slowly, 'and I think this is an island.'

'They're all dead,' said Piggy, 'an' this is an island. Nobody don't know we're here. Your dad don't know, nobody don't know—'

His lips quivered and the spectacles were dimmed with mist. 'We may stay here until we die.'

With that word the heat seemed to increase till it became a threatening weight and the lagoon attacked them with a blinding effulgence.

'Get my clothes, muttered Ralph. 'Along there.'

WILLIAM GOLDING

TASK

1 The opening description here is very effective. Read it through again.

Now think of a world in which you would like to live and write no more than a side of description.

Make your writing as vividly descriptive as you can, paying special attention to the vocabulary you use. Don't be satisfied with your first draft.

Down on the Funny Farm

(1 hour 30 minutes)

Read the article printed below.

The person who wrote this article clearly does not belong on a farm.

Down on the Funny Farm

My husband and I had always dreamt of growing all our own food. Before buying our farm, I imagined myself passing dishes of fresh young vegetables across our table, along with the modest message, 'Our own.' But today the two of us stagger, lugging half-hundredweight sacks of grub to a crowd of 45 fat animals who do little but exist in a digestive trance. How did I, a townie, get stuck running a hotel for idle beasts?

We began with 'our own' garden, a disaster from which we learned nothing. After a season of rotavating, fertilising, putting up fencing and back-breaking labour, we produced the £400 tomato. It was a good tomato – spared by the wild creatures who left their dental impressionns on all the others.

The goats came next. We had always loved goat's cheese and imagined a few dainty goats would supply us with chèvre or feta while cavorting as adorable pets. Thus, I accepted delivery of two demented goat sisters, Lulu and Lulubelle.

While I knew goats didn't simply extrude neat white logs of Montrachet, I had not known that the 'goat person' must become involved with milking platforms, teat problems and, most significantly, sexual liaisons. Goats won't give milk unless they have been mated, and in our town the only billy around was Bucky, a horned and whiskered creature with an odour that seemed visible. On his initial conjugal visit, he and 'the girls' kicked up such a fuss that they did £1,000 worth of damage to the barn before eating the window-sills. The romance was cancelled.

Lulu and Lulubelle occasionally entertain us with a frolic on our front lawn, banging heads and performing a few choreographed moves that recall some Dionysian rite. But most of the time, the girls simply munch and relieve themselves.

Next came the dream of fresh eggs, gathered in the mornings – a dream that gave way to the reality of 38 irritable Rhode Island Reds. After several hundred pounds' worth of chicken feed, there was, one morning, an egg – brown, silky and warm – under the hen who almost took my hand off when I reached for it.

Hens, I learned, are cranky creatures. Even the cock has let us down. We expected him to wake us with his proud crow. But on the Phony Farm (as we call our smallholding), the cock must be roused at noon.

With the chickens came the geese. We ordered them on impulse from a poultry catalogue.

Goslings. The word had a nursery-rhyme appeal. But my five chartreuse-fuzzed baby geese soon quacked and snacked themselves into twenty-one-pound fatties. For a time, I laboured under the delusion they would fly south for the winter. I had seen a documentary, 'The Incredible Flight of the Snow Geese.' But they fly about as well as I do – skidding a few feet down to their plastic kiddies' paddling pool.

I became resigned to running a goose spa, but my husband had other ideas. 'Christmas is coming and the goose is getting fat,' he hissed with a Jack Nicholson glint in his eye. I was appalled. How could he consider roasting an animal that thought of me as Mother Goose?

The goslings had followed me to a nearby pond, where neighbours assured me I could relocate them ('Once they hit that water, they'll never leave'). But when I left, so did they – in single file. I turned around and saw them, their daft grey heads raised above the high grass, seeking only to walk in my footsteps.

I was touched. Their fuzz gone, their voices raucous, the geese have become a kind of repulsive pet. The only male, Arnold, even goosed me when I turned my back on him. The bad news is, they can live to over 30.

Today I buy my 'farm-fresh' fare. I pick up my goose from a high class butcher and find free-range eggs and natural goat's cheese at the delicatessen. The eggs cost £1.40 for half a dozen, but they're still cheaper than my own eggs, which cost £170 each if you factor in such costs as hen-houses.

But the best news is that I can roast a goose, baste it, enjoy the smell and know: *It's not Arnold.* Arnold is out in the paddling pool.

LAURA CUNNINGHAM

TASKS

2 Explain why the writer is a failure as a farmer.

3 Imagine that, for a while, you have to live in a world in which you do not belong. (You may be completely non-sporting and find yourself in an outward-bound sports camp; you may find yourself in the middle of the desert when you are someone who cannot cope with the heat.)

Write about one day in your life.

Lessons on the Mountains

(1 hour)

Printed below is a description of how people can learn a whole new way of seeing and hearing things when they are in a completely new environment, in this case on a mountain.

Lessons on the Mountains

Something happens to your mind in the mountains. You are freed from the numbing odour of combustion, alive again to the scents of wood mould and pine. There are spectacular novelties. Thunder shakes you to your bones. Ice cleaves the wordless rock. Waterfalls roar, melting snow gurgles. To see and hear such things is to feel new, to start life again.

It is not just that mountains are unpeopled. Mountains are sensual. There is a sharp outline, vivid texture and the warmth of an unhazed sun. You must exert yourself, if not to keep warm, then to see what lies over the next ridge. Lifting yourself over rocks and fallen trees, you feel the pleasure of muscle telling bone, and rediscover the child's joy of body leading mind. The dappling of sunlight through pine bough becomes hypnotic.

Your analytical mind lets go and an older part of the brain decides where to put a foot or how far to extend an arm in balance. You become incapable of tallying accounts or addressing letters. If you push harder, the mind changes even more. The oxygen-thin air shuts down your cogitative circuits. Your brain cranks out endorphins – chemicals that make you feel euphoric. Mountain climbers grow addicted to this euphoria; it makes them feel like gods. Hikers struggling over mountain passes and fishermen standing for hours in cold streams feel bits of the same elation.

The mind wanders and drifts into the world of spirits. The silence is eloquent. Clouds veil the peaks. Imagination, squeezed by the lack of oxygen, loses its critical edge. Our thoughts ride the winds and we see ghosts wandering. Mountains have always been the roosting place of spirit. The Greeks housed their gods on Mount Olympus. Hindus say the god Siva came down from Mount Kailas. Muhammad saw the Angel Gabriel while meditating on Mount Hira, and Moses received the Ten Commandments on top of Mount Sinai.

Critic John Ruskin held that men ought to be knocked off balance now and then, so the emotions would be 'strong enough to vanquish, partly, the intellect.' What better way to be knocked off balance than to walk on mountains? As playwright John Dennis crossed the Alps in 1688, he spoke of feeling 'delightful Horror' and 'terrible Joy.'

Travellers have flocked to the mountains to discover the sublime, the lofty passions elicited by nature that were evidence of magnificence in God and man. Mountains became places to explore rapture. US President Thomas Jefferson said of Virginia's Natural Bridge: 'It is impossible for the emotions arising from the sublime to be felt beyond what they are here... The rapture of the spectator is really indescribable.'

Mountains continue to be part of the way we find out who we are. They are an opportunity to exert ourselves, to see things in a clearer light, to feel things we have not felt, to explore latitudes not yet drawn on maps. That gives us great joy. That is why we stride over the ridge tops and down the slopes, probing the secrets of wooded valleys and the haughty shapes of summits. We want to open our hearts to the sun, to see the bones inside the clouds. We want to look into the spirit of things and see there hints of our own character.

PETER STEINHART

TASK

4 Think of a place which is very special for you but which probably wouldn't mean much to the majority of people.

In a similar style to the article you have just read, try to describe and explain the place to one of your friends.

1984

(1 hour 30 minutes)

In your classbook we explained how George Orwell imagined a world in his future and the result was *1984*. Re-read the extract to remind yourself of it.

1984

The Ministry of Truth – Minitrue, in Newspeak – was startlingly different from any other object in sight. It was an enormous pyramidal structure of glittering white concrete, soaring up, terrace after terrace, 300 metres into the air. From where Winston stood it was just possible to read, picked out on its white face in elegant lettering, the three slogans of the party:

WAR IS PEACE

FREEDOM IS SLAVERY

IGNORANCE IS STRENGTH

The Ministry of Truth contained, it was said, 3,000 rooms above ground level, and corresponding ramifications below. Scattered about London there were just three other buildings of similar appearance and size. So completely did they dwarf the surrounding architecture that from the roof of Victory Mansions you could see all four of them simultaneously. They were the homes of the four Ministries between which the entire apparatus of government was divided. The Ministry of Truth, which concerned itself with news, entertainment, education, and the fine arts. The Ministry of Peace, which concerned itself with war. The Ministry of Love, which maintained law and order. And the Ministry of Plenty, which was responsible for economic affairs. Their names, in Newspeak: Minitrue, Minipax, Miniluv, and Miniplenty.

The Ministry of Love was the really frightening one. There were no windows in it at all. Winston had never been inside the Ministry of Love, nor within half a kilometre of it. It was a place impossible to enter except on official business, and then only by penetrating through a maze of barbed-wire entanglements, steel doors, and hidden machine-gun nests. Even the streets leading up to its outer barriers were roamed by gorilla-faced guards in black uniforms, armed with jointed truncheons.

Winston turned round abruptly. He had set his features into the expression of quiet optimism which it was advisable to wear when facing the telescreen. He crossed the room into the tiny kitchen. By leaving the Ministry at the time of day he had sacrificed his lunch in the canteen, and he was aware that there was no food in the kitchen except a hunk of dark-coloured bread which had got to be saved for tomorrow's breakfast. He took down from the shelf a bottle of colourless liquid with a plain white label marked victory gin. It gave off a sickly, oily smell, as of Chinese rice-spirit. Winston poured out nearly a teacupful, nerved himself for a shock, and gulped it down like a dose of medicine.

Instantly his face turned scarlet and the water ran out of his eyes. The stuff was like nitric acid, and moreover, in swallowing it one had the sensation or being hit on the back of the head with a rubber club. The next moment, however, the burning in his belly died down and the world began to look more cheerful. He took a cigarette from a crumpled packet marked victory cigarettes and incautiously held it upright, whereupon the tobacco fell out on to the floor. With the next he was more successful. He went back to the living-room and sat down at a small table that stood to the left of the telescreen. From the table drawer he took out a penholder, a bottle of ink, and a thick, quarto-sized blank book with a red back and a marbled cover.

For some reason the telescreen in the living-room was in an unusual position. Instead of being placed, as was normal, in the end wall, where it could command the whole room, it was in the longer wall, opposite the window. To one side of it there was a shallow alcove in which Winston was now sitting, and which, when the flats were built, had probably been intended to hold bookshelves. By sitting in the alcove, and keeping well back, Winston was able to remain outside the range of the telescreen, so far as sight went. He could be heard, of course, but so long as he stayed in his present position he could not be seen. It was partly the unusual geography of the room that had suggested to him the thing that he was now able to do.

But it had also been suggested by the book that he had just taken out of the drawer. It was a peculiarly beautiful book. Its smooth creamy paper, a little yellowed by age, was of a kind that had not been manufactured for at least 40 years past. He could guess, however, that the book was much older than that. He had seen it lying in the window of a frowsy little junk-shop in a slummy quarter of the town (just what quarter he did not now remember) and had been stricken immediately by an overwhelming desire to possess it. Party members were supposed not to go into ordinary shops ('dealing on the free market', it was called), but the rule was not strictly kept, because there were various things, such as shoelaces and razor blades, which it was impossible to get hold of in any other way. He had given a quick glance up and down the street and then had slipped inside and bought the book for two dollars fifty. At the time he was not conscious of wanting it for any particular purpose. He had carried it guiltily home in his brief-case. Even with nothing written in it, it was a compromising possession.

The thing that he was about to do was to open a diary. This was not illegal (nothing was illegal, since there were no longer any laws), but if detected it was reasonably certain that it would be punished by death, or at least by 25 years in a forced-labour camp. Winston fitted a nib into the penholder and sucked it to get the grease off. The pen was an archaic instrument, seldom used even for signatures, and he had procured one, furtively and with some difficulty, simply because of a feeling that the beautiful creamy paper deserved to be written on with a real nib instead of being scratched with an ink-pencil. Actually he was not used to writing by hand. Apart from very short notes, it was usual to dictate everything into the speak-write which was of course impossible for his present purpose. He dipped the pen into the ink and then faltered for just a second. A tremor had gone through his bowels. To mark the paper was the decisive act. In small clumsy letters he began to write.

GEORGE ORWELL

TASK

5 Think of the world as it is now and use your imagination to project forward 50 years or so.

Write a story entitled '2055'.

Russia's Lake Baikal

(1 hour 30 minutes)

Lake Baikal is the largest, deepest body of fresh water on Earth – and its pollution is a great tragedy to those who live on its shores.

Russia's Lake Baikal

'I remember too clearly for my own good,' Sergei Vasiliev said sadly. The slight, gently spoken ship's captain was reminiscing about his career at the helm of the *Albatross,* a scientific-research vessel.

Suddenly he wondered aloud, perhaps for the first time in almost 40 years, whether he could have found the courage to speak his mind that fateful July day in 1954. But the government officials did not ask his opinion of their plan – and to volunteer it would have been unthinkable. Barely a year had passed since Stalin's death, and the dictator's hand still lay heavy on the land.

Vasiliev knew little about the officials, only that they were 'very serious, very powerful men' who had arranged to use his ship for their first look at Lake Baikal in south-eastern Siberia. They were of course, well-informed. All Soviet schoolchildren were taught that Baikal is special.

It is the deepest lake on earth, measuring more than a mile from top to bottom, and one of the largest, 395 miles long by 50 miles wide. It holds one-fifth of the planet's fresh water – more than all North America's Great Lakes combined. And it is so immense that if all its 336 tributaries dried up, its volume – some 5,520 cubic miles of water – could keep its one outflowing river, the Angara, moving for close to 400 years.

At school, these men had traced Baikal's elegant crescent shape and learnt to call it the Pearl of Siberia and the Sacred Sea. Yet as days passed, Vasiliev overheard enough of their conversation to know that they weren't admiring the lake so much as evaluating it, probing its shores for a place to put something.

The officials were convinced that the lake's sparkling-clear, nearly mineral-free water, when run through the pulp of Siberian pines, would produce 'super' cellulose for jet-aircraft

tyres. Some pollution of the Sacred Sea would result. But that was the price of keeping up with the Americans. Soviet leader Nikita Khrushchev is said to have declared, 'Baikal too must work.'

Thirty-eight summers later, Sergei Vasiliev is still haunted by the sight of the Baikalsk Cellulose-Paper Plant. 'Helping to bring that monster to Lake Baikal,' he says, 'is the one great regret of my life.'

I got my first glimpse of Lake Baikal at daybreak in late June 1990, from the patio of a hilltop hotel on the south-western shore. Reflecting a clear summer sky, the lake was luminous and blue, framed against granite crags and evergreens. I had heard Baikal likened to America's Grand Canyon – its scale and beauty too vast to imagine. Renowned Russian author Valentin Rasputin, who has written his best fiction in a cabin by Lake Baikal, once told me, 'Man does not have enough feelings to respond to this wonder.'

I could see ships passing, leaving faint trails of foam. I paid close attention, for I was about to spend the next month on board the *Obruchev,* a 59-foot-long research vessel.

Our group would include Sasha Timonin, a 35-year-old wildlife biologist and the expedition guide, and the ship's first-rate crew: Victor, the self-possessed young captain; Slava, chief engineer; Yuri, his assistant; deck-hand Wovchek; and Galya, the cook. We planned first to explore the remote upper reaches of Baikal – a region rarely seen by foreigners – then work our way south towards Baikalsk and the cellulose plant.

Also on board – in a photograph on the bulkhead – was the hawk-eyed man after whom the ship was named. Vladimir Obruchev, the father of Siberian geology, first came to Baikal in 1888. His conclusion that the lake was formed by faulting of the earth's crust represented the first modern theory of Baikal's creation.

Lake Baikal sits in the planet's deepest land depression, a rift more than five miles deep that has been opening for at least 25 million years. Judging by the thickness of sediment at the bottom, Baikal has been here for much of that time, which makes it the world's oldest body of fresh water – and its most interesting.

'Imagine what science could learn from a 100,000-year-old man,' says Mikhail Grachev, director of the Limnological Institute in Irkutsk, where more than 100 scientists study all aspects of the lake. 'That's what Baikal is like to a biologist – a natural laboratory for the study of evolution.'

Baikal is a living museum of aquatic plants and animals, incredibly rich in life at all depths.

One of its mysteries is how *nerpa*, the Baikal seal, ended up here some 2,000 miles from its nearest relative, the Arctic ringed seal. The most plausible theory, explains seal expert Sasha Timonin, is that they were pushed southwards by advancing polar ice during the Pleistocene Epoch, eventually moving up rivers to the lake.

Fifty-two species of fish and more than 250 varieties of freshwater shrimp inhabit the waters of Lake Baikal. *Epischura baicalensis*, a tiny crustacean, renders the water strikingly clear by straining our algae and bacteria. But water at the southern end of the lake tells a different story. Around Baikalsk, bacteria discharged by the cellulose plant contaminate some 75 square miles of water.

DON BELT

TASK

6   Carry out the following tasks:

   a   Describe Lake Baikal in as much detail as you can.

   b   Explain Sergei Vasiliev's one great regret and the reason why it was allowed to happen.

   c   Explain why the lake exists.

   d   What is special about the wildlife in the lake?

Secrets of A–Grade Pupils

(1 hour 30 minutes)

In your classbook we printed an article which gave advice about work and revision techniques.

We have printed it again below.

Secrets of A-Grade Pupils

Everyone knows about super-achieving pupils. They get excellent grades all right, but only by becoming boring swots, their noses always stuck in a book. They're useless at sport and failures when it comes to the opposite sex.

How, then, do we account for Alex Rodgers or Amanda Parr?

Alex, now a first-year student in natural sciences at Magdalene College, Cambridge,

played rugby for William Hulme's Grammer School in Manchester and Wilmslow Rugby Club. In the lower-sixth form he directed the school production of a Dylan Thomas radio play which he'd adapted for the stage. Alex left school with five A-level grade As.

Amanda, reading English at Bristol University, acted in plays at the Weald of Kent Grammar School for Girls in Tonbridge, played badminton and did aerobics regularly. Yet she still managed to get nine grade As in her GCSEs and three As at A level. The orchestral piece she composed as part of her A-level course was short-listed for the prestigious Boosey and Hawkes music prize.

Both she and Alex won coveted medals awarded to outstanding students by the Associated Examining Board (AEB).

How do super-achievers like these do it? Brains aren't the only answer. 'The most academically gifted pupils do not necessarily perform best in exams,' says George Turnbull, senior administrator at the AEB. Knowing how to make the most of your innate abilities counts for much more. Sometimes learning comes too easily for high-IQ pupils and they never find out how to buckle down.

Hard work isn't the whole story either. 'It's not how long you sit there with the books open,' said one of the high-achieving pupils we interviewed. 'It's what you do while you're sitting.' Some of these pupils actually put in fewer hours than their lower-scoring classmates. The kids at the top of the class get there by mastering a few basic techniques that others can readily learn. Here, according to education experts and students themselves both in this country and the US, are the secrets of A-grade pupils.

1 Set priorities. Top students brook no intrusions on study time. Once the books are open, phone calls go unanswered, TV unwatched, snacks ignored. Study is business; business comes before recreation.

2 Study anywhere – or everywhere. Claude Olney, a university business professor in Arizona assigned to tutor underachieving college athletes, recalls a cross-country runner who exercised daily. Olney persuaded him to use the time to memorise biology terms. Another student stuck a vocabulary list on the bathroom cabinet. He learned a new word every day while brushing his teeth.

Among the students we spoke to, study times were strictly a matter of personal preference. Some of them worked late at night when the house was quiet. Others woke early. Still others studied as soon as they came home when the day's work was fresh in their minds. All agreed, however, on the need for consistency. 'Whatever I was doing, I kept a slot free every day for studying,' says New Jersey college student Ian McCray.

3 Get organised. At school, Ian did athletics, played rugby and was in the band and orchestra. 'I was so busy, I couldn't waste time looking for a pencil or missing paper. I kept everything just where I could get my hands on it,' he says.

Paul Melendres, a student in New Mexico, maintains two folders –one for the day's assignments, another for homework completed and marked. High-achieving pupil Traci Tsuchiguchi has another system. She immediately files the day's school work in colour-coded folders by subject so they'll be available for review at exam time.

Even pupils who don't have a private study area remain organised. A rucksack or drawer keeps essentials together and cuts down on time-wasting searches.

4 Learn how to read. 'I used to wade through heaps of irrelevant material,' remembers Amanda Parr. 'But then I got used to reading quickly; if the first sentence of a paragraph wasn't relevant, I'd move on to the next paragraph.'

'The best course I ever took', says Oklahoma student Christopher Campbell, 'was speed-reading. I not only increased my words per minute but also learned to look at a book's table of contents, graphs and pictures first. Then, when I began to read, I had a sense of the material and I retained a lot more.'

In his book *Getting Straight As*, Gordon Green says the secret of good reading is to be 'an active reader – one who continually asks questions that lead to a full understanding of the author's message'.

5 Schedule your time. When a teacher set a long essay, Alex Rodgers would spend a couple of days reading round the subject and making notes, then he'd do a rough draft and write up the essay. He would aim to finish a couple of days before the assignment was due in so that if it took longer than anticipated, he'd still make the deadline.

When preparing for exams, both Alex and Amanda handled revision in manageable blocks. 'Give yourself about eight weeks,' recommends Amanda. 'Set a small amount each day. If you just sit down to a huge file, you'll never get through it.'

Of course, even the best students procrastinate occasionally. But when that happens, they face up to it. 'Sometimes it comes down to late nights,' admits Christi Anderson, a pupil from South Dakota. 'Still, if you want good grades, you have to make the deadline.'

6 Take good notes. 'Before writing anything, I divide my page into two columns,' says Amanda. 'the left section is about a third of the page wide; the right, two-thirds. I write my notes in the wider column, and jot down the significance of each point on the left. During revision, this is very useful because you can see immediately why the material is relevant, rather than being daunted by great chunks of information.'

Just before the end-of-lesson bell rings, most pupils close their books, put away papers, talk to friends and get ready to leave. Christi Anderson uses those few minutes to write a two- or three-sentence summary of the lesson's principal points, which she scans before the next day's class.

7 Clean up your act. Neat papers are likely to get higher marks than sloppy ones. 'The student who hands in a tidy essay,' says Professor Olney, 'is on the way to an A grade.'

8 Speak up. 'If you ask questions, you know immediately whether you have grasped the point or not,' states Alex Rodgers. Being sure that you understand everything throughout the year makes preparing for exams easier, he says. Class participation goes beyond merely asking questions, though. It's a matter of showing intellectual curiosity.

In a lecture on economics, for example, Paul Melendres asked how the Chinese economy could be both socialist and market-driven, without incurring some of the problems that befell the former Soviet Union. 'I don't want to memorise information for tests only,' he says. 'Better grades come from better understanding.'

9 Study together. The value of working together was shown in an experiment at the University of California at Berkeley. While a postgraduate there, Uri Treisman observed a first-year calculus course in which Asian-Americans on average did better than other minority students from similar academic backgrounds. Treisman found that the Asian-Americans discussed homework, tried different approaches and explained their solutions to one another.

The others, by contrast, studied alone, spent most of their time reading and rereading the text, and tried the same approach time after time even if it was unsuccessful. On the basis of his findings. Treisman suggested teaching group-study methods in the course. Once that was done, the groups performed equally well.

10 Test yourself. Domenica Roman, at school in West Virginia, highlights any points she thinks may be covered in the exam as part of her note-taking. During revision she frames tentative test questions based on those points and gives herself a written examination. 'If I can't answer the question satisfactorily, I go back and review,' she says.

Experts confirm what Domenica has worked out for herself. Pupils who make up possible test questions often find many of them come up in the real exam and thus do better.

11 Do more than you're asked. If her maths teacher sets five problems, Christi Anderson does ten. If the history teacher assigns 8 pages of reading, she reads 12. 'Part of learning is practising,' advises Christi. 'And the more you practise, the more you learn.'

The most important 'secret' of superior students is not so secret. For almost all A-grade pupils, the contribution of their parents was crucial. From infancy, the parents imbued them with a love of learning. They set high standards for their children, and held them to those standards. They encouraged them in their studies, tested them when asked, but did not do the work for them.

In short, the parents impressed the lessons of responsibility on their children, and they delivered.

EDWIN KIESTER
SALLY VALENTINE KIESTER

TASKS

7 Using the information and tips from the article, spend some time devising a work schedule for yourself.

Decide that you're going to stick with it!

8 Persuade your parents to read the article and discuss it with them, sharing your opinions with them.

Flying on a Wing and a Prayer
(2 hours 30 minutes)

Printed below is quite a complicated article which tells the story of a veteran space probe travelling into the depths of space further than any probe has travelled before.

Read the article carefully to make sure you understand it.

Flying on a Wing and a Prayer

Step outside after nightfall and look above the western horizon into the Milky Way. The gaseous blue-green planet Neptune will be hiding among that spray of stars, and spacecraft Voyager 2 will be speeding towards it. On 25 August, in the small hours, Voyager will swing past the eighth planet, its final checkpoint on a four-planet 'grand tour' of the outer solar system. After that, eternity beckons.

Voyager 2, originally designed for a 4-year probe of 2 planets, but still going after 11 years and 3 planets, is a superstar of America's space programme. On occasion, electronics have fizzled and gears have locked, but Voyager's operators have repaired them by remote control, or learned to work around them. Along with sister ship Voyager 1, Voyager 2 has a good chance of surviving to make measurements beyond the solar system, where no man-made craft has gone before.

More than 200 scientists and engineers keep the Voyagers productive. Most work at the California Institute of Technology's Jet Propulsion Laboratory (JPL) in Pasadena, a contractor for NASA. JPL has managed unmanned trips to the Moon, Mars, Mercury and Venus. But it is especially proud of the Voyagers.

They have revealed the sulphur volcanoes of Jupiter's moon Io and the tortured landscape of the Uranian moon Miranda. They photographed Jupiter's titanic storms, and their reports on the strange braids and dark spokes in Saturn's rings sent planetary scientists diving for answers.

Visualise this black-and-white contraption, speeding towards Neptune at more than ten miles per second. Twin whip antennae point outwards to tap planetary radio aurae. A third antenna, a 12-foot dish, points back towards Earth. At the base of the dish is a round tank of hydrazine manoeuvring fuel.

Surrounding the tank is a thick, ten-sided ring nearly six feet in diameter. It holds six computers, a tape recorder, radio, gyroscopes and tiny electric heaters that wink on and off to keep the interior slightly above freezing. Attached to the exterior of the ring is a gold-coated disc offering recorded sounds and pictures of Earth to whatever finds it. (Aliens: set your player to 16⅔ rpm.)

Voyager also bristles with booms. One 43-foot tower holds devices that measure magnetic fields. Another boom carries five scientific instruments on a swivelling scan platform. Two are television cameras. A third boom holds three thermo-electrical generators. Every year, a decrease in radioactive decay of

Voyager 2's plutonium fuel robs it of about seven watts of power.

The spacecraft has suffered other bruises at the hands of time. The worst is damage to a gearbox, or actuator, which rotates the scan platform. As Voyager 2 swung past Saturn in 1981, the activator seized up and caused cameras to gaze off into deep space. Diagnostic work pointed to a lubricant loss in a bearing. The actuator was restarted, but tests indicated it had only 100 or so complete turns before it would fail, crippling half of Voyager's instruments.

'We've used about 99 revolutions already,' says engineer George Cox. Consequently, any proposal to activate the actuator comes under heavy scrutiny. Most of its remaining life is being saved for Neptune.

Like the actuator, the two flight-data computers on Voyager have their problems; twice they've lost chunks of memory because of age. Still, the remaining memory works well enough to compress information coming from the cameras. (This is necessary because of the brief time available for radio transmission – Voyager will zoom past Neptune in about one hour.)

The data compression wasn't needed in the beginning. JPL had to reprogramme the computers in mid-flight. They also had to educate the spacecraft to keep the cameras locked on the planet. Steady time exposures are needed in the feeble Neptunian sunlight. High noon on Neptune is as dim as the last rays of sunset on Earth.

Another problem is navigation. Neptune revolves around the sun roughly once every 165 years. 'It's not even been observed for one complete orbit since its discovery in the 1840s,' says navigation-team chief Donald Gray. Because nobody knows the exact period of its orbit, the team is less sure of the exact moment Voyager will arrive.

They also don't know the precise strength of Neptune's gravity, which will determine how much the planet will warp Voyager's course. Navigators are depending on this warp to send Voyager sharply south after passing Neptune, to pass closely by the moon Triton. Using gravity to set Voyager's course is no afterthought. Without a gravity boost from Jupiter, the trip would have been impossible.

Meanwhile, voyager is maintaining its own orientation. Its principal reference points are the Sun, and the star Canopus. Sensors focused on the two stars keep Voyager stable in flight; when a planet eclipses these stars, gyroscopes take over.

For all its abilities, Voyager needs regular instruction by radio, and herein lies a potentially fatal problem. JPL put two radio receivers on board, but only the back-up works now – and not well. JPL forgot to make a scheduled call to Voyager 2 in April 1978 while everyone was focusing on a Voyager 1 problem; the craft switched over to back-up because it thought the main receiver had failed. Then, 30 minutes after Voyager switched back again, an electrical jolt knocked out the main receiver permanently.

JPL was horrified to find that the back-up receiver had another problem: a short circuit had narrowed the band of frequencies over which it could receive signals. Instead of 200,000 hertz (the width of 20 AM radio stations), the window was 1,000 times narrower. And it wouldn't stay still: heating the receiver just one-eighth of a degree slides the window nearly half its own width. After firing the thrusters for a trajectory correction, JPL can't send long transmissions for two days.

The Neptune encounter promises additional communications difficulties. Voyager will be so distant that radio signals, travelling 186,00 miles per second, will take more than 4 hours to get there. If Voyager falters, a lot of data will be lost before JPL can react. And Voyager will have to send information as fast as possible to include all the scientific results. The on-board tape recorder holds just 100 video pictures, and the imaging team plans 90 times that many. Every second, two typewritten pages of information will have to squeeze through a transmitter with the total power of five CB radios.

Some of this will be accomplished with elaborate computer processing, but it wouldn't be possible without NASA's Deep Space Network, which listens and talks to spacecraft by means of huge dish antennae in Spain, Australia and California. For Neptune, one of those with a good view will be California's Goldstone facility.

Goldstone is a three-hour drive from Los

Angeles, deep in the Mojave Desert. The rotating part of its largest dish weighs 4,000 tons. Recently that dish was widened to make it more sensitive for the Neptune encounter. Covering an area one-third that of a football field, it will try to make out a signal 400,000 million times weaker than the wattage of a digital watch. The feat will require an accuracy of one-eighth of an inch in moving this huge dish.

Besides receiving, the antenna will transmit. The transmission energy – up to 100 kilowatts for Voyager – might endanger anything overhead. Two employees are charged with keeping aircraft out of the way.

After flooding scientists with its bounty, Voyager 2 will plummet into the dark fringes of the solar system at 36,000 mph. With nothing more to focus them on, JPL will shut off Voyager's cameras for ever.

For years, both Voyagers will remain in the solar system. Its boundary, the heliopause, is where the solar wind – the burst of subatomic particles from the sun – is finally lost in random motions of interstellar dust, hydrogen and other particles from the galaxy. Crossing the heliopause, the Voyagers' instruments will give humanity its first direct knowledge of that realm. No one knows where the boundary lies, but the radio equipment will probably start sniffing it by the late 1990s.

The Voyagers might not be working when they get there, though. According to JPL, there won't be enough power to operate the craft by 2017. Manoeuvring fuel will be low, and the spacecraft can't hold steady without it. These obstacles look insurmountable but, given the project's brilliant record, the operators may come up with a way to squeeze out a few more years of life. Finally, cold and inert, speeding on for millions of years, the Voyagers will continue to sail the sea of stars.

JAMES CHILES

TASKS

9   Explain carefully in your own words the journey of the space probe.
You should mention:
- the purpose of the mission;
- the problems which have arisen and how they have been coped with;
- the hopes for what might be achieved.

10   It is at some point in the future. You are a scientist on duty. Suddenly a signal comes through which seems to come from a Voyager space probe. Develop the story.
(Use ideas from the extract to help you get started.)

Watership Down

(1 hour 30 minutes)

Re-read the extract from *Watership Down* which we have printed below.

Watership Down

The next day was bright and dry, with a fresh wind that cleared up what remained of the wet. The clouds came racing over the ridge from the south as they had on the May evening when Hazel first climbed the down. But now they were higher and smaller, settling at last into a mackerel sky like a beach at low tide. Hazel took Bigwig and Blackberry to the edge of the escarpment, whence they could look across to Nuthanger on its little hill. He described the approach and went on to explain how the rabbit-hutch was to be found. Bigwig was in high spirits. The wind and the prospect of action excited him and he spent some time with Dandelion, Hawkbit and Speedwell, pretending to be a cat and encouraging them to attack him as realistically as they could. Hazel, whose talk with Fiver had somewhat clouded him, recovered as he watched them tussling over the grass and ended by joining in himself, first as an attacker and then as the cat, staring and quivering for all the world like the Nuthanger tabby.

'I shall be disappointed if we don't meet a cat after all this,' said Dandelion, as he waited for his turn to run at a fallen beech branch from one side, claw it twice and dash out again. 'I feel a really dangerous animal.'

'You vatch heem, Meester Dando,' said Kehaar, who was hunting for snails in the grass near-by. 'Meester Pigvig, 'e vant you t'ink all vun peeg yoke; make you prave. Cat 'e no yoke. You no see 'im, you no 'ear 'im. Den yomp! 'E come.'

'But we're not going there to eat Kehaar,' said Bigwig. 'That makes all the difference. We shan't stop watching for cats the whole time.'

'Why not eat the cat?' said Bluebell. 'Or bring one back here for breeding? That ought to improve the warren stock no end.'

Hazel and Bigwig had decided that the raid should be carried out as soon after dark as the farm was quiet. This meant that they would cover the half mile to the outlying sheds at sunset, instead of risking the confusion of a night journey over ground that only Hazel knew. They could steal a meal among the swedes, halt till darkness and cover the short distance to the farm after a good rest. Then – provided they could cope with the cats – there would be plenty of time to tackle the hutch; whereas if they were to arrive at dawn they would be working against time before men came on the scene. Finally, the hutch rabbits would not be missed until the following morning.

'And remember,' said Hazel, 'it'll probably take these rabbits a long time to get to the down. We shall have to be patient with them. I'd rather do that in darkness, elil or no elil. We don't want to be messing about in broad daylight.'

'If it comes to the worst,' said Bigwig, 'we can leave the hutch rabbits and bolt. Elil take the hindmost, don't they? I know it's tough, but if there's real trouble we ought to save our own rabbits first. Let's hope that doesn't happen, though.'

RICHARD ADAMS

TASK

11 You have read in your classbook how writers sometimes give animals human characteristics in their stories. Write a story for young children in which you do just that.

You must:
- decide on the animals you are going to use;
- think about a suitable plot;
- think about your audience;
- be careful to use suitable vocabulary and language.

A Poet and His Country

(2 hours)

Printed below is a short article about William Butler Yeats, together with one of his poems. Yeats was an Irish poet who spent much of his life apart from his native country.

A Poet and His Country

William Butler Yeats, Ireland's great poet and dramatist, spent much of his life away from his native country. Yet wherever he was, he dreamed of returning, and drew constant inspiration from the Irish countryside, people and legends. In a letter assuring some Ipswich schoolgirls that the Innisfree of his celebrated poem was a real lake isle, he wrote: 'I lived in Sligo when I was young, and longed... to build myself a cottage on this island and live there always. Later on I lived in London and felt very homesick and made the poem.'

Eldest son of the Anglo-Irish painter John Butler Yeats, William was born in Dublin in June 1865. For several years he went to the Godolphin School in Hammersmith, but spent holidays with his mother's family in Sligo – an area to which he returned time and again in his poems.

From the start of his literary career, Yeats determined to produce distinctively Irish work for an Irish audience. He helped found Dublin's renowned Abbey Theatre in 1904, wrote several plays for the theatre and worked as its production manager until 1910.

For many years Yeats divided his time between London, Dublin – where in 1922 he was elected a Senator in the newly independent Irish Parliament – and Galway.

He was a frequent visitor at Coole Park, home of Lady Gregory, his patron, and later bought a near by ruined Norman castle, Thoor Ballylee, the 'Tower' which features in much of his best work.

Described by T S Eliot as 'the greatest poet of our time,' Yeats was awarded the Nobel prize for Literature in 1923. He died in southern France in 1939 and was later buried at Drumcliff, as foretold in one of his last poems, *Under Ben Bulben.*

The Lake Isle of Innisfree

I will arise and go now, and go to Innisfree,
And a small cabin build there, of clay and wattles made:
Nine bean-rows will I have there, a hive for the honey-bee,
And live alone in the bee-loud glade.

And I shall have some peace there, for peace comes
   dropping slow,
Dropping from the veils on the morning to where the
   cricket sings;
There midnight's all a glimmer, and noon a purple glow,
And evening full of the linnet's wings.

I will arise and go now, for always night and day
I hear lake water lapping with low sounds by the shore;
While I stand on the roadway, or on the pavements grey,
I hear it in the deep heart's core.

TASKS

12 Spend some time in the library and research the life of William Butler Yeats further. Write a short biography of him.

13 Read the poem again, *The Lake Isle of Innisfree,* and write about it, giving your opinion of it.

5

THE WORLD OF WORK

James Herriot

(1 hour)

James Herriot was a vet and a number of his books have provided the basis for a very successful television series.

The extract printed below is from his book *Let Sleeping Vets Lie* and tells the story of an occasion when trying to do his work made him very uneasy.

Let Sleeping Vets Lie

As the faint rumbling growl rolled up from the rib cage into the ear pieces of my stethoscope the realisation burst upon me with uncomfortable clarity that this was probably the biggest dog I had ever seen. In my limited past experience some Irish Wolfhounds had undoubtedly been taller and a certain number of Bull Mastiffs had possibly been broader, but for sheer gross poundage this one had it. His name was Clancy.

It was a good name for an Irishman's dog and Joe Mulligan was very Irish despite his many years in Yorkshire. Joe had brought him into the afternoon surgery and as the huge hairy form ambled along, almost filling the passage, I was reminded of the times I had seen him out in the fields around Darrowby enduring the frisking attentions of smaller animals with massive benignity. He looked like a nice friendly dog.

But now there was this ominous sound echoing round the great thorax like a distant drum roll in a subterranean cavern, and as the chest piece of the stethoscope bumped along the ribs the sound swelled in volume and the lips fluttered over the enormous teeth as though a gentle breeze had stirred them. It was then that I became aware not only that Clancy was very big indeed but that my position, kneeling on the floor with my right ear a few inches from his mouth, was infinitely vulnerable.

I got to my feet and as I dropped the stethoscope into my pocket the dog gave me a cold look – a sideways glance without moving his head; and there was a chilling menace in his very immobility. I didn't mind my patients snapping at me but this one, I felt sure, wouldn't snap. If he started something it would be on a spectacular scale.

I stepped back a pace. 'Now what did you say his symptoms were, Mr Mulligan?'

'Phwaat's that?' Joe cupped his ear with his hand. I took a deep breath. 'What's the trouble with him?' I shouted.

The old man looked at me with total incomprehension from beneath the straightly adjusted cloth cap. He fingered the muffler knotted immediately over his larynx and the pipe which grew from the dead centre of his mouth puffed blue wisps of puzzlement.

Then, remembering something of Clancy's past history, I moved close to Mr Mulligan and bawled with all my power into his face. 'Is he vomiting?'

The response was immediate. Joe smiled in great relief and removed his pipe. 'Oh aye, he's womitin' sorr. He's womitin' bad.' Clearly he was on familiar ground.

Over the years Clancy's treatment had all been at long range. My young boss, Siegfried Farnon, had told me on the first day I had arrived in Darrowby two years ago that there was nothing wrong with the dog, which he had described as a cross between and Airedale and a donkey, but his penchant for eating every bit of rubbish in his path had the inevitable result. A large bottle of bismuth, mag carb mixture had been dispensed at regular intervals. He had also told me that Clancy, when bored, used occasionally to throw Joe to the ground and worry him like a rat just for a bit of light relief. But his master still adored him.

Prickings of conscience told me I should carry out a full examination. Take his temperature, for instance. All I had to do was to grab hold of that tail, lift it and push a thermometer into his rectum. The dog turned his head and met my eye with a blank stare; again I heard the low booming drum roll and the upper lip lifted a fraction to show a quick gleam of white.

'Yes, yes, right, Mr Mulligan.' I said briskly. 'I'll get you a bottle of the usual.'

In the dispensary, under the rows of bottles with their Latin names and glass stoppers I shook up the mixture in a ten ounce bottle, corked it, stuck on a label and wrote the directions. Joe seemed well satisfied as he pocketed the familiar white medicine but as he turned to go my conscience smote me again. The dog did look perfectly fit but maybe he ought to be seen again.

'Bring him back again on Thursday afternoon at two o'clock,' I yelled into the old man's ear. 'And please come on time if you can. You were a bit late today.'

I watched Mr Mulligan going down the street, preceded by his pipe from which regular puffs rose upwards as though from a departing railway engine. Behind him ambled Clancy, a picture of massive clam. With his all-over covering of tight brown curls he did indeed look like a gigantic Airedale.

Thursday afternoon, I ruminated. That was my half day and at two o'clock I'd probably be watching the afternoon cinema show in Brawton.

JAMES HERRIOT

TASKS

1 Explain James Herriot's cowardice in the face of this dog. Give at least three examples of his cowardice during the extract.

2 When the dog is brought back on Thursday afternoon it is seen by one of the other vets. Given what you have read, write your own possibly amusing account of this second visit.

The Carpenter

(2 hours)

You have already studied some poems in your classbook about people working. Here is a poem called *The Carpenter* in which Clifford Dyment writes about his father. The poem is written in quite simple four–line verses.

The Carpenter

With a jack plane in his hands
My father the carpenter
Massaged the wafering wood,
Making it white and true.

He was skilful with his saws,
Handsaw, bowsaw, hacksaw,
And ripsaw with fishes' teeth
That chewed a plank in a second.

He was fond of silver bits,
The twist and countersink –
And the auger in its pit
Chucking shavings over its shoulder.

I remember my father's hands,
For they were supple and strong
With fingers that were lovers –
Sensuous strokers of wood:

He fondled the oak, the strong-man
Who holds above his head
A record-breaking lift
Of thick commingled boughs;

And he touched with his finger tips
Dark boards of elm and alder,
Spruce, and cherry for lathes
That turned all days to spring.

My father's hands were tender
Upon my tender head,
But they were massive on massive
Beam for building a house,

And delicate on the box wood
Leaning against the wall
As though placed there in a corner
For a moment and then forgotten,

And expert as they decoded
Archives unlocked by the axe –
The pretty medullary rays
Once jammed with a traffic of food

To a watched and desired tree
That he marked and felled in the winter,
The tracks of tractors smashing
The ground where violets grew,

The bound in chains and dragged
To the slaughtering circular saw:
A railway dulcimer
Rang the passing bell

Of my father's loved ones,
Though there was no grief in him
Caressing the slim wood, hearing
A robin's piccolo song.

CLIFFORD DYMENT

TASK

3 a Using the ideas from the poem, explain how Clifford Dyment views his father.

   b Pick out three of the ideas from the poem which you find particularly effective. (You might pick out three phrases or even words.)

   Write down each of your choices and explain why you find them particularly effective.

   c Think of a person you know (it might be your father) and write a similar poem about them.

Job Advertisements

(1 hour 30 minutes)

In your classbook we printed a selection of advertisements from the paper called *Appointments*. On the next page you will find some more for you to study.

TASKS

4 The advertisements here are for a variety of jobs. Look at the way in which the advertisements are set out and the language used.

Pick two of the advertisements and write about the layout and language. You should mention:

■ The order in which things are mentioned.
■ The size of the print.
■ The style of the print.
■ What sort of person the advertisement is aimed at.
■ Whether the language used is clear for the target audience.

5 Write a letter of application for one of the jobs.

6 Imagine you are one of the interviewers for the job applied for above. Use ideas from the advertisements to devise three questions which you would ask when conducting the interview for this post.

Fishing for Gold in Ghana

(2 hours)

Here is an article from *The Grocer* about the development of tuna fishing and its marketing in Ghana and the involvement of British firms. Read the article.

Fishing for Gold in Ghana

Clive Beddall reports from West Africa on a multi-million dollar investment in tuna

Last weekend, the people of the Ghanaian port of Tema flocked to the quayside to welcome home their fishermen. But as they clamoured to view the catch borne by scores of traditional wooden canoes which paddle the nearby ocean, a more significant arrival for the economic prosperity of the West African state was taking place a quarter of a mile away.

Next to the container port which serves the capital, Accra, and its well established gold and cocoa exporting business, Ghana's new and rapidly expanding high-tech tuna fleet was set to unload a consignment of skipjack.

The canoes have been paddling in and out of Tema for centuries with supplies of inshore fish to feed the expanding local populace. But the sight of the more modern tuna boats is new. So, too, are the visits by supermarket quality control executives from the UK, France and Germany, as they fly into nearby Kotoka International Airport preparing to buy product from one of the industry's newest producers for Europe.

Until recently, Ghana did not appear on the statistical profile of UK skipjack imports. In the West African region, its tuna packing performance was overshadowed by shipments from the other main areas – the Ivory Coast and Senegal. But since a new initiative by the Star-Kist division of Heinz, its exports graph has been rising. Currently, the annual estimate for the country is some 2.3 million cases (48/halves).

Catering and retail size Ghanaian tuna in vegetable oil and brine under the Heinz label have been listed by UK multiples and cash and carries and now, thanks to a major investment in a cannery at Tema, Heinz-Star-Kist is bidding to become an even stronger player in Europe.

According to the company's own figures, Ghanaian supplies to the UK between last November and October 1 this year, were 474,840 cartons (basis 48/halves). And Heinz is claiming an 8% share of the UK retail market, after two Neilsen periods, for its branded and private label business.

Star-Kist went to Ghana in the mid sixties, setting up a fish procurement base for its Puerto Rican packers. It joined the local Mankoadze Fisheries firm as a joint processing partner in a small tuna canning plant in the seventies, trading as Pioneer Food Cannery. However, in 1987, due to marketing difficulties with MF, increasing competition from Thailand, and industrial worker problems, the US group withdrew support and canning ceased.

But, in October 1990, it reopened Pioneer in an agreement with Mankoadze, funding factory costs, including fish, with the unit paid a per tonne fee for processing tuna loins.

The emergence of today's operation began in 1993 when several important market and wider economic factors combined to make a larger plant viable. The company recognised the potential of Ghana's new investment regulations, and the terms of the Lomé Convention which allows, under certain conditions, the duty-free export of canned tuna into the EU. It also saw the chance to source and produce at low costs, as well as the advantages of a newly realistic exchange rate for the Ghanaian cedi (the local currency). Thus Star-Kist bought out its joint venture partner and began an expansion and refurbishment programme. This started with an initial investment of $16 million in plant and machinery with more recent spends, including investment in tuna boats and fishing equipment, virtually doubling the initial outlay.

Significantly, all product from Tema is prominently labelled 'Dolphin safe', and currently some 70% of the fish is caught by pole and line.

Initially aimed at packing 90 tonnes a day, the plant's production estimate was revised last year to 150 tonnes of skipjack, in an operation employing about 1,800. As a result, during the fiscal year 1996, it is budgeted to produce some 37,500 tonnes, 56% of the total Star-Kist Europe volume. The canner's target for the UK is 700,000 cases in the fiscal year May 1995 to April 1996.

Despite the commodity nature of the tuna business, Ted Morgado, general manager of Star-Kist International's West African operations, claims that his unit enjoys advantages when trading with supermarket buyers.

'We have received a good response from the UK. We enjoy a "plus" in that we are close to the customer. It is three weeks sailing time from Tema to Felixstowe. In addition, we can prove that our fish are canned more rapidly than much of the tuna which is sourced around the world. While some will be packed from fresh raw material, the quantities frozen at sea are in Tema within three weeks of being hauled aboard the vessels, whereas in some regions, fish can remain frozen for months before reaching a cannery.

'For us, it is unlikely to be longer than six weeks from "catch to can", and some Euro buyers have already commented on the fresh taste of our fish compared to other suppliers,' he claimed.

While the world price for tuna has soared to nearly $1,100 tonne (landed Bangkok) – mainly as a result of poor fishing in the massive South West Pacific grounds – Morgado says catches off Ghana have been improving.

But he believes the Bangkok rate must fall soon. Pacific fishing is expected to be better at the turn of the year, and he predicts the world price will fall to $970 tonne early in 1996.

Meanwhile, with the prospect of more European business, Ghana's tuna fishing fleet is being expanded. Some 70% of the cannery's requirements come from the home fleet, with the rest bought from Spanish and French vessels. The Ghanaian percentage will grow as more boats are commissioned, and, significantly, Carnaud metalbox sets up a can making facility nearby.

Europe accounts for the largest slice of the world canned tuna market, with 40%. Thus it was inevitable that Star-Kist, while best known in its home base of the US, should rapidly develop a canning and procurement arm to supply the region. Unconfirmed evidence of its intentions came earlier last year when it was linked with the purchase of john West Foods after the sector brand leader had been put up for sale by Unilever. However, no deal was forthcoming and JWF was withdrawn from the market by its multi-national parent.

Meanwhile, for the first time in the Heniz Corporation's history, it is developing a category management organisation on top of its local sales networks in European markets. Thus Tema has been integrated within Star-Kist Europe, which already includes a tuna and fish processing facility at Douarnenez, in Brittany, from which much of the company's French food market expansion has been developed since if bought the Paul Poulet operation in 1981. Following that deal it has expanded the firm's share of the French canned fish market from 6% to 18%. In addition, in 1983 it bought the Marie Elisabeth sardine packing canneries at Peniche and Matosinhos in Portugal, later closing the latter to develop a single site. Now a fourth wing to the business is being completed in the Seychelles, where Star-Kist is taking a 60% share, and management control, of a cannery specialising in yellowfin.

The group's tuna category director, Arnaud Raillard, says a pan-European strategy pays dividends. 'In these days of due diligence it is important to have an integrated approach – from boat to the supermarket shelf.'

Under Larry Krogsdale, director of operations, this group has established a strong presence across European markets. It has been especially creative in France, building a range of 70 lines with the accent firmly on added value. Now, thanks to Tema, this process is being extended to the UK.

Raillard sees further potential for the group, citing figures which project that, by the year 2000, the total world market will be 167 million cartons, compared with the current 140m. And, significantly, the statistics suggest that Europe will account for the biggest slice – 57m cartons.

He estimates the British trade at around eight million cartons, with the business split between retail, with 70%, and catering with 30%.

In addition, the company is aware of the growth of strong brands in the EU's largest market, Italy, and Raillard hinted that the Star-Kist development in that area will be by acquisition.

There were plenty of smiling faces in Ghana last week. The state president, FL Lt Jerry Rawlings, has been in the US wooing Wall Street with details of his programme for improving the nation's economic performance, and the country has won praise from abroad as it bids to attract more foreign developers to its shores. In addition, its economy is proving to be healthier as the accent on exports broadens from the traditional, profitable areas of cocoa and gold.

Star-Kist is confident that its new European sales initiative will see tuna swimming with the major foreign currency earners.

TASK

7 You work as an advertising executive for the Star-Kist division of Heinz and it is your job to devise an advertising campaign for tins of tuna.

You can use information and ideas from this article.

For instance it would be good publicity to be able to say that the fish are caught by rod and line and thus the fishing method does not harm dolphins.

Your campaign should include:

■ A letter to be sent to retailers.
■ The wording of a leaflet which could be handed out to shop customers.
■ The wording of an advertisement to be placed in several newspapers.

Remember you want to be very positive but you must not criticise rivals in your campaign.

Controversy

(1 hour 30 minutes)

You have already read the story about catching frogs by John Steinbeck. We have printed it below as a reminder.

Catching Frogs

Two hours later they recalled what they had come for. The frog pool was square – 50 feet wide and 70 feet long and 4 feet deep. Lush soft grass grew about its edge and a little ditch brought the water from the river to it and from it little ditches went out to the orchards. There were frogs there all right, thousands of them. Their voices beat the night, they boomed and barked and croaked and rattled. They sang to the stars, to the waning moon, to the waving grasses. They bellowed love songs and challenges. The men crept through the darkness towards the pool. The captain carried a nearly-filled pitcher of whisky and every man had his own glass. The captain had found them flash-lights that worked. Hughie and Jones carried gunny-sacks. As they drew quietly near, the frogs heard them coming. The night had been roaring with frog song and then suddenly it was silent. Mack and the boys and the captain sat down on the ground to have one last short one and to map their campaign. And the plan was bold.

During the millennia that frogs and men have lived in the same world, it is probable that men have hunted frogs. And during that time a pattern of hunt and parry has developed. The man with net or bow or lance or gun creeps noiselessly, as he thinks, towards the frog. The pattern requires that the frog sit still, sit very still and wait. The rules of the game require the frog to wait until the final flicker of a second, when the net is descending, when the lance is in the air, when the finger squeezes the trigger, then the frog jumps, plops into the water, swims to the bottom and waits until the man goes away. That is the way it is done, the way it has always been done. Frogs have every right to expect it will always be done that way. Now and then the net is too quick, the lance pierces, the gun flicks and that frog is gone, but it is all fair and in the frame-work. Frogs don't resent that.

But how could they have anticipated Mack's new method? How could they have foreseen the horror that followed? The sudden flashing of lights, the shouting and squealing of men, the rush of feet. Every frog leaped, plopped into the pool, and swam frantically to the bottom. Then into the pool plunged the line of men, stamping, churning, moving in a crazy line up the pool, flinging their feet about. Hysterically the frogs, displaced from their placid spots, swam ahead of the crazy thrashing feet and the feet came on. Frogs are good swimmers, but they haven't much endurance. Down the pool they went until finally they were bunched and crowded against the ends. And the feet and wildly-plunging bodies followed them. A few frogs lost their heads and floundered among the feet and got through and these were saved. But the majority decided to leave this pool for ever, to find a new home in a new country where this kind of thing didn't happen. A wave of frantic, frustrated frogs, big ones, little ones, brown ones, green ones, men frogs and women frogs a wave of them broke over the bank, crawled, leaped, scrambled. They clambered up the grass, they clutched at each other, little ones rode on big ones. And then – horror on horror – the flashlights found them. Two men gathered them like berries. The line came out of the water and closed in on their rear and gathered them like potatoes. Tens and fifties of them were flung into the gunny-sacks and the sacks filled with tired, frightened, and disillusioned frogs, with dripping, whimpering frogs. Some got away, of course, and some had been saved in the pool. But never in frog history had such an execution taken place. Frogs by the pound, by the fifty pounds. They weren't counted, but there must have been six or seven hundred. Then happily Mack tied up the necks of the sacks. They were soaking, dripping wet and the air was cool. They had a short one in the grass before they went back to the house, so they wouldn't catch cold.

It is doubtful whether the captain had ever had so much fun. He was indebted to Mack and the boys. Later when the curtains caught fire and were put out with the little towels, the captain told the boys not to mind it. He felt it was an honour to have them burn his house clear down, if they wanted to. 'My wife is a wonderful woman,' he said in a kind of peroration. 'Most wonderful woman. Ought to of been a man. If she was a man I wouldn' of married her.' He laughed a long time over that and repeated it three or four times and resolved to remember it, so he could tell it to a lot of other people. He filled a jug with whisky and gave it to Mack. He wanted to go to live with them in the Palace Flophouse. He decided that his wife would like Mack and the boys if she only knew them. Finally, he went to sleep on the floor with his head among the puppies. Mack and the boys poured themselves a short one and regarded him seriously.

Mack said: 'He give me that jug of whisky, didn't he? You heard him?'

'Sure he did,' said Eddie. 'I heard him.'

'And he give me a pup?'

'Sure, pick of the litter. We all heard him. Why?'

'I never did roll a drunk and I ain't gonna start now,' said Mack. 'We got to get out or here. H'es gonna wake up feelin' lousy and it's goin' to be all our fault. I just don't want to be here.' Mack glanced at the burned curtains, at the floor glistening with whisky and puppy dirt, at the bacon grease that was coagulating on the stove front. He went to the pups, looked them over carefully, felt bone and frame, looked in eyes and regarded jaws, and he picked out a beautifully-spotted bitch with a liver-coloured nose and a fine dark-yellow eye. 'Come on, darling,' he said.

They blew out the lamp because of the danger of fire. It was just turning dawn as they left the house.

'I don't think I ever had such a fine trip,' said Mack. 'But I got to thinkin' about his wife coming back and it gave me the shivers.' The pup whined in his arms and he put it under his coat. 'He's a real nice fella,' said Mack. 'After you get him feelin' easy, that is.' He strode on toward the place where they had parked the Ford. 'We shouldn't go forgettin' we're doin' all this for Doc,' he said. 'From the way things are pannin' out, it looks like Doc is a pretty lucky guy.'

JOHN STEINBECK

In your classbook we associated this extract with some topics which involve working with animals and which are controversial. You have already worked on one of these topics in class.

Printed below is the list which appeared in the classbook:

- zoos
- circuses
- animal testing
- blood sports
- export of live animals
- farming – the meat trade

TASK

8 Choose a different topic from the one you chose before and plan, draft and write an essay on the subject.

Just the Job

(2 hours)

A very large number of people at some times in their lives find themselves unemployed.

'Just the Job' is the title of a booklet produced by the Employment Department Group. It is aimed at people who are out of work and it is designed to outline ways in which the unemployed can be helped and can themselves.

Just the Job

Jobcentres

Jobcentres are very good places to start your job search – whether you're looking for your first job or want to get back into the job market after being made redundant.

The first thing you notice is how job vacancies are clearly displayed on cards. You just write down the ones that interest you and, if you want to know more, ask at the reception desk. In fact, our receptionist will have more ideas about where you can look for work in your area such as local papers, local employers, and private employment agencies.

It's worthwhile dropping into your Jobcentre frequently because new jobs are coming in all the time.

And if you have been unemployed for a while there are plenty of other ways Jobcentres can help your job search such as seminars and Jobclubs to boost your confidence, help brush up your interview technique, prepare your cv and plenty more. And you'll have a Client Adviser to talk to about the kind of work you want and advise you about what benefits you can claim while looking.

Jobcentres are run by the Employment Service, part of the Employment Department, to offer you what you need to find a job – it's all here under the one roof.

All Jobcentres are listed in your local phonebook under Employment service or Jobcentre.

Job search seminars

If you're still looking for work after three months a great way to boost your chances is to attend one of our **job search seminars**. These last four days, spread over five weeks, and are a great way to improve your chances of finding a good job.

The seminar looks at things such as the way you come over in job interviews and helps with the practical details of applying for work – such as letter writing, preparing your cv, making calls, typing and even helping with postage. You'll have plenty of time to make use of the services. Attending the seminar doesn't affect your benefit and we'll pay your fares to and from the seminar. During the seminar you'll also learn about any other help that is available locally.

In fact, not everyone has to wait for three months to apply to attend the seminar. People with disabilities, people returning to work, people who have been on Training programmes, ex-offenders and ex-regulars may be able to join before three months.

Jobclub

There are all sorts of advantages in joining a Jobclub. In fact, belonging to a Jobclub is often described by people looking for work as one of the most rewarding and helpful things they get involved with.

For one thing, Jobclubs sometimes hear about jobs that don't get advertised. Secondly, you have direct help from your Jobclub leader on your telephone and interview techniques.

Your Jobclub leader will also help you prepare job applications that really stand out from the crowd. Meanwhile you'll have access to stamps, telephones, newspapers and stationery – free of charge.

And you'll benefit from the support and encouragement of your fellow jobseekers.

Being a member of a Jobclub won't affect how much benefit you receive and your fares to and from the Jobclub will be paid for you. To qualify you need to have been out of work for six months or more. However, you can join sooner if you've been on Training For Work, have a disability, or are an ex-offender, an ex-regular or are returning to the labour market.

TASK

9 You are going to your first meeting of the Jobclub and are rather nervous.

At the meeting there are four or five other people in much the same position as you.

Write about what happens at the meeting in the form of a playscript.

Try to make your characters different, from different backgrounds with different experiences, so that your scene is lively and varied.

(You may go on later to rehearse the scene with others and use it as the basis for a speaking and listening assessment.)

Great Expectations

(1 hour 30 minutes)

Pip in *Great Expectations*, by Charles Dickens, doesn't want to be a blacksmith. Pip has been brought up by his sister and her husband, Joe Gargery, who is a blacksmith and who teaches Pip how to follow in his footsteps. Pip confides to his friend Biddy that he doesn't want to pursue this way of life.

Great Expectations

You are one of those, Biddy,' said I, 'who make the most of every chance. You never had a chance before you came here, and see how improved you are!'

Biddy looked at me for an instant, and went on with her sewing. 'I was your first teacher, though; wasn't I?' said she, as she sewed.

'Biddy!' I exclaimed in amazement. 'Why, you are crying!'

'No I am not,' said Biddy, looking up and laughing. 'What put that in your head?'

What could have put it in my head, but the glistening of a tear as it dropped on her work?

I sat silent, recalling what a drudge she had been until Mr. Wopsle's great-aunt successfully overcame that bad habit of living, so highly desirable to be got rid of by some people. I recalled the hopeless circumstances by which she had been surrounded in the miserable little shop and the miserable little noisy evening school, with that miserable old bundle of incompetence always to be dragged and shouldered. I reflected that even in those untoward times there must have been latent in Biddy what was now developing, for, in my first uneasiness and discontent I had turned to her for help, as a matter of course. Biddy sat quietly sewing, shedding no more tears, and while I looked at her and thought about it all, it occurred to me that perhaps I had not been sufficiently grateful to Biddy. I might have been too reserved, and should have patronised her more (though I did not use that precise word in my meditations) with my confidence.

'Yes, Biddy,' I observed, when I had done turning it over, 'you were my first teacher, and that at a time when we little thought of ever being together like this, in this kitchen.'

'Ah, poor thing!' replied Biddy. it was like her self-forgetfulness to transfer the remark to my sister, and to get up and be busy about her, making her more comfortable; 'that's sadly true!'

'Well!' said I, 'we must talk together a little more, as we used to do. And I must consult you a little more, as I used to do. Let us have a quiet walk on the marshes next Sunday, Biddy, and a long chat.'

My sister was never left alone now, but Joe more than readily undertook the care of her on that Sunday afternoon, and Biddy and I went out together. It was summertime, and lovely weather. When we had passed the village and the church and the churchyard, and were out on the marshes and began to see the sails of the ships as they sailed on, I began to combine Miss Havisham and Estella with the prospect, in my visual way. When we came to the river-side and sat down on the bank, with the water rippling at our feet, making it all more quiet than it would have been without that sound, I resolved that it was a good time and place for the admission of Biddy into my inner confidence.

'Biddy,' said I, after binding her to secrecy, 'I want to be a gentleman.'

'Oh, I wouldn't, if I was you!' she returned. 'I don't think it would answer.'

'Biddy,' said I with some severity, 'I have particular reasons for wanting to be a gentleman.'

'You know best, Pip; but don't you think you are happier as you are?'

'Biddy,' I exclaimed impatiently, 'I am not at all happy as I am. I am disgusted with my calling and with my life. I have never taken to either, since I was bound. Don't be absurd.'

'Was I absurd?' said Biddy, quietly raising her eyebrows; 'I am sorry for that; I didn't mean to be. I only want you to do well, and to be comfortable.'

'Well then, understand once for all that I never shall or can be comfortable – or anything but miserable – there, Biddy! – unless I can lead a very different sort of life from the life I lead now.'

'That's a pity!' said Biddy, shaking her head with a sorrowful air.

Now, I too had often thought it a pity, that, in the singular kind of quarrel with myself which I was always carrying on, I was half inclined to shed tears of vexation and distress when Biddy gave utterance to her sentiment and my own. I told her she was right, and I knew it was much to be regretted, but still it was not to be helped.

'If I could have settled down,' I said to Biddy, plucking up the short grass within reach, much as I had once upon a time pulled my feelings out of my hair and kicked them into the brewery wall, 'if I could have settled down and been but half as fond of the forge as I was, when I was little, I know it would have been much better for me. You and I and Joe would have wanted nothing then, and Joe and I would perhaps have gone partners when I was out of my time, and I might even have grown up to keep company with you, and we might have sat on this very bank on a fine Sunday, quite different people. I should have been good enough for *you*; shouldn't I, Biddy?'

Biddy sighed as she looked at the ships sailing on, and returned for answer, 'Yes; *I* am not over-particular.' It scarcely sounded flattering, but I knew she meant well.

'Instead of that,' said I, plucking up more grass and chewing a blade or two, 'see how I am going on. Dissatisfied and uncomfortable, and – what would it signify to me, being coarse and common, if nobody had told me so!'

Biddy turned her face suddenly towards mine, and looked far more attentively at me than she had looked at the sailing ships.

'It was neither a very true nor a very polite thing to say,' she remarked, directing her eyes to the ships again. 'Who said it?'

I was disconcerted, for I had broken away without quite seeing where I was going. It was not to be shuffled off now, however, and I answered, 'The beautiful young lady at Miss Havisham's, and she's more beautiful than anybody ever was, and I admire her dreadfully, and I want to be a gentleman on her account.' Having made this lunatic confession, I began to throw my torn-up grass into the river, as if I had some thoughts of following it.

'Do you want to be a gentleman, to spite her or to gain her over?' Biddy quietly asked, after a pause.

'I don't know,' I moodily answered.

'Because, if it is to spite her,' Biddy pursued, 'I should think – but you know best – that might be better and more independently done by caring nothing, for her words. And if it is to gain her over, I should think – but you know best – she was not worth gaining over.'

Exactly what I myself had thought, many times. Exactly what was perfectly manifest to me at the moment. But how could I, a poor dazed village lad, avoid that wonderful inconsistency into which the best and wisest of men fall every day?

'It may be all quite true,' said I to Biddy, 'but I admire her dreadfully.'

In short, I turned over on my face when I came to that, and got a good grasp on the hair on each side of my head, and wrenched it well. All the while knowing the madness of my heart to be so very mad and misplaced, that I was quite conscious it would have served my face right, if I had lifted it up by my hair, and knocked it against the pebbles as a punishment for belonging to such an idiot.

CHARLES DICKENS

TASKS

10 Answer the following questions to test that you have read the extract carefully.

    a How do you feel about Pip here? Do you sympathise with him or feel that he is ungrateful?

    b How would Joe feel if he overheard what Pip says here?

11 Write a scene between Pip and Joe in which Pip tries to explain to Joe what his feelings are. Pip should try not to hurt Joe's feelings.

Boozer's Labourer

(2 hours)

The extract printed on the following pages describes the work situation of a teenager which has begun to turn into a nightmare.

He started the job as a live-in full-time barman but he is required to do a whole variety of menial tasks in addition.

Read the extract which is the beginning of the story.

Boozer's Labourer

I got a job as the full-time barman, living in, at a fair-sized pub called The Mailbag Hotel.

'It's the meanest kip on earth,' the outgoing barman told me. But if you're smart you'll be able to make some bunce on the side.'

It was certainly a mean kip.

There were four of us in the lower staff: Fanny, Polly, Hilda and me; and at breakfast Hilda used to sneak into the family dining room when the Shoutworth twins had gone to school – to see if they had left any toast. Sometimes we got a slice or two to share amongst us (they always gave me the biggest piece), though again she'd come back with a dropped face and sigh: 'Eaten the bloody lot!'

Apart from fetching twelve buckets of coal, chopping firewood, lighting five fires, cleaning the whole bar, taps, glasses and all, and doing the big door plates, I had to wash and polish thirty-one brass spittoons every morning. (Somebody had pinched one, and I often prayed that he'd come back and pinch the lot.) I hated that job worse than anything – except washing the dogs. I suppose that I did get used to the spittoons, in a bitter begrudging fashion, but the dogs I never got used to.

They were four soft slippery spaniels, with flopping ears and melancholy faces, and the way their backs sagged right down when I was scrubbing them made me nervous that they might suddenly collapse in the middle. But worse than that was the heartrending atmosphere they created, for though they never barked, growled or bit, they completely unnerved me by their looks of ghastly misery.

'Don't stare at me like that!' I used to scream at them when I could no longer stand it. 'I don't want to wash you! I hate washing you!' And like as not I'd burst out crying, and sit me down on the floor while the four of them gathered round and watched me, joining in now and again with plaintive moans.

At night too, I often had a bit of a weep when I was all alone and watching the trams from the window of my dark room.

The D tram went to Debmoor Hill, where my girl Sally lived. Night after night I'd watch those trams go sailing by, and when the very last D had gone I'd go into my bed at the Mailbag and have a good scrike on my hard little pillow.

Shoutworth, the landlord, was a purple-faced geezer of nineteen stone or thereabouts, with a pair of piggy eyes that put the fear of kingdom come in me – right from the very first day when he had bellowed:

'D'you call that brass polished, boy? Give me the flannel and paste, and I'll show you what a finished tap should look like.'

He fair made the pub shudder with the weight he put on that tap – though I had to admit that I'd never seen brass gleam so brilliant in all my life. As try as I might I couldn't get the others to approach it in brightness, though come to that I had ten to clean to his one, and I was only nine stone to his nineteen.

He had what Fanny called 'elaphantisis of the legs' – and according to the gossip she was in a position to know – that kept him stuck supping whiskey on his stool for most of the opening hours. And it may have been this weighing-down disease that gave him a curious notion about the speed normal human beings should move at, especially barmen.

'Bring down two soups,' he would suddenly bawl at me around midday and the bar quiet. 'You can have your own dinner while cook is pouring them out.'

Cook was a flurried little soul, and there would be a stack of steak puddings that had collapsed in her shaky fingers, hidden away in some corner of the oven for my dinner, and I had to scoff than standing on my toes, and then flash down with the soups. If he chanced to send me up for another order I might get a slab of collapsed suet pudding, and if not I got none.

Of course, like a lad will, I had a few dodgy strokes of getting my own back. One was a practice of nipping along the counter of the public bar and filling all the pint pots without any charge – whenever old Shoutworth used to shuffle to the Gents. About forty navvies would have their eyes pinned on him, waiting for him to rise, and the very moment he did make a move they would drain their pots, and I'd fill them on the house.

Another habit I took up was that of swigging brandy of an afternoon. When the pub shut at three o'clock I had the job of cleaning all the mirrors and pictures, and I can tell you that there is something depressing about cleaning enormous Victorian overmantels in a closed public house on a sunny afternoon. One occasion I smuggled a bottle of Martell's three-star cognac into the Commercial Room, and before setting into the work I sat down for twenty minutes, during which I meditated upon eternity and drank a pint mug of brandy. The liquor so charged me with energy that I dispensed with the usual stepladder, and taking a short run across the room I leapt clean on the mantelpiece. Unfortunately, when leaning back to clean the bronze eagle on the top, I fell backwards and knocked myself dateless. A fearful thundering in my ears awoke me, and when I rushed to the front door the forty navvies were hammering away with horny fists, because opening time was ten minutes overdue.

My life, I realised, could not go on like this.

BILL NAUGHTON

TASKS

12 Write character studies of the landlord and the young barman.

■ Use information from the passage.
■ Make clear contrasts between the two characters.

13 What you have read is the opening of the story. The extract ended with the words, 'my life, I realised, could not go on like this.'

Continue the story.

6

MISFITS

Feeling Different

(1 hour)

Here are two articles, one about being young and one about being old.

We are not a sub-species...

The worst thing about being a teenager is the word 'teenager.' Being a teenager doesn't feel any different to being a normal person. I don't seem to be undergoing any emotional traumas, or identity crises – I must be letting somebody down. The word teenager prevents some people from treating adolescents as young adults; in their eyes we become a kind of sub-species.

My sixth form used to be regularly visited by various speakers. One week the local insurance man came. In an unfortunate effort to obtain group participation and yet remain in control of the talk, he treated 200 intelligent 18-year-olds like a load of morons. Smiling benignly, he said: 'Now what do we find under roads?' The answers he received – worms, moles, and dead insurance men – were not what he was looking for. Actually it was pipelines. Ask a stupid question! The point is, that man would not have spoken to adults in the same way, so why to teenagers? If you treat people like idiots, they act like idiots.

There might not be that much difference between a 34-year-old and a 38-year-old, but there's a hell of a lot of difference between a 14-year-old and an 18-year-old. When I was 13, I thought being in the fifth year was the ultimate

in maturity: I could wear a navy jumper instead of the putrid regulation royal blue. Now at the worldly age of 18, 16 seems a mere nothing.

The word teenager is misleading because it leads to generalisations and it is so derogatory. For many adults there is no such thing as a teenager who doesn't like discos – if you happen not, as many teenagers don't – they label you as an awkward, anti-social adolescent. For a short time I was a waitress in a restaurant. The average age of the staff was 19, that of the clientele about 40. We, the staff, used to watch amused and slightly disgusted as overweight middle-aged swingers, who in the light of day would claim that discos were a load of nonsense, jerked violently around to the latest hits – as they say. (They were either dancing or having heart attacks – I couldn't quite tell.) If, in the eyes of adults, 'teenage culture' is such a contemptible thing, why, given the opportunity, do they throw themselves into it with so much enthusiasm and a lot less style?

I may be cynical, but I think it is partly due to jealousy. Some adults patronise teenagers because they are envious of their youth and because the respect they don't get from their peers they demand from their juniors.

Even on the lofty level of our local tennis club, this type of jealousy rears its head, or rather, swings its racket. If we were to put forward our strongest women's team, it would consist entirely of teenage girls. Of course, this never happens. The elder women play by virtue of their age, not skill. After all, teenage girls don't count as women.

It always seems like sour grapes to me, when I say something predictable like 'I won't get married,' and the adults smile knowingly and say equally as predictably 'you'll soon change.' Whether they believe I'll change or not, doesn't matter, what they don't like is that I'm indirectly criticising their way of life. Also I'm enjoying a freedom of opinion and expression which they never had. What their 'you'll soon change' actually means is: 'shut up you stupid girl, you don't know what you're talking about. We know best.' I don't think you would find such narrow mindedness in an adolescent.

If there is such a thing as a teenager, it refers to a state of mind and not a particular age range. At 20, you don't automatically become an adult because you've dropped the 'teen' in your age. Unfortunately 'teenager' has come to connote things like selfishness, irresponsibility, and arrogance. This means there are a lot of adults around who are still teenage. Equally, if maturity is measured by attributes such as compassion and tolerance, and not merely the number of years you've totted up, then there are a lot of adult teenagers around.

I would like the word 'teenager' to be banned, but I suppose that will never happen, as a lot of people would stop making a lot of money.

LOIS MCNAY

We are Survivors

For all those born before 1940 we celebrate today because we are here. Consider the changes we have witnessed...

For all those born before 1940 we celebrate today because we are here. Consider the changes we have witnessed....

We were born before the TV age, before polio shots, frozen food, plastics, contact lenses, frisbees and the pill.

We were before refrigerators, dish-washers, tumble dryers, electric blankets, air conditioners, credit cards, split atoms, laser beams, ballpoint pens and before man walked on the moon.

We got married first and then lived together. How quaint can you be?

In our time, closets were for clothes, not for 'coming out of'. Bunnies were small rabbits and dishes were for washing, not receiving programmes from outer space. Designer Jeans were scheming girls, and having a meaningful relationship meant getting along well with your cousins.

We thought fast food was what you ate during Lent and cold turkey was what you ate on Boxing Day.

We were before house-husbands, gay rights, computer dating, dual careers and commuter marriages. Divorce was something that happened to film stars. We were before day-care centres, group therapy and nursing homes. We played with Dinky toys, wore liberty-bodices, and took a daily dose of cod liver oil and malt. We drank Ovaltine, ate porridge, and listened to Dick Barton, the Goon Show, Workers' Playtime and Housewives' Choice.

We had never heard of Radio 1, tape decks, electric typewriters, artificial hearts, word processors or yoghurt. For us, time-sharing meant togetherness, not Spanish holiday homes; a chip meant a piece of wood, hardware meant a shop where you bought hammers and nails, and software wasn't even a word!

In 1940 'Made in Japan' meant poor quality and the Koreans and Taiwanese hadn't even started production. Pizzas, McDonalds and instant coffee were unheard of.

We were born when everything in Woolworths cost one penny. For sixpence, you could take a tram ride, go to the cinema and buy an ice cream.

In our day cigarette smoking was fashionable, grass was mowed, Coke was a cold drink, and pot was something you cooked in. Rock music was a lullaby and AIDS were for those with hearing difficulties.

We were certainly not before the difference between the sexes we discovered, but we were surely before the sex change; we made do with what we had and we were the last generation to think you needed a husband to have a baby!

We typed letters with manual typewriters, and computations by hand, and used carbon paper to make copies. We used telephones without buttons or dials and Fax was something you looked up in an encyclopaedia. We did business with handshakes and trust and somehow it all worked and we survived.

TASK

1 Answer the following questions clearly and concisely.

   a In your own words say what is the point of view of each writer.

   b What is it that Lois McNay dislikes about the way teenagers are treated?

   c The writer of *We are Survivors* does not actually complain about the way the old are treated. But what is it, do you think, that he finds so annoying?

   d Write your own version of one of these articles, either drawing on your own experience or by talking to adults.

Roll of Thunder, Hear My Cry

(1 hour)

Printed below is the extract from *Roll of Thunder, Hear My Cry* which you have already studied in class. Read the extract again.

Roll of Thunder, Hear My Cry

We stood patiently waiting behind the people in front of us and when our turn came, T J handed his list to the man. 'Mr Barnett, sir,' he said, 'I got me this here list of things my mama want.'

The storekeeper studied the list and without looking up asked 'You one of Mr Granger's people?'

'Yessir,' answered T J.

Mr Barnett walked to another counter and began filling the order, but before he finished a white woman called, 'Mr Barnett, you waiting on anybody just now?'

Mr Barnett turned around. 'Just them,' he said, indicating us with a wave of his hand. 'What can I do for you, Miz Emmaline?' The woman handed him a list twice as long as T J's and the storekeeper, without a word of apology to us, proceeded to fill it.

'What's he doing?' I objected.

'Hush, Cassie,' said Stacey, looking very embarrassed and uncomfortable. T J's face was totally bland, as if nothing at all had happened.

When the woman's order was finally filled, Mr Barnett again picked up T J's list, but before he had gotten the next item his wife called, 'Jim Lee, these folks needing help over here and I got my hands full.' And as if we were not even there, he walked away.

'Where's he going?' I cried.

'He'll be back,' said T J, wandering away.

After waiting several minutes for his return, Stacey said, 'Come on Cassie, let's get out of here.' He started toward the door and I followed. But as we passed one of the counters, I spied Mr Barnett wrapping an order of pork chops for a white girl. Adults were one thing; I could almost understand that. They ruled things and there was nothing that could be done about them. But some kid who was no bigger than me was something else again. Certainly Mr Barnett had simply forgotten about T J's order. I decided to remind him and, without saying anything to Stacey, I turned around and marched over to Mr Barnett.

'Uh...'scuse me, Mr Barnett,' I said as politely as I could, waiting a moment for him to look up from his wrapping. 'I think you forgot, but you was waiting on us 'fore you was waiting on this girl here, and we been waiting a good while now for you to get back.'

The girl gazed at me strangely, but Mr Barnett did not look up. I assumed that he had not heard me. I was near the end of the counter so I merely went to the other side of it and tugged on his shirt sleeve to get his attention.

He recoiled as if I had struck him.

'Y-you was helping us,' I said, backing to the front of the counter again.

'Well, you just get your little black self back over there and wait some more,' he said in a low, tight voice.

I was hot. I had been as nice as I could be to him and here he was talking like this. 'We been waiting on you for near an hour,' I hissed, 'while you 'round here waiting on everybody else. And it ain't fair. You got no right –'

'Whose little nigger is this!' bellowed Mr Barnett.

Everyone in the store turned and stared at me. 'I ain't nobody's little nigger!' I screamed, angry and humiliated. 'And you ought not be waiting on everybody 'fore you wait on us.'

'Hush up, child, hush up,' someone whispered behind me. I looked around. A woman who had occupied the wagon next to ours at the market looked down upon me. Mr Barnett, his face red and eyes bulging, immediately pounded on her.

'This gal yourn, Hazel?'

'No, suh,' answered the woman meekly, stepping hastily away to show she had nothing to do with me. As I watched her turn her back on me, Stacey emerged and took my hand.

'Come on, Cassie, let's get out of here.'

'Stacey!' I exclaimed, relieved to see him by my side. 'Tell him! You know he ain't fair making us wait –'

'She your sister, boy?' Mr Barnett spat across the counter.

Stacey bit his lower lip and gazed into Mr Barnett's eyes. 'Yessir.'

'Then you get her out of here,' he said with hateful force. 'And make sure she don't come back till yo' mammy teach her what she is.'

'I already know what I am!' I retaliated. 'But I betcha you don't know what you are! And I could sure tell you, too, you ole –'

Stacey jerked me forward, crushing my hand in the effort, and whispered angrily, 'Shut up, Cassie!' His dark eyes flashed malevolently as he pushed me in front of him through the crowd.

MILDRED TAYLOR

TASK

2 Use your imagination and write about another event in Cassie's life.

As in the extract, write as if you were Cassie.

Going Home

(1 hour)

In this extract from *Life Drawing* (a short story by Bernard MacLaverty) Liam Diamond goes to visit his sick father.

Life Drawing

The snow, thawed to slush and refrozen quickly, crackled under his feet and made walking difficult. For a moment he was not sure which was the house. In the dark he had to remember it by number and shade his eyes against the yellow glare of the sodium street lights to make out the figures on the small terrace doors. He saw Fifty-six and walked three houses farther along. The heavy wrought-iron knocker echoed in the hallway as it had always done. He waited, looking up at the semi-circular fan-light. Snow was beginning to fall, tiny flakes swirling in the corona of light. He was about to knock again or look to see if they had got a bell when he heard shuffling from the other side of the door. It opened a few inches and a white-haired old woman peered out. Her hair was held in place by a net a shade different from her own hair colour. It was one of the Miss Harts but for the life of him he couldn't remember which. She looked at him, not understanding.

'Yes?'

'I'm Liam,' he said.

'Oh, thanks be to goodness for that. We're glad you could come.'

Then she shouted over her shoulder, 'It's Liam.'

She shuffled backwards, opening the door and admitting him. Inside she tremulously shook his hand, then took his bag and set it on the ground. Like a servant, she took his coat and hung it on the hall stand. It was still in the same place and the hallway was still a dark electric yellow.

'Bertha's up with him now. You'll forgive us sending the telegram to the College but we thought you would like to know,' said Miss Hart. If Bertha was up the stairs then she must be Maisie.

'Yes, yes, you did the right thing,' said Liam. 'How is he?'

'Poorly. The doctor has just left – he had another call. He says he'll not last the night.'

'That's too bad.'

By now they were standing in the kitchen. The fireplace was black and empty. One bar of the dished electric fire took the chill off the room and no more.

'You must be tired,' said Miss Hart, 'It's such a journey. Would you like a cup of tea? I tell you what, just you go up now and I'll bring you your tea when it's ready. All right?'

'Yes, thank you.'

When he reached the head of the stairs she called after him,

'And send Bertha down.'

Bertha met him on the landing. She was small and withered and her head reached to her chest. When she saw him she started to cry and reached out her arms to him saying,

'Liam, poor Liam.'

She nuzzled against him, weeping. 'The poor old soul,' she kept repeating. Liam was embarrassed feeling the thin arms of this old woman he hardly knew about his hips.

'Maisie says you have to go down now,' he said, separating himself from her and patting her crooked back. He watched her go down the stairs, one tottering step at a time, gripping the banister, her rheumatic knuckles standing out like limpets.

He paused at the bedroom door and for some reason flexed his hands before he went in. He was shocked to see the state his father was in. He was now almost completely bald except for some fluffy hair above his ears. His cheeks were sunken, his mouth hanging open. His head was back on the pillow so that he strings of his neck stood out.

'Hello, it's me, Liam,' he said when he was at the bed. The old man opened his eyes flickeringly. He tried to speak. Liam had to lean over but failed to decipher what was said. He reached out and lifted his father's hand in a kind of wrong handshake.

'Want anything?'

His father signalled by a slight movement of his thumb that he needed something. A drink? Liam poured some water and put the glass to the old man's lips. Arcs of scum had formed at the corners of his sagging mouth. Some of the water spilled on to the sheet. It remained for a while in droplets before sinking into dark circles.

'Was that what you wanted?' The old man shook his head. Liam looked around the room, trying to see what his father could want. It was exactly as he had remembered it. In twenty years he hadn't changed the wallpaper, yellow roses looping on an umber trellis. He lifted a straight-backed chair and drew it up close to the bed. He sat with his elbows on his knees, leaning forward.

'How do you feel?'

The old man made no response and the question echoed around and around the silence in Liam's head.

Maisie brought in tea on a tray, closing the door behind her with her elbow. Liam noticed that two red spots had come up on her cheeks. She spoke quickly in an embarrassed whisper, looking back and forth between the dying man and his son.

'We couldn't find where he kept the teapot so it's just a tea-bag in a cup. Is that all right? Will that be enough for you to eat? We sent out for a tin of ham, just in case. He had nothing in the house at all, God love him.'

'You've done very well,' said Liam. 'You shouldn't have gone to all this trouble.'

'If you couldn't do it for a neighbour like Mr Diamond – well? Forty-two years and there was never a cross word between us. A gentleman we always called him, Bertha and I. He kept himself to himself. Do you think he can hear us?' The old man did not move.

'How long has he been like this?' asked Liam.

'Just three days. He didn't bring in his milk one day and that's not like him y'know. He'd left a key with Mrs Rankin, in case he'd ever lock himself out again – he did once, the wind blew

the door shut – and she came in and found him like this in the chair downstairs. He was frozen, God love him. The doctor said it was a stroke.'

Liam nodded, looking at his father. He stood up and began edging the woman towards the bedroom door.

'I don't know how to thank you, Miss Hart. You've been more than good.'

'We got your address from your brother. Mrs Rankin phoned America on Tuesday.'

'Is he coming home?'

'He said he'd try. She said the line was as clear as a bell. It was like talking to next door. Yes, he said he'd try but he doubted it very much.' She had her hand on the door knob. 'Is that enough sandwiches?'

'Yes thanks, that's fine.' They stood looking at one another awkwardly. Liam fumbled in his pocket. 'Can I pay you for the ham... and the telegram?'

'I wouldn't dream of it,' she said. 'Don't insult me now, Liam.' He withdrew his hand from his pocket and smiled his thanks to her.

'It's late,' he said, 'perhaps you should go now and I'll sit up with him.'

'Very good. The priest was here earlier and gave him...' she groped for the word with her hands.

'Extreme Unction?'

'Yes. That's twice he has been in three days. Very attentive. Sometimes I think if our ministers were half as good....'

'Yes, but he wasn't what you could call gospel greedy.'

'He was lately,' she said.

'Changed times.'

She half turned to go and said, almost coyly, 'I'd hardly have known you with the beard.' She looked up at him, shaking her head in disbelief. He was trying to make her go, standing close to her but she skirted round him and went over to the bed. She touched the older man's shoulder.

'I'm away now, Mr Diamond. Liam is here, I'll see you in the morning,' she shouted into his ear. Then she was away.

BERNARD MACLAVERTY

TASK

3 Write about Liam's feelings here. You might like to consider
- ■ what we learn about the past;
- ■ the way Liam is treated when he reaches the house;
- ■ the writer's use of setting and description.

Uniform

(3 hours)

Look up the word 'uniform' in a dictionary. What does the word mean as an adjective? What does the word mean as a noun?

Here are two articles about school uniform.

Schools return to classical mode

Britain's comprehensive schools are turning to traditional values to brush up their public image in the face of increased competition. School uniforms, strong disciplinary policies, streaming and the classics are on the increase.

School uniform retailers report a surge in business from the state sector in the past two years. Kinch and Lack, the country's largest independent retailer of school uniforms, has seen a 20 per cent increase in trade from state schools over the past two years.

Les Stephens, the managing director, said: 'We have certainly noticed this. State schools are tending to introduce a basic uniform with a tie and a blazer-badge, and are becoming relatively strict about what children should wear.'

Classics are also making a come-back. The Joint Association for Classical Teachers, which watches the welfare of classics in both state and independent schools, has noticed more interest from comprehensive schools.

Jeannie Cohen, the association's secretary, said that three years ago the outlook for the subject had been gloomy, with the National Curriculum threatening to squeeze them out of the timetable.

Now, more were finding space for them, she said. In Harrow, north London, four comprehensives and a sixth-form college had all recently reintroduced classics.

A few years ago Latin was introduced as an experiment in inner-city Harlem in New York,

she said. After three months, the pupils' reading ages had gone up by 13 months and their mathematics ages by 11 months.

'It would be wonderful if it had a similar effect at English schools,' she said.

At Holland Park Comprehensive in west London, regarded as a flagship of progressive education, staff plan to end mixed-ability teaching for fourth and fifth years, reintroduce Latin and begin teaching the three sciences separately instead of as a single subject. The school's headteacher, Maggie Pringle, said that parents had raised the issue of bringing in Latin and had supported other changes, but she added that schools should be cautious about bowing to competitive urges.

'You have to be careful about making changes according to the market. If you do that, you will just lose some of your own integrity and become a school of confused values,' she said.

But according to Phil Woods, principal investigator of a £250,000 Open University study, many schools have turned to traditionalism precisely because of market forces. Recent reforms aimed at increasing parental choice and forcing schools to compete with one another have linked funding to the numbers of pupils they attract.

Mr Woods plans to question 6,000 parents about their choice of secondary school in the next 3 years in a study funded by the Economic and Social Research Council. Preliminary research which he began in 1990 highlighted a trend towards traditionalism in some schools.

Mr Woods said: 'We found that schools were tending to make certain changes such as tightening up homework policies and streaming children broadly by ability. They are familiar with competition and with the fact that parents can go to different schools.'

In one case, a school which was losing pupils because their parents felt they were not being stretched had introduced ability streams to stop them leaving, he said. Others had responded to the new air of competition by emphasising their caring atmosphere.

One school selling itself through traditional values is Highbury Grove in Islington, north London. A reputation for strict discipline and high standards under former headmaster Rhodes Boyson, who went on to become an education minister, was severely tarnished last year when the headteacher, Peter Searl, was suspended after two critical inspectors' reports.

From now on the school is turning its back on trendiness and emphasising classics, tidiness and good behaviour. Latin will be compulsory in the first two years, all pupils will be in full uniform, and attendance will be monitored electronically. Staff are receiving training in how to enforce good discipline.

Highbury Grove is one of a very few inner-city schools that never abandoned Latin. Now it is making the subject compulsory for 11- and 12 year-olds, and will offer it to all pupils.

When they return to school this week, pupils will be given a behaviour guide explaining rules and sanctions, and a headmasters' detention, introduced by the acting head, John Phillips, will be imposed on serious offenders.

Baseball caps and training shoes will no longer be permitted, and children's presence will be registered on a computer at the start of each lesson to combat truancy.

Judy Bedawi, a parent governor at the school, said that all the changes were sought by parents worried that standards of discipline and dress had been slipping.

'Parents are really pleased because they want their kids to get a good education, and for that you need a safe, disciplined and decent environment,' she said.

Pupils at Castle Hall School in West Yorkshire will also see changes when they arrive back for the new term this week. The school, which used to take pupils aged from nine to 13, has become an 11–16 comprehensive after plans to select pupils by ability were rejected by the former Secretary of State for Education, John Patten.

Pupils must turn up this week wearing blazers and ties, and will be placed in sets for all subjects according to their abilities.

The school, which has opted out of local-authority control, has a new discipline policy and the headteacher, Mike Bell, is keeping a 'watching brief' on the introduction of classics.

He said: 'We are, to quote a cliché, consumer-driven. But, having said that, we would have felt it was important to present these things as part of a package anyway.'

However, these types of changes will not necessarily persuade parents to send their children to a particular school, according to Mr Woods of the Open University. He believes they may prefer a caring atmosphere.

'It is wrong to characterise parents as simply wanting high examination results and strict discipline,' Mr Woods said. 'Some do, but many are more sophisticated than that.'

Dress Sense

Why expect children to think for themselves and then tell them what to wear? A teacher writes of his opposition to school uniforms.

It's that time of year again, the time when I find it hard to believe that I am not going mad. It's a few weeks into term and the powers-that-be have decided to hold a 'uniform blitz'. Horror of horrors, it has been noticed that some pupils are walking around 'unacceptably' dressed and it's the duty of all of us staff to inspect them and see that they're brought up to scratch.

That's 'all of us', you notice. For some reason, this particular topic is deemed to be of such vital importance that staff are reminded, in a specially convened meeting, of their 'corporate responsibility' with regard to uniform enforcement. Nobody can opt out, and trouble will ensue if this is attempted. This presents a problem for those, like me, who see uniform as not merely unimportant and unnecessary, but positively wrong and evil. For now, it seems, I am obliged to spend my time examining shirts to see whether they are dotted or striped, to make a value judgement about whether a pullover is royal or navy blue and, gulp, decide whether the girls' skirts are of an 'acceptable' length. And I'm not going to do it.

This is not to say however, that I am above a bit of deception for the sake of an easy life. If challenged about any alleged lack of uniformity among the pupils in my tutor group, I will tut-tut and pretend that I intend to do something about it. In fact, there is no way that I am prepared to degrade both the pupils and myself by telling them what they ought to look like.

A more courageous colleague who holds similar views recently told the deputy head what he thought. The result was astonishing. If you're not prepared to toe the line, he was told, it might be as well to seek employment elsewhere. It seems that this crazy issue has assumed such paramount importance that it has become a sacking matter.

My colleague is a language teacher. So am I. You'll find that many anti-uniform teachers are linguists and the reason is obvious: most of them have taught abroad and found that the wearing of uniform has no effect whatsoever in the improvement of discipline or learning. The only effect it ever has is to create unnecessary conflict and tension between staff and pupils. I am personally still smarting from the annual humiliation of having to attempt to explain to colleagues from the French and German schools with whom we have exchanges just why we in this country continue to insist on it.

Well, er, it's tradition. And, er, if you didn't have a uniform, the less well-off pupils would stand out because of their shabbiness. And there would be dreadful competition between pupils trying to outdo each other in the fashion stakes. All nonsense, of course, because in the continental schools, all the students wear functional jeans and sweaters, bought inexpensively from their local C&A store, and there is absolutely no way that you can work out the financial status of the wearers. And then there's the chestnut that school uniform 'fosters a sense of belonging and pride in the institution'. In fact it fosters a sense of resentment at being denied a basic freedom. A fine institution will engender a sense of pride in its members for far better reasons than an artificial imposition of notional standards of dress.

The uniform issue is a serious one in education because it stands out as an anomaly in a movement of pupil-centred reforms. The GCSE, profiling, the growth of personal and social education; all are designed to increase the emphasis on individual development, to encourage and assist children to think and to make decisions for themselves. Yet, in something as fundamental and personal as clothing, we seek to deny them any rights whatsoever and to impose upon them artificial and outdated 'standards'. Not that any of these arguments will sway those senior staff for whom uniform enforcement is a way of life and of crucial educational importance.

Meanwhile, I wonder what the European Court of Human Rights would have to say about the issue? I intend to find out.

TASKS

4 Summarise the reasons, according to the first article, why schools are turning to school uniform.

5 Write a pamphlet (to be sent to parents of new children) explaining all the advantages of school uniform.

   You will need to think carefully about the size of the pamphlet and its layout, as well as the content.

6 Explain, in your own words, the teacher's point of view in the second article.

7 Imagine the teacher has a full interview with his deputy head about this issue. Write the conversation.

8 Prepare for a debate in your class on the usefulness of school uniform. Either in full or in note form prepare your speech – are you for, against or undecided?

Ha' penny

(2 hours 30 minutes)

You will find that we have used material written by Alan Paton elsewhere in the classbook. For quite a long time he was Principle of a large, boys' reformatory in Johannesburg.

Ha' penny

Of the six hundred boys at the reformatory, about one hundred were from ten to fourteen years of age. My Department had from time to time expressed the intention of taking them away, and of establishing a special institution for them, more like an industrial school than a reformatory. This would have been a good thing, for their offences were very trivial, and they would have been better by themselves. Had such a school been established, I should have liked to be Principal of it myself, for it would have been an easier job; small boys turn instinctively towards affection, and one controls them by it, naturally and easily.

Some of them, if I came near them, either on parade or in school or at football, would observe me watchfully, not directly or fully, but obliquely and secretly; sometimes I would surprise them at it, and make some small sign of recognition which would satisfy them so that they would cease to observe me, and would give their full attention to the event of the moment. But I knew that my authority was thus confirmed and strengthened.

The secret relations with them were a source of continuous pleasure to me. Had they been my own children I would no doubt have given a greater expression to it. But often I would move through the silent and orderly parade, and stand by one of them. He would look straight in front of him with a little frown of concentration that expressed both childish awareness and manly indifference to my nearness. Sometimes I would tweak his ear, and he would give me a brief smile of acknowledgement, or frown with still greater concentration. It was natural, I suppose, to confine these outward expressions to the very smallest, but they were taken as symbolic, and some older boys would observe them and take themselves to be included. It was a relief, when the reformatory was passing through times of turbulence and trouble, and when there was danger of estrangement between authority and boys, to make those simple and natural gestures, which were reassurances to both me and them that nothing important had changed.

On Sunday afternoons when I was on duty I would take my car to the reformatory and watch the free boys being signed out at the gate. This simple operation was watched by many boys not free, who would tell each other, 'In so many weeks I'll be signed out myself.' Among the watchers were always some of the small boys, and these I would take by turns in the car. We would go out to the Potchefstroom Road with its ceaseless stream of traffic, and to the Baragwanath cross-roads, and come back by the Van Wyksrus road to the reformatory. I would talk to them about their families, their parents, their sisters and brothers, and I would pretend to know nothing of Durban, Port Elizabeth, Potchefstroom, and Clocolan, and ask them if these places were bigger than Johannesburg.

One of the small boys was Ha'penny, and he was about twelve years old. He came from Bloemfontein and was the biggest talker of them all. His mother worked in a white person's house, and he had two brothers and two sisters. His brothers were Richard and Dickie, and his sisters Anna and Mina.

'Richard and Dickie?' I asked.

'Yes, meneer.'

'In English,' I said, 'Richard and Dickie are the same name.'

When we returned to the reformatory, I sent for Ha'penny's papers; there it was plainly set down, Ha'penny was a waif, with no relatives at all. He had been taken in from one home to another, but he was naughty and uncontrollable, and eventually had taken to pilfering at the market.

I then sent for the Letter Book, and found that Ha'penny wrote regularly, or rather that others wrote for him till he could write himself, to Mrs Betty Maarman, of 48 Vlak Street, Bloemfontein. but Mrs Maarman had never once replied to him. When questioned, he had said, perhaps she is sick. I sat down and wrote at once to the Social Welfare Officer at Bloemfontein, asking him to investigate.

The next time I had Ha'penny out in the car I questioned him again about his family. And

he told me the same as before, his mother, Richard and Dickie, Anna and Mina. But he softened the 'D' of Dickie, so that it sounded now like Tickie.

'I thought you said Dickie,' I said.

'I said Tickie,' he said.

He watched me with concealed apprehension, and I came to the conclusion that this waif of Bloemfontein was a clever boy, who had told me a story that was all imagination, and had changed one single letter of it to make it safe from any question. And I thought I understood it all too, that he was ashamed of being without a family and had invented them all, so that no one might discover that he was fatherless and motherless and that no one in the world cared whether he was alive or dead. This gave me a strong feeling for him, and I went out of my way to manifest towards him that fatherly care that the State, though not in those words, had enjoined upon me by giving me this job.

Then the letter came from the Social Welfare Officer in Bloemfontein, saying that Mrs Betty Maarman of 48 Vlak Street was a real person, and that she had four children, Richard and Dickie, Anna and Mina, but that Ha'penny was no child of hers, and she knew him only as a derelict of the streets. She had never answered his letters, because he wrote to her as 'Mother', and she was no mother of his, nor did she wish to play any such role. She was a decent woman, a faithful member of the church, and she had no thought of corrupting her family by letting them have anything to do with such a child.

But Ha'penny seemed to me anything but the usual delinquent; his desire to have a family was so strong, and his reformatory record was so blameless, and his anxiety to please and obey so great, that I began to feel a great duty towards him. Therefore I asked him about his 'mother'.

He could not speak enough of her, nor with too high praise. She was loving, honest, and strict. Her home was clean. She had affection for all her children. It was clear that the homeless child, even as he had attached himself to me, would have attached himself to her; he had observed her even as he had observed me, but did not know the secret of how to open her heart, so that she would take him in, and save him from the lonely life that he led.

'Why did you steal when you had such a mother?' I asked.

He could not answer that; not all his brains nor his courage could find an answer to such a question, for he knew that with such a mother he would not have stolen at all.

'The boy's name is Dickie,' I said, 'not Tickie.'

And then he knew the deception was revealed. Another boy might have said, 'I told you it was Dickie,' but he was too intelligent for that; he knew that if I had established that the boy's name was Dickie, I must have established other things too. I was shocked by the immediate and visible effect of my action. His whole brave assurance died within him, and he stood there exposed, not as a liar, but as a homeless child who had surrounded himself with mother, brothers, and sisters, who did not exist. I had shattered the very foundations of his pride, and his sense of human significance.

He fell sick at once, and the doctor said it was tuberculosis. I wrote at once to Mrs Maarman, telling her the whole story, of how this small boy had observed her, and had decided that she was the person he desired for his mother. But she wrote back saying that she could take no responsibility for him. For one thing, Ha'penny was a Mosuto, and she was a coloured woman; for another, she had never had a child in trouble, and how could she take such a boy?

Tuberculosis is a strange thing; sometimes it manifests itself suddenly in the most unlikely host, and swiftly sweeps to the end. Ha'penny withdrew himself from the world, from all Principals and mothers, and the doctor said

there was little hope. In desperation I sent money for Mrs Maarman to come.

She was a decent, homely woman, and, seeing that the situation was serious, she, without fuss or embarrassment, adopted Ha'penny for her own. The whole reformatory accepted her as his mother. She sat the whole day with him, and talked to him of Richard and Dickie, Anna and Mina, and how they were all waiting for him to come home. She poured out her affection on him, and had no fear of his sickness, nor did she allow it to prevent her from satisfying his hunger to be owned. She talked to him of what they would do when he came back, and how he would go to the school, and what they would buy for Guy Fawkes night.

He in his turn gave his whole attention to her, and when I visited him he was grateful, but I had passed out of his world. I felt judged in that I had sensed only the existence and not the measure of his desire. I wished I had done something sooner, more wise, more prodigal.

We buried him on the reformatory farm, and Mrs Maarman said to me, 'When you put up the cross, put he was my son.'

'I'm ashamed,' she said, 'that I wouldn't take him.'

'The sickness,' I said, 'the sickness would have come.'

'No,' she said, shaking her head with certainty. 'It wouldn't have come. And if it had come at home, it would have been different.'

So she left for Bloemfontein, after her strange visit to a reformatory. And I was left too, with the resolve to be more prodigal in the task that the State, though not in so many words, had enjoined upon me.

ALAN PATON

TASKS

9 Describe Mrs Maarman's feelings when she recieved the money to visit Ha'penny.

10 Imagine that you are Ha'penny at the moment when 'the deception was revealed'. What are you thinking? What do you want to do? (Remember that Ha'penny is a misfit who desparately wants to fit in.)

11 Imagine that you are Alan Paton standing by Ha'penny's grave. What are you thinking?

12 Give your opinion of this story in no more than a page of writing.

Dickens

(1 hour 30 minutes)

During your classbook study you have looked at two extracts from *Great Expectations* by Charles Dickens. Below you will find one of them reprinted to remind you.

Great Expectations

He conducted me to a bower about a dozen yards off, but which was approached by such ingenious twists of path that it took quite a long time to get at; and in this retreat our glasses were already set forth. Our punch was cooling in an ornamental lake, on whose margin the bower was raised. This piece of water (with an island in the middle which might have been the salad for supper) was of a circular form, and he had constructed a fountain in it, which, when you set a little mill going and took a cork out of a pipe, played to that powerful extent that it made the back of your hand quite wet.

'I am my own engineer, and my own carpenter, and my own plumber, and my own gardener, and my own Jack of all Trades,' said Wemmick, in acknowledging my compliments. 'Well, it's a good thing, you know. It brushes the Newgate cobwebs away, and pleases the Aged. You wouldn't mind being at once introduced to the Aged, would you? It wouldn't put you out?'

I expressed the readiness I felt, and we went into the castle. Then, we found, sitting by a fire, a very old man in a flannel coat: clean, cheerful, comfortable, and well cared for, but intensely deaf.

'Well, aged parent,' said Wemmick, shaking hands with him in a cordial and jocose way, 'how am you?'

'All right, John; all right!' replied the old man.

'Here's Mr Pip, aged parent,' said Wemmick, 'and I wish you could hear his name. Nod away at him, Mr Pip; that's what he likes. Nod away at him, if you please, like winking!'

'This is a fine place of my son's, sir,' cried the old man, while I nodded as hard as I possibly could. 'This is a pretty pleasure-ground, sir. This spot and these beautiful works upon it ought to be kept together by the Nation, after my son's time, for the people's enjoyment.'

'You're as proud of it as Punch; ain't you, Aged?' said Wemmick, contemplating the old man, with his hard face really softened; 'there's a nod for you;' giving him a tremendous one; 'there's another for you;' giving him a still more tremendous one; 'you like that, don't you? If you're not tired, Mr Pip – though I know it's tiring to strangers – will you tip him one more? You can't think how it pleases him.'

I tipped him several more, and he was in great spirits. We left him bestirring himself to feed the fowls, and we sat down to our punch in the arbour; where Wemmick told me as he smoked a pipe, that it had taken him a good many years to bring the property up to its present pitch of perfection.

'Is it your own, Mr Wemmick?'

'O yes,' said Wemmick. 'I have got hold of it, a bit at a time. It's a freehold, by George!'

'Is it, indeed? I hope Mr Jaggers admires it?'

'Never seen it,' said Wemmick. 'Never heard of it. Never seen the Aged. Never heard of him. No; the office is one thing, and private life is another. While I go into the office, I leave the Castle behind me, and when I come into the Castle, I leave the office behind me. If it's not in any way disagreeable to you, you'll oblige me by doing the same. I don't wish it professionally spoken about.'

Of course I felt my good faith involved in the observance of his request. the punch being very nice, we sat there drinking it and talking, until it was almost nine o'clock.

'Getting near gun-fire,' said Wemmick then, as he laid down his pipe; 'it's the Aged's treat.'

Proceeding into the Castle again, we found the Aged heating the poker, with expectant eyes, as a preliminary to the performance of this great nightly ceremony. Wemmick stood with his watch in his hand until the moment was come for him to take the red-hot poker from the Aged, and repair to the battery. He took it, and went out, and presently the Stinger went off with a bang that shook the crazy little box of a cottage as if it must fall to pieces, and made every glass and teacup in it ring. Upon this the Aged – who I believe would have been blown out of his arm-chair but for holding on by the elbows – cried out exultingly, 'He's fired! I heerd him!' and I nodded at the old gentleman until it is no figure of speech to declare that I absolutely could not see him.

The interval between that time and supper, Wemmick devoted to showing me his collection of curiosities. They were mostly of a felonious character; comprising the pen with which a celebrated forgery had been committed, a distinguished razor or two, some locks of hair, and several manuscript confessions written under condemnation – upon which Mr Wemmick set particular value as being, to use his own words, 'every one of 'em Lies, sir.' These were agreeably dispersed among small specimens of china and glass, various neat trifles made by the proprietor of the museum, and some tobacco-stoppers carved by the Aged. They were all displayed in that chamber of the Castle into which I had been first inducted, and which served, not only as the general sitting-room, but as the kitchen too, if I might judge from a saucepan on the hob, and a brazen bijou over the fireplace designed for the suspension of a roasting-jack.

There was a neat little girl in attendance, who looked after the Aged in the day. when she had laid the supper-cloth, the bridge was lowered to give her the means of egress, and she withdrew for the night. The supper was excellent; and though the Castle was rather subject to dry-rot, insomuch that it tasted like a bad nut, and though the pig might have been farther off, I was heartily pleased with my whole entertainment. Nor was there any drawback on my little turret bedroom, beyond there being such a very thin ceiling between me and the flagstaff, that when I lay down on my back in bed, it seemed as if I had to balance that pole on my forehead all night.

Wemmick was up early in the morning, and I am afraid I heard him cleaning my boots. After that, he fell to gardening, and I saw him from my gothic window pretending to employ the Aged, and nodding at him in a most devoted manner. Our breakfast was as good as the supper, and at half-past eight precisely we started for Little Britain. By degrees, Wemmick got dryer and harder as we went along, and his mouth tightened into a post-office again. At last, when we got to his place of business and he pulled out his key from his coat-collar, he looked as unconscious of his Walworth property as if the Castle and the drawbridge and the arbour and the lake and the fountain and the Aged, had all been blown into space together by the last discharge of the Stinger.

CHARLES DICKENS

TASK

13 Like Pip, you are going to visit someone you are not sure about. It might be a friend's aged grandmother or your mother's old aunt who you have never met before.

Describe the visit and make the person you are visiting a Dickensian character.

■ You will need to get the physical description of the character right.
■ You will need to think carefully about the way in which they behave.

Stephen Hawking

(1 hour 30 minutes)

You have already read an extract from the story of Stephen Hawking's life. We have reprinted it below to remind you.

A Brief History of Stephen Hawking

In an upmarket restaurant near Cambridge city centre one lunchtime during December 1988, 12 graduates are sitting around a large table. To one side, slumped in a wheelchair and being spoon-fed by a nurse, is a man in his mid-forties.

His neat open-necked shirt and plain jacket contrast favourably with the general scruffiness of the young men and women, and behind steel-rimmed spectacles his clear blue eyes are alert. But he looks terribly frail, almost withered away to nothing.

He cannot talk because of a tracheotomy; set into the centre of his sinewy throat is a plastic breathing device about two inches in diameter. So when the young people make a flippant remark in his direction, he painstakingly moves two fingers of one hand – almost his last vestige of bodily freedom – to spell out his reply with the computer control on his lap, and a voice-synthesiser, connected to the computer, turns the words into speech. His metallic reply brings peals of mirth from the whole table.

Then, excitement: the arrival in the restaurant of the guest of honour, a glamorous redhead in a fake-fur coat. 'Sorry I'm late,' she says. 'My car was wheel-clamped in London.'

She adds, laughing, 'There must be some cosmic significance in that!'

The man's eyes light up. What has been called 'the greatest smile in the world' envelopes his boyish face. The redhead crouches in front of him.

'Professor Hawking, I'm delighted to meet you. I'm Shirley MacLaine.'

For the rest of the meal the Oscar-winning Hollywood actress, who is deeply interested in metaphysics and spiritual matters, and has strong beliefs about the meaning of life, plies Hawking with questions, wanting his views. When she asks: 'Do you believe there is a God who created the Universe and guides His creation?' Hawking smiles momentarily. The Star Wars voice says, 'No.'

It is not what Shirley MacLaine wants to hear and she doesn't agree; she has already spoken to holy men and teachers in many countries. But she can only listen and take note, for if nothing else, Stephen Hawking's views have to be respected. His field is theoretical cosmology: the study of the Universe at large – in terms of ideas the biggest of big science.

His fundamental breakthroughs, pushing forward our understanding of the origin of the Universe, the laws which govern its existence and the eventual fate of everybody and everything, have made Hawking arguably the greatest physicist of our time.

He has been proclaimed 'the finest mind alive' and 'the greatest genius of the late twentieth century'; even 'Einstein's heir'.

Moreover, he is known to millions, far and wide, for his science book *A Brief History of Time*. aimed at the lay reader, it is a publishing phenomenon. An instant bestseller in Britain and America, it has earned a place in the Guinness Book of Records for spending 184 weeks in The Sunday Times 'top-ten' lists, and has sold more than five million copies worldwide.

How did all this happen? How has a man who is almost completely paralysed and weighs less than six and a half stone overcome every obstacle and achieved far more than most able-bodied people ever dream of accomplishing?

Stephen William Hawking was a healthy baby, born to intellectual, eccentric parents. His father Frank, a doctor specialising in tropical diseases, and his mother Isobel, a Glasgow doctor's daughter, had a large rambling house in St Albans, Hertfordshire, cluttered with books. Carpets and furniture stayed in use until they fell apart; wallpaper was allowed to dangle where it had peeled through old age. The family car was a London taxi, bought for £50.

Hawking, who has two younger sisters and a younger adopted brother, is fascinated by his birthdate: January 8, 1942. It was the three hundredth anniversary of the death of Galileo, the Italian mathematician and astronomer who revolutionised astronomy and was persecuted by the Inquisition for maintaining that the Sun is the centre of our planetary system – not the Earth, as ancient astronomers believed.

'Galileo', says Hawking, 'was the first scientist to start using his eyes, both figuratively and physically. In a sense, he was responsible for the age of science we now enjoy.'

Hawking went to St Albans School, a private school noted for academic excellence. By the end of his third year, when he won the school divinity prize, he was part of a small group, the brightest of the bright students, who hung around together. They listened to classical music (pop was infra dig) and read only the 'smart' authors: Kingsley Amis, Aldous Huxley and Hawking's hero, Bertrand Russell, at once intellectual giant and liberal activist.

Hawking spent very little time on maths homework, yet got full marks. A friend recalls: 'While I would be worrying away at a complicated problem, he just knew the answer. He didn't have to think about it.'

This instinctive insight also impressed his teachers. In 1958, during a science lesson in the sixth form (where Hawking and his friends built a rudimentary computer, at a time when only a few large companies and universities had computers), the teacher posed the question: 'Does a cup of hot tea reach a drinkable temperature more quickly if you put the milk in first, or add the milk after pouring?' While the rest of the class struggled with a muddle of concepts, Hawking almost instantly announced the correct answer: 'Add the milk after pouring, of course,' (the hotter the tea, initially, the faster it will cool).

Hawking the schoolboy was a typical swot, awkward, skinny and puny. His grey uniform always looked a mess and he jabbered rather than talked clearly, having inherited a slight lisp from his father. His friends dubbed his speech 'Hawkingese'.

It had nothing to do with early signs of illness; he was just that sort of kid – a figure of classroom fun, respected by his friends, avoided by most.

All this changed when Hawking went up to Oxford, winning a scholarship to read Natural Science, a course which combined mathematics and physics, at University College. He found much of the work easy and averaged only one hour's work a day. Once, when his tutor set some physics problems from a textbook, Hawking did not even bother to do them. Asked why, he spent 20 minutes pointing out errors in the book.

Hawking was feeling bored, and in danger of sliding into apathy, when luckily he found an interest: the Boat Club. His wraithlike physique was perfectly suited to coxing. He had a loud voice with which he enjoyed barking instructions, and he cultivated a daredevil image when navigating on the river. Many times he returned to shore with bits of the boat knocked off and oar blades damaged, having tried to guide his crew through an impossible narrow gap. Norman Dix, his rowing trainer, suspects, 'Half the time, he was sitting in the stern with his head in the stars, working out mathematical formulae.'

Hawking has never been interested in observational astronomy. While at Oxford he did a vacation course at the Royal Greenwich Observatory, helping the then Astronomer Royal, Sir Richard Woolley, with research into binary stars. However, upon looking through the telescope and seeing merely a couple of hazy dots, he was convinced that theoretical cosmology would be much more interesting.

MICHAEL WHITE, JOHN GRIBBIN

TASK

14 Many people would regard some of Stephen Hawking's ideas eccentric. He has stated that he has come to believe in the possibility of time travel. To travel forward or backwards in time must be a classic way of turning yourself into a misfit.

Write your own story where you do just that – you travel in time – it is up to you whether you go forwards or backwards.

(You are being asked to write a science fiction story. Remember that the most effective science fiction can be believed in.)

Making a Speech

(2 hours)

Sometimes you find yourself completely out of step with other people in your view of something. It often takes courage to put a point of view to a group when this is the case. It takes even more courage when people are against you rather than just indifferent.

Writing a speech needs good control of punctuation. The following punctuation marks are often very important:

! (exclamation mark) for emphasis.
? (question mark) for rhetorical questions.

Of course commas, full stops and so on must be used properly too.

TASKS

15 Write a speech in which you put the case for a topic you believe in. Remember your audience does not share your point of view.

Here are some suggestions:
- Tougher punishment for crime.
- Supporting Aid Agencies in the Third World.
- Housing for the homeless.
- Action on drugs.
- Animal Rights.

16 Take the speech you have written and use it as the basis for further writing. This time begin by setting the scene and inventing characters. Describe the situation. Include the speech and the reactions of the listeners. Describe how it all ended.

Punctuation
This time you will need to use speech marks (inverted commas) as well as the other punctuation marks you have already used. Remember speech marks indicate which words are actually spoken (the spoken words may only be part of a sentence so the whole sentence needs proper punctuation).

Bleak House

(1 hour)

You have already studied the opening of *Bleak House* by Charles Dickens in your classbook. You will find it reprinted below to remind you.

Bleak House

LONDON. Michaelmas Term lately over, and the Lord Chancellor sitting in Lincoln's Inn Hall. Implacable November weather. As much mud in the streets as if the waters had but newly retired from the face of the earth, and it would not be wonderful to meet a Megalosaurus, 40 feet long or so, waddling like an elephantine lizard up Holborn Hill. Smoke lowering down from chimney-pots, making a soft black drizzle, with flakes of soot in it as big as full-grown snowflakes – gone into mourning, one might imagine, for the death of the sun. Dogs, undistinguishable in mire. Horses, scarcely better – splashed to their very blinkers. Foot passengers, jostling one another's umbrellas, in a general infection of ill-temper, and losing their foothold at street corners, where tens of thousands of other foot passengers have been slipping and sliding since the day broke (if this day ever broke), adding new deposits to the crust upon crust of mud, sticking at those points tenaciously to the pavement, and accumulating at compound interest.

Fog everywhere. Fog up the river, where it flows among green aits and meadows; fog down the river, where it rolls defiled among the tiers of shipping and the waterside pollutions of a great (and dirty) city. Fog on the Essex marshes, fog on the Kentish heights. Fog creeping into the cabooses of collier-brigs; fog lying out on the yards and hovering in the rigging of great ships; fog drooping on the gunwales of barges and small boats. Fog in the eyes and throats of ancient Greenwich pensioners, wheezing by the firesides of their wards; fog in the stem and bowl of the afternoon pipe of the wrathful skipper, down in his close cabin; fog cruelly pinching the toes and fingers of his shivering little 'prentice boy on deck. Chance people on the bridges peeping over the parapets into a nether sky of fog, with fog all round them, as if they were up in a balloon, and hanging in the misty clouds.

Gas looming through the fog in divers places in the streets, much as the sun may, from the spongy fields, be seen to loom by husbandman and ploughboy. Most of the shops lighted two hours before their time – as the gas seems to know, for it has a haggard and unwilling look.

The raw afternoon is rawest, and the dense fog is densest, and the muddy streets are muddiest, near that leaden-headed old obstruction, appropriate ornament for the threshold of a leaden-headed old corporation – Temple Bar. And hard by Temple Bar, in Lincoln's Inn Hall, at the very heart of the fog, sits the Lord High Chancellor in his High Court of Chancery.

Never can there come fog too thick, never can there come mud and mire too deep, to assort with the groping and floundering condition which this High Court of Chancery, most pestilent of hoary sinners, holds, this day, in the sight of heaven and earth.

On such an afternoon, if ever, the Lord High Chancellor ought to be sitting here – as here he is – with a foggy glory round his head, softly fenced in with crimson cloth and curtains, addressed by a large advocate with great whiskers, a little voice, and an interminable brief, and outwardly directing his contemplation to the lantern in the roof, where he can see nothing but fog. On such an afternoon, some score of members of the High Court of Chancery bar ought to be – as here they are – mistily engaged in one of the ten thousand stages of an endless cause, tripping one another up on slippery precedents, groping knee-deep in technicalities, running their goat-hair and horse-hair warded heads against walls of words, and making a pretence of equity with serious faces, as players might. On such an afternoon, the various solicitors in the cause, some two or three of whom have inherited it from their fathers, who made a fortune by it, ought to be – as are they not? – ranged in a line, in a long, matted well (but you might look in vain for Truth at the bottom of it), between the registrar's red table and the silk gowns, with bills, cross-bills, answers, rejoinders, injunctions, affidavits, issues, references to masters, masters' reports, mountains of costly nonsense, piled before them. Well may the court be dim, with wasting candles here and there; well may the fog hang heavy in it, as if it would never get out; well may the stained-glass windows lose their colour, and admit no light of day into the place; well may the uninitiated from the streets, who peep in through the glass panes in the door, be deterred from entrance by its owlish aspect, and by the drawl languidly echoing to the roof from the padded dais where the Lord High Chancellor looks into the lantern that has no light in it, and where the attendant wigs are all stuck in a fog bank! This is the Court of Chancery, which has its decaying houses and its blighted lands in every shire; which has its worn-out lunatic in every madhouse, and its dead in every churchyard; which has its ruined suitor, with his slipshod heels and threadbare dress, borrowing and begging through the round of every man's acquaintance; which gives to moneyed might the means abundantly of wearying out the right; which so exhausts finances, patience, courage, hope, so overthrows the brain and breaks the heart, that there is not an honourable man among its practitioners who would not give – who does not often give – the warning, 'Suffer any wrong that can be done you, rather than come here!'

CHARLES DICKENS

TASK

1 What you have just re-read is the opening of the novel and Dickens has taken great care to create an atmosphere.

You are about to start writing a novel which is set in the place where you live. The plot of your novel is going to be very sad and perhaps frightening.

Write the first couple of pages of your novel in which you set the scene.

Shelter

(2 hours)

Dickens often wrote about unfortunate people who were forced to live in squalid conditions in nineteenth-century London.

Some people would argue that things haven't changed much today and there are still unfortunate people in much the same situation.

Printed on the next page is a message from the organisation 'Shelter' and an extract from one of their leaflets. They are an organisation which help the homeless, who are still too frequently on the streets of towns and cities.

Shelter URGENT MESSAGE

THE NATIONAL CAMPAIGN FOR HOMELESS PEOPLE

Recent winters have brought temperatures as low as -9°c to many parts of the country as well as snow and icy weather. Can you imagine the appalling risk to people living in damp, decaying homes, or out on the streets this winter, if we are faced with the same freezing conditions? Your money really is desperately needed now to help save more lives; so please, give what you can.

Thank you again.   Chris Holmes

Company No. 1038133. Charity No. 263710

Your gift now could help us save people's lives this Winter

The Winter Nights appeal is a response to Shelter's increasing concern for the thousands of people who are homeless – or living in damp, decaying homes not worthy of the name – during the winter months. They can be at the mercy of rain, snow and the freezing cold.

Sometimes the conditions they live in can kill.

Winterwatch, an initiative we launched together with the charity Crisis, aims to create enough emergency accommodation across the country, so that no one is left without a bed in cold weather.

Our 40 Housing Aid Centres around the country help people living in appalling conditions to fight for decent housing, and also help people threatened with the prospect of losing their homes.

Our Nightline emergency telephone advice line gives vital help to desperate and homeless people who might otherwise spend nights on the freezing streets.

We simply can't let these things happen. So please, give what you can to our Winter Nights appeal today – and help us to prevent suffering and death in the cold winter nights ahead. Thank you.

Homeless and desperate on the freezing city streets…

Shelly had been beaten up by her partner, again. It was midnight, freezing cold, and she had nowhere to go.

Standing in a call box, with her little girl Kate by her side, she managed to get through to Shelter's Nightline… who found them both a bed in an emergency hostel. Now they're safe and warm, in a flat of their own.

After fighting for his life in hospital, 5lb baby Simon faced death in his own home…

Simon weighed only 5lb when he was born. After he came home he developed a nasty cough. His parents' home was damp and mouldy, with broken windows and doors that let in freezing winds. The private landlord did no repairs. Imagine how Simon's parents felt as winter drew near… But with help from a Shelter Housing Aid Centre they've now found a warm, dry home to live in.

TASKS

2 Look carefully at the appeal and write briefly what effect it has on you.

You should consider:

- why particular people are mentioned
- the tone of the appeal
- the layout of the leaflet
- the purpose of the separate note

3 Imagine you want to raise money in school for this charity. You are allowed to produce a poster and are given three minutes in which to make an appeal in assembly.

- Design a poster.
- Write your appeal.

The National Trust

(1 hour 30 minutes)

You will find reprinted below the extract from the National Trust leaflet which you have used as the basis for some work in the classbook. Read the material through again.

Land under National Trust protection within The National Park

Protecting traditional buildings

Of course with so many working hill farms along with the 250 Lake District cottages owned by the Trust there is an awful lot of building work to be done.

Rebuilding, renovation and repair of these important properties has to be carried our regularly with the added complication of maintaining traditional appearances. This means specially skilled professionals to do the work and expensive traditional materials to complete the appearance.

Lime mortar is used as a weather coating to walls as opposed to unsuitable sand and cement render. The dressing of slate, the use of wooden pegs in place of nails and the adzing of riven oak for fencing or rafters are all more costly and time consuming methods, but are longer lasting and necessary in retaining the character of Lakeland property.

Fells, valleys & lakes

The National Trust now protects and cares for over a quarter of the Lake District National Park. In all 12 valleys the Trust protects large areas and there is access for everyone along both public and National Trust footpaths.

Borrowdale 15,000 acres including 9 farms, half of Derwentwater including the main islands, the hamlets of Watendlath and Seathwaite, woodlands and popular sites such as the Bowder Stone, Friars's Crag and Ashness Bridge.

Buttermere – the lakes of Buttermere, Crummock and Loweswater, farms in Buttermere village and land around the lakes themselves.

Coniston – 4 miles of lakeshore, 865 acres of woodland, 8 farms, 50 cottages, campsites and even the gracious Steam Yacht Gondola.

Duddon – 8 working farms covering nearly 6,000 acres, including Cockley Beck, the Trust's first fell farm, given in 1929.

Ennerdale – in this remote valley the Trust protects 7,700 acres, including the 5,000 acres of the wild and solitary Kinniside Common.

Eskdale – the 3,300 acres of Brotherilkeld Farm bought to prevent afforestation of the valley head, and another 5 working farms in upper Eskdale and the 7,900 acres of Eskdale Common.

Grasmere – the bed of the lake itself, 3 fell farms with a total of 800 acres of enclosed land plus several thousand acres of fell common and half of Rydal Water.

Hawkshead – extensive woodland along the west side of Windermere with public access to the shore and 5 farms. The Beatrix Potter Gallery, Hill Top and Hawkshead Courthouse are important buildings protected by the Trust.

Langdale – a favourite valley for visitors; the Trust has 9 farms, 22 cottages, a major campsite, the Old Dungeon Ghyll Hotel and a Youth Hostel.

Ullswater – Gowbarrow Park was acquired in 1906. Trust ownership now extends to 12,500 acres including 6 farms and Brotherswater.

Wastwater – the Trust protects virtually all the valley, 16,000 acres with 5 farms, the lake itself and the magnificent mountains that overlook it on all sides. Also, the Nether Wasdale estate comprising 1,000 acres with 7 farms and 420 acres of important woodland.

Windermere (Crosthwaite), Troutbeck and Ambleside – shore fields on Windermere, Townend in Troutbeck, and in total 12 farms, 12 cottages and 320 acres of woodland.

Lakeshores

Lakeshores always appear so unchanging but they too need constant care. Wave action can often undercut vegetation making bank reinforcements necessary, but of course these must be visually unobtrusive; in other places alders may be planted to help stabilise a shoreline.

At Yew Tree Tarn a geological fault led to the periodic draining of the Tarn. Thanks to the contributions of the Lake District Appeal a team of workers has rebuilt the dam to solve the problem and re-landscaped the area to preserve its beauty for generations to come.

Footpaths

One of the great pleasures of the Lake District, shared by local people and visitors alike, is to escape the pressures of life by walking the fells. In many places, however, paths have been turned into rivers of scree up to 100 feet (30 metres) wide in places, by the constant pounding of thousands of feet combined with the ravages of Lakeland weather. The Lake District Appeal has enabled the National Trust to take on people to form 4 footpath repair gangs in Borrowdale, Langdale, Grasmere and Wasdale. These dedicated individuals have fought doggedly against time and the elements over recent years to restore over 50 miles (80 kilometres) of the most eroded footpaths by the ancient method known as 'pitching'. This is slow, labour-intensive work, using only local materials – often averaging a mere 18 yards (15 metres) a day – but with continued maintenance this work will ensure that these paths last for hundreds of years to come.

TASK

4 Think of a place which you have visited and which you know well and like.

You believe that this place should be turned into a National Park.

You have the chance to prepare your case and present it at a meeting of the national committee of the National Trust.

Prepare your case. You should consider all of the data you have read and carefully analyse your reasons for proposing this place.

Urban Development and Planning

(2 hours)

Printed below is an extract from a book called *Urban Development and Planning*, by John Hancock.

Comprehensive redevelopment of central areas: Birmingham

Birmingham, the second largest city in Great Britain, is a regional shopping centre for the five million people living in the West Midlands.

In the last thirty years, massive physical changes have been made to the central area. The largely Victorian core has been transformed into one of the most modern cities in Europe. A programme of large-scale slum clearance has made space in the city centre for new highways and major shopping and commercial projects. This section focuses on the new shopping centre.

The most significant change in shopping in the last thirty years has been the decline in the total number of shops, especially the 'street corner' type of shop. Changing shopping habits such as using the supermarket, and new methods of retailing, such as by national multiple stores like Sainsbury, Tesco and Boots, have encouraged investment in the city centre. By using the central area, the shopper has a choice of style, quality, service and price. Studies of customer movement by the big chain stores, such as Marks and Spencer and Littlewoods, show how the cluster of shops in the centre offers the shopper maximum choice for minimum effort.

In Birmingham two new shopping schemes have been completed: the Bull Ring Centre and the Birmingham Shopping Centre over New Street Station. The Bull Ring redevelopment was linked with the first major road redevelopment, Smallbrook Ringway, a section of the inner ring road. The Bull Ring Centre includes shops and offices. It was built on the site of Birmingham's old market, on the edge of the old central core. The local authority stated its requirement for shopping space, car parking, bus stations, and other uses. Tenders were invited from probate developers, who were given freedom of design

and shopping arrangement. In 1959 Laing Developments won the contract for the centre, which opened in 1964. This massive centre, on five interlocking levels, is now linked to a newer scheme over New Street Station. Shoppers move through warm, covered shopping halls on seven floors. The other main shopping streets nearby have been pedestrianised. There are 25,000 car-parking spaces, in recognition of the increased use of the car to reach the most economic and attractive shopping site.

Redevelopment in this scale presupposes courage and commitment. In 1944 an Act of Parliament allowed local authorities comp-ulsorily to purchase blitz areas of the very expensive city centre. Birmingham, Coventry and Plymouth acted; but some cities hesitated, and lost the opportunity, as the 1944 Act was withdrawn in 1947. In 1946 Birmingham received permission for its plans for major redevelopment of the city centre. There are many critics of the new centre. Reconstruction causes dirt, blight, disruption, the loss of familiar landmarks; and it takes a long time. Critics suggest that Birmingham has lost its atmosphere and individuality. Even today, with so much achieved, new worries about competition from out-of-town shopping centres have emerged. The City Council has responded, actively promoting its city centre to luxury shop-owners in their determination to make Birmingham an international city. They believe that city-centre shops will attract customers so long as environmental standards are high and the range and quality of shops continues to improve.

Some areas have been cleared of housing and then left to await redevelopment for many years. The traffic circulation system is being constantly changed because some key sections are incomplete.

TASKS

5 Imagine that you are the planning officer who has been responsible for the development of Birmingham city centre.

You have been invited to give a talk to other planning officers explaining what you have achieved in Birmingham.

Prepare your talk.

6 Think about where you live. The planning officer in your area is talking about a major redevelopment project. There is going to be a public meeting.

Prepare three questions which you would want to ask at the public meeting.

7 Describe a town centre which you know well. Make sure that you refer to those things which you like about it and explain anything which you dislike.

Touch and Go

(1 hour)

You will find reprinted below the extract from *Touch and Go* in which Emma Rowlands was involved in a hunt for rats.

Touch and Go

'Right then, let's get started. Where's Harry?'

There was now a restless mass of dogs in front of the barn. A brown-and-white surge of Jack Russells with a scattering of sharp lean terriers. Whimpering and barking in anticipation, they strained at their leashes, tails going, paws scrabbling with excitement.

Ivor had told her that a pack of twenty could kill as many as a hundred rats on a good day.

It was a big storage barn with a tiled roof and openings on either side, room for haycarts to be driven in back in the old days. Three hundred years old, at a guess. Nowadays it was used for grain storage, in bins.

Emma shivered at the thought of the carnage to come, wandered inside, leaned against the wall and looked around her. It had a gloom and quietness that cut off the confused din from outside. A sturdy geometric symmetry of huge oak beams supported the length and breadth of the walls and the soaring inverted Vs that braced the shadowy roof. Daylight shafted in through cubes and rectangles left by a few shattered tiles. Long rods of dusty light pierced that upper darkness

and diffused into daylight halfway down.

Harry passed her, an executioner's figure in his red rubber gloves and black knitted cap pulled well down over his ears. his black sweater had one scarlet word knitted into it. HOSANNA. He carried a chainsaw without the blade; instead a pipe had been fixed.

'This'll smoke 'em out, see?' he flung over his shoulder as he made for the further wall.

A group of youths ran in and started beating the huge grain containers with staves. It seemed as if a heavy-metal band filled the barn. Emma slipped out before she was ordered to do so. She was nearly tripped up by the dogs, now released. And all hell broke out. Rats were suddenly everywhere, swarming over the tops of the containers, running across the floor, leaping up at the walls, dashing for exit holes.

The dogs were on them, urged by the shouts; they pounced, shook, left the dead and went on joyfully to despatch the living. The floor heaved with a black, white, brown tide, splashed with red. A shout from above as Glyn, astride a beam, flailing an iron bar, beat down rats on to the men and dogs below. Yelping, squealing, savage laughter, fear and a hot excited rage and exhilaration filled the barn from floor to roof as the sun rose higher and the frost melted on the ground outside.

Emma's hand trembled as she slashed swiftly at her pad with a stick of charcoal. It was a hopeless task, but it kept her from being sick. She retreated further from the opening and watched a line of four youngsters with their dogs, who had been set to stop that escape route. As a squealing tide of terrified rats poured out they beat about them with pitchforks and heavy sticks while their dogs finished off the crawling wounded. One boy had an airgun and pot-shotted dangerously at escapees.

'Daft bugger, leave it to Scorcher or you'll hit him!' yelled an undersized lad with huge kicking boots. The boy with the gun had RATS painted on his motor-cycle helmet and out of bravado fired up into the air.

'Scares 'em, though, dunnit?' he yelled back, hate blazing in his eyes.

Then a huge rat, as big as a size 12 wellington boot, ran across Emma's foot. From its pointed muzzle came blood and a keening sound. Up dashed a small Jack Russell and seized it behind the ears. He got it down on the ground, but it gave a convulsive jerk, and twisting upwards bit hard into the dog's throat, hanging on as it was thrown from side to side.

'Come on, Scorcher, shake 'im, boy! Kill 'im!'

But the rat was nearly as big as the dog and Emma watched, terrified, unable to move. This was a nightmare. At that moment Ivor ran past her and she grasped his arm.

'That dog will be killed, oh –'

Ivor snatched the pitchfork from the yelling boy and neatly skewered the rat as it clung, not touching the dog. The jaws relaxed, the rat twitched in its last agony on the prongs and the dog sank on to the ground, shaking its head groggily.

'It's a monster and Scorcher got it. It's a monster an'–' The lad was pulling the rat off the prongs of the pitchfork by its tail, when Ivor, his face mottled with anger, hit him hard. The lad toppled over sideways, rat in hand, landing by his coughing dog.

'What's that for then?' he asked. 'Scorcher got it. It's Scorcher's.'

'It damn nearly got Scorcher, you young fool!

That dog's too young for the hunt. I told you not to bring him. Glyn'd say the same. Now he's bitten. He might die. Stupid little git. Now get him to the vet.'

The boy's mouth drew down at the corners. He couldn't be more than twelve. He stretched out a hand to the shivering dog, looked up at Ivor, but Ivor flung off back into the barn.

'I'll miss the rest of it – ' he said, torn. Emma saw that the little dog was only half grown.

'I'll take you,' she said, helping the boy up. 'What's your name? You carry Scorcher.'

'Scorcher would've finished 'im off. We get prize money for the biggest rat. I'd better hide it else someone'll pinch it off me. I'm Dewi.'

He shoved the rat under the stone wall and piled stones on it. Then he picked up his dog and followed Emma to the car. It didn't cross his mind to thank her, but as he sank on the seat, the dog in his lap, he caressed its head and gave a long sigh. There was blood on his boots.

'You won't peg out, will you, Scorcher? Not you. You're a champion you are. In't he, missis?'

They were driving at a fair pace across the field. Emma could have kissed Dewi. She had been able to retreat with dignity, with a purpose. They negotiated the overgrown lane, and the chained-up dog gave its mournful greeting as they passed the farmhouse. The day was clear and blue now, warm for November. Across the fields the sound of church bells blew towards them. Sunday, a day of prayer.

She followed Dewi's directions, hoping the vet was in, his midday Sabbath dinner finished. The time had fled.

'Ivor probably saved his life,' said Emma, and Dewi grunted.

Morgan Griffiths was in, playing a small harmonium in the front room for his mother and sisters. One of those born to bachelorhood, was Emma's first impression as he led the way to the surgery. He looked well-fleshed and docile, but his manner changed as he closed the door between his work and the rest of the house. He looked keenly through his spectacles, his hands touched the little dog with professional firmness.

'Put him up on here, Dewi,' he said. 'Ratting, were you? This fellow's got a bit to go to his full strength. He's like you, bach, got to fill out, get some muscles.' He reached over and squeezed

Dewi's upper arm. 'Get some biceps, man. Duw, plenty of porridge.'

He cleaned the torn throat. 'Nasty bite that –'

'He near killed a monster, big as your boot –'

'I'll have to give him an injection. Hold him still now.'

While he swabbed a place on the dog's backside, then deftly slid in the needle, pushing the plunger down, Emma asked whether a rat's bite was poisonous.

Mr Griffiths withdrew the syringe, swabbed again and looked at her directly for the first time.

'Ever heard of Weil's disease?' She shook her head.

'Carried in rat's saliva, and its urine. A rat urinates every thirty seconds. Contaminates everything it touches.' He turned again to Dewi. 'Come you now, boy, and wash your hands while I wash – what's this fellow's name?'

'Scorcher,' said Dewi.

'Scorcher's neck and head and belly. See what I'm doing? You do the same, soap around the nails, now, then use a paper towel. Particular you have to be. How about you, missis?'

'I'm Emma Rowlands. I've moved back to Bryntanat.'

'Good of you to bring the lad here. Better wash your hands, just in case. And you, my lad, should be wearing rubber gloves.'

As she and Dewi did as they were told, Mr Griffiths dried his patient with paper towels and went on talking.

'Rats. Need a Pied Piper to get rid of them. Warfarin's meat and drink to them, especially now some farmers are growing maize. Love maize, those creatures, makes 'em immune to Warfarin.'

'It's good fun, ratting,' said Dewi. 'We'll get near a hundred today, counting the old pigsties after the barn. You should have seen Glyn, Tregaron, up on the beam. Grand he was.' He looked at his dog lying obediently on the table. 'Scorcher'll be a champion, won't he, Mr Griffiths, when he gets better?'

'*If* he gets better, Dewi. If luck and the Lord agree. Then he won't get poisoned again. Once bitten, no more trouble. Have to watch, mind. Keep him quiet, warm bread and milk.' Abruptly he turned to Emma, adjusting his spectacles with a large, soft, very clean hand. 'Know why the men carry pheasants home from a shoot by the necks, Mrs Rowlands?' So he had spotted her wedding ring. Should she after all keep it on? Looking down at it now, as she dried her fingers, it seemed like a forged passport. 'Dewi knows, ask him. His father beats for Talycoed.'

As they left, Mr Griffiths said again, 'Straight home with him now, and let me know how he goes on. Quiet and comfy he needs to be for a day or two.'

ELIZABETH BERRIDGE

TASK

8 Emma writes a letter to a friend in London telling her about her experience.

Write her letter. (Remember that, as well as telling her about the rat hunt, Emma will want to tell her friend a little about her new life.)

London's Crossroads

(1 hour 30 minutes)

Below is part of an article from the *Geographical* magazine about London and some of the problems of this large city.

It is quite a detailed article and you will have to read it carefully.

London's Crossroads

London's global status and quality of life continues to slip, although less severely and for different reasons than many allege. Does the recent establishment of a government committee to develop a strategic plan for London signal a change of heart? Senior Correspondent **Richard Evans** *reports.*

Perhaps Londoners just love complaining. Or maybe they just enjoy turning minor inconveniences into major dramas. Whatever the reason, a host of professional surveys and reports in the last two years have found that London's future as a cosmopolitan centre for culture and business is threatened by worsening living conditions and a chronic lack of urban investment and planning.

Separate research reports by the consultants Coopers and Lybrand Deloitte and the Corporate Resources Group maintain that not only is London a very expensive place to live but it also lacks decent transport, education and training.

Award-winning British architect Richard Rogers wrote in his latest book *A New London* that the city presents 'a dismal contrast' to many of its European counterparts. Margaret Hodge, chairman of the Association of London Authorities, warned last year that 'London is on the slide and is in need of some intensive repair.'

London's residents have certainly noticed a number of disturbing trends in recent years: the growing legion of homeless in streets and parks; traffic-clogged roads at all hours of the day; crowded and unreliable Underground trains; potholes and cracked pavements; ubiquitous rubbish; and gas and water leaks galore. The accelerating decay of the British capital is particularly striking when returning from a holiday or business trip in Paris, Geneva, Amsterdam or any other European city where public transport runs smoothly and the pavements are comparatively spotless.

Environmental pollution is yet another symptom of this decline. Today, London's poor air quality regularly exceeds World Health Organisation guidelines. Two rubbish-fired incinerators and two sewage sludge incinerators scheduled for completion in the London area by 1998 can only make things worse. Especially singled out for criticism has been the giant rubbish incinerator built on a derelict site in Bexley, south-east London. The Bexley incinerator will burn 1.5 million tonnes of refuse each year and could generate enough electricity to power a large town. But environmentalists and local residents claim that its emissions will pose a very real health hazard for those living in the region.

'South-east London will be turned into a toxic sacrifice zone.' warned Greenpeace campaigner Madeleine Cobbing. 'Even considering building an incinerator of this scale in such a heavily populated area shows irresponsibility beyond belief.' Building four incinerators in the same part of London, environmentalists maintain, is sheer insanity.

Industrialists make the counter-claim that such incinerators will generate far cleaner electricity than do existing coal-fired power stations. London's rubbish is currently dumped in huge landfill sites in the home counties, rotting down to create methane, a powerful 'greenhouse' gas contributing to global warming. The planned sewage sludge incinerators are needed to dispose of the huge quantities of sewage which are currently dumped in the English Channel. European

Community legislation ensures that all sea dumping will be outlawed by 1998.

Defenders of the incinerator projects maintain that they must be built somewhere, and that criticisms are typical of the so-called NIMBY (not in my back yard) syndrome whereby local residents simply want them to be built elsewhere.

All the waste incinerator projects in question are funded and will be run by private industry. This is in line with current government practice which has entrusted such redevelopment schemes as Docklands, Canary Wharf, the now-abandoned Battersea power station and the area around King's Cross and Paddington stations to the private sector. But critics argue that the future of London cannot be safely left to profiteers who have no real stake in the capital.

TASKS

9 In your own words carefully summarise what is being said about London in this article. (Your summary should be between 200 and 250 words long.)

10 Write one paragraph defending incinerator projects and another paragraph attacking them.

Slough

(1 hour)

During your classbook study you worked on three poems, *Town and Country* by Gordon Symes, *Wind* by Ted Hughes and *God's Grandeur* by Gerard Manley Hopkins. Printed below is another poem for you to read which gives John Betjeman's view of a particular town.

Slough

Come, friendly bombs, and fall on Slough
It isn't fit for humans now,
There isn't grass to graze a cow
Swarm over, Death!

Come, bombs, and blow to smithereens
Those air-conditioned, bright canteens,
Tinned fruit, tinned meat, tinned milk, tinned beans
Tinned minds, tinned breath.

Mess up the mess they call a town –
A house for ninety-seven down
And once a week a half-a-crown
For twenty years,

And get that man with double chin
Who'll always cheat and always win,
Who washes his repulsive skin
In women's tears,

And smash his desk of polished oak
And smash his hands so used to stroke
And stop his boring dirty joke
And make him yell.

But spare the bald young clerks who add
The profits of the stinking cad;
It's not their fault that they are mad,
They've tasted Hell.

It's not their fault they do not know
The birdsong from the radio,
It's not their fault they often go
To Maidenhead

And talk of sports and makes of cars
In various bogus Tudor bars
And daren't look up and see the stars
But belch instead.

In labour-saving homes, with care
Their wives frizz out peroxide hair
And dry it in synthetic air
And paint their nails.

Come, friendly bombs, and fall on Slough
To get it ready for the plough.
The cabbages are coming now;
The earth exhales.

JOHN BETJEMAN

TASK

11 As one of your classbook tasks you chose one of the three poems mentioned on the previous page and studied it in detail.

Compare the poem which you chose in class with *Slough*.

You should compare:

■ the poets' intentions
■ the language they use
■ how effective you consider each poem to be

AA Book of the British Countryside

(1 hour)

You will find reprinted below the extract from the *AA Book of the British Countryside* which you have already used in your classbook study.

Where wildlife hides in the heart of a town

For the town dweller, the world of nature begins before he reaches his front door. Up to 50 species of plants and animals may live in and around his house, and beyond the door there is an even greater wealth of wildlife.

Over the centuries roads, buildings and industry have gradually submerged large areas of Britain's natural landscape. Nevertheless, wildlife has not been exterminated in towns – it exists even in the heart of great conurbations; and while it can be argued that London's starling flocks and the Trafalgar Square pigeons, not to mention the pelicans of St James' Park, are merely grace-and favour residents fed by man, many species of insects, invertebrates, mammals, birds and plants have displayed nature's ability to overcome even the most unpromising of man-made habitats.

Most towns have parks, commons or other open spaces which provide 'mini-countrysides' especially attractive to birds: more than 100 different species have been recorded in London's Regent's Park in one year. But even if migrant birds settle and are able to breed in such areas, they do not become part of the town's natural history in the strict sense for, without the artificial habitat created by man, they would not survive.

True town wildlife exists because of its

ability to adapt and live in close proximity to man. Wild flowers in towns have to overcome the following handicaps: reduced light caused by the screening effect of smoke, dust and fog; choked pores from oily deposits; sour soil and reduced soil bacteria; the corrosive effects of sulphates absorbed through the leaves; and limited water. In spite of all this, some thrive.

Within a space of seven years a bombed site in the City of London turned from barren rubble to a teeming haven of wildlife. A study carried out between 1946 and 1953 showed that the first plants to arrive were those which reproduce by airborne spores: algae, mosses and ferns. The came the plants with light seeds borne by 'parachutes' – dandelion and sycamores, fruiting thistles, rosebays and Oxford ragwort.

Grasses followed: seaside species came from the contents of sandbags and fodder plants from food for horses stabled in London. Apple, tomato, plum, date and cherry plants developed from food remnants. Plants with hooked fruits were carried in by man. Pellitory-of-the-wall and ivy grew in the dry cracks of walls, and Canadian fleabane, brambles and buddleia also appeared. Before the blitz, only pellitory-of-the-wall was firmly established in the City, but by 1952 there were 269 species of wild flowers, grasses and ferns on record.

Where previously few wild animals were seen in the City, apart from pigeons, starlings and rats, by the end of the 7-year study, 4 mammals, 31 birds, 56 insects and 30 other invertebrates had been noted. They included snails, slugs, woodlice, centipedes, aphids, spiders, caterpillars, moths and butterflies. The cat, mouse and rat population was augmented by hedgehogs, lizards, snakes and tortoises, and other lost pets.

Ornithological history was made when the black redstart, formerly a rare summer migrant, bred in the ruins. It now nests regularly in factory yards, sidings and power stations.

Railways and canal embankments reach into the centres of most cities bringing wildlife with them. Embankments, covered with grass, flowers, shrubs and a variety of trees, harbour insects, birds, mice, voles, shrews and rabbits and provide foraging ground for hedgehogs, foxes, badgers and squirrels.

The fish in canals attract a variety of birds, including herons, and many aquatic plants thrive in disused waterways.

Sewage farms and rubbish tips are an important source of food for birds and animals on the fringe of towns. It had been estimated that 40 million flies feed on each acre of filter beds. This attracts wagtails, flycatchers, warblers and starlings.

Reservoirs contain bacteria, algae, small crustaceans and insect larvae. Pike, perch, roach and trout are often introduced for sport, and herons, grebes and cormorants appear, together with visiting waders, ducks, geese and swans. Common, herring and blackheaded gulls roost on the water after spending the winter days scavenging on rubbish tips.

Open rubbish dumps also provide a ready supply of food for insects, invertebrates, birds and even rats, foxes, hedgehogs, rabbits and badgers.

Away from town centres, suburban gardens form an ideal habitat for birds, particularly where man stocks bird tables and provides nest boxes. In addition to the ubiquitous house sparrow and starling, robins, blue and great tits, greenfinches, chaffinches, dunnocks, wood pigeons, blackbirds, song and mistle thrushes are common suburbanites. Swifts and house martins are numerous, feeding on flying insects.

While squirrels and hedgehogs have long been known as visitors to the garden, in recent years, possibly because of the decline in rabbits since 1953, foxes have become a nuisance in some areas, tearing open modern paper-bag type dustbins. Most gardens contain a large number of insects and, if neglected, soon display a variety of weeds. In return, many attractive 'wild' flowers, such as the michaelmas daisy and lupin, have spread from gardens to grow wild.

In many places, old churchyards survive and are often neglected. Colonies of lichen grow on tombstones, the older ones carrying more species since aerial pollution, particularly sulphur dioxide, has killed off less hardy forms. Owls and weasels may sometimes be found, preying on rats and mice.

Dockland is an area where wildlife can flourish, with foreign plants growing among the native wild flowers. The food produced by spillage attracts insects, rats, mice, hedgehogs, weasels and rabbits, which are preyed on by owls, kestrels and even foxes. In addition, linnets, goldfinches, wrens, blackbirds, song thrushes and gulls live and breed in the area.

The average householder would be surprised if it were possible for him to count the number of wild creatures which shelter under his roof; there are at least 50 species which are often found indoors. Rats, mice or bats are usually eradicated as soon as discovered, and common toads hibernating in basements and cellars are usually removed promptly. But a whole range of insects, including houseflies, silverfish, and scavenging beetles are not so conspicuous. Minute spores can produce mould on neglected food, clothing or walls, and dry rot fungi can germinate in suitable places. Open windows let in moths and other night-flying insects, and garden insects are often brought into the house on clothes or flowers.

Some animals show a remarkable ability to adapt to specialised urban environments:
brown rats and mice living and breeding in sub-zero temperatures at a refrigerated store developed thicker fur and a protective layer of fat. Moths have developed darker colours to merge with sooty backgrounds – a process known as industrial melanism.

As man changes the environment, some species of plants and animals are driven out, while others thrive. In this process man's waste products have come to form an important link or supplement to the natural food chain in urban areas.

In watching for changes in urban wildlife, it is important not to be misled by oddities mentioned from time to time in the Press, such as peregrines hunting over Big Ben, a stone curlew resting in a child's sandpit or field mice appearing in an uncompleted office block. While no doubt interesting additions to town wildlife, they are merely freak occurrences.

TASK

12 Write a letter to the leader of your town council asking for the preservation of a small derelict site near the city centre.

You will need to argue your case strongly and will need to give examples of the wildlife and plant development which you think should be preserved.

Kuala Lumpur

(2 hours)

Kuala Lumpur is probably a town which few of you have had the opportunity to visit. Imagine that you have won the chance to spend some time there. You have very little information.

Printed on the next few pages are some bits and pieces of information which you have found on the back of a map of the city.

Dining/eating out/restaurants

Eden Village (*Steak & Seafood Cuisine*)
Jalan Raja Chulan, Tel: 2414027

Eden Airport Restaurant
(*Dim Sum & Mandarin Cuisine*)
1st Fl Fima Airtel,
Komplek Subang International Airport
Tel: 7463495

Eden Seafood Village
(*Seafood & Mandarin Cuisine*)
Jln SS22/23 Damansara Jaya, Petaling Jaya
Tel: 7193225

Eden Good Food People
(*Steak & Seafood Cuisine*)
Jln SS22/23 Damansara Jaya, Petaling Jaya
Tel: 7193184

Owing to Malaysia's diverse racial background, the variety of culinary spread available is endless. Especially when there is a comprehensive range of superb international restaurants, popular fastfood chains, quaint local restaurants and fascinating open-air hawker stalls to excite one's taste buds. Have a feast. Tuck into spicy Malay dishes, exotic Indian fare, delicious Chinese cuisine or relish European delights. There are also numerous Japanese and Korean and Thai Restaurants.

Restoran Oversea (*Chinese*)
Lot Lg 2 Central Market Jalan Hang Kasturi

No 84-88 Jalan Imbi

Spices Restaurant (*Asian*)
Concorde Hotel Jalan Sultan Ismail

Xin Cuisine Chinese Restaurant
Concorde Hotel Jalan Sultan Ismail

Blues Cafe
Lot 10 Shopping Centre
50 Jalan Sultan Ismail

Shopping at Subang International Airport

Syarikat Sriwani (M) Sdn Bhd
Terminal 1 (Nth & Sth Wings)
Tel: 7462450

Gurun Duty Free (M) Sdn Bhd
Lot 52 Duty Free Plaza

Isetan Duty Free Shop Sdn Bhd
Lot 48 Palza Bebas Cukai

Parkson Duty Free Centre Sdn Bhd
Lot 51 Plaza Bebas Cukai

Selberan Co Sdn Bhd
Lot 41 Duty Free Plaza North Wing,
Terminal 1

Agate Group Malaysia
Terminal 1 N & S Wings

Pernas Sime Darby Duty Free Sdn Bhd
Duty Free Plaza, Terminal 1

Dewana Duty Free Sdn Bhd
Duty Free Plaza, Terminal 1

Choc Stop
Lot 38 Terminal 1 North Wing

Colours and Fragrances Sdn Bhd
Lot 42 Terminal 1 North Wing

Guardian Pharmacy
North & South Wing

Ruang Prima Duty Free Sdn Bhd
Departure Hall, Terminal 1

K.I. Production (Karl Iskandar)
Southern Wing, Duty Free Plaza, Terminal 1

Calan Duty Free Shoppers
No F1, International Departure
Lounge Airport

Selamat Datang Ke Malaysia!

That means 'Welcome to Malaysia' in our national language. You are in Malaysia, a land of enchantment and a diverse racial background with Malay, Chinese and Indian races forming the majority of the population.

Malaysians live and work in harmony regardless of race and its is natural that they extend this admirable quality to visitors to the country. Bahasa Malaysia is the official national language and English the second language, while Chinese and Indian dialects are widely spoken. Being culturally diverse, visitors to the country will be intrigued by the many facets of local heritage.

The Federal Capital of Malaysia is Kuala Lumpur and although being a metropolis, it has managed to keep a fine balance between multi-storey buildings, historical edifices and luscious greenery. Even more fascinating, Kuala Lumpur is a shopper's paradise with products ranging from internationally renowned brands to local handicrafts.

Tickle your taste buds! Malaysian food will entice you with its exotic flavour and it'll leave you asking for more. Apart from the local fare there are multifarious restaurants located within the city.

Don't wait! Book yourself on a tour of the city and discover for yourself the charms of Kuala Lumpur, whether a tour organised by your hotel or travel agency, or by car rental.

So enjoy what Kuala Lumpur has to offer, and you might just want to stay a day longer.

Useful Information

Climate
It is hot and humid throughout the year, with plenty of sunshine and temperatures ranging from 21°C to 32°C. The average rate of annual rainfall is quite high: 2000 mm to 2500 mm. The rainy seasons are August – September along the West Coast, and November – February on the East Coast as well as in northern Borneo, with much of the rain concentrated in the late afternoons.

Time
Malaysian time is 8 hours ahead of GMT and 16 hours ahead of the US Pacific Standard Time.

Monetary transactions
There are more than 40 commercial banks in Malaysia. Travellers' cheques are accepted by all banks, hotels and large departmental stores. And most establishments accept the American Express © Card. There are also foreign exchange vending machines at the Subang International Airport. The Malaysian currency is the Ringgit Malaysia (RM) or Malaysian Dollar which divides into 100 sen. To assist you during your stay in Malaysia, the foreign exchange rates are listed below:

US $1.00	= RM2.70
UK £1	= RM4.20
¥100	= RM1.970
DM$ 1.00	= RM1.61

(The exchange rate quoted is indicative only. Please refer to your financial institution's daily rates)

Telephone
Telephone cards are used in Kuala Lumpur and most major towns in Malaysia. These cards are available at all Telekom shops, 7–11 outlets, Petronas petrol kiosks and other distribution agents. You can use your American Express Card at all Uniphone and Telephone Machine Credit Card phones – please look for the decals or signs.

Business hours
Departmental stores/supermarkets are usually opened from 10am to 10pm and shops from 9am to 7pm. In Kuala Lumpur, there are several 24-hour stores and in most towns, you can find 24-hour petrol kiosks. A Thursday – Friday weekend is observed in Johor, Terengganu, Kelantan, Kedah and Perlis. Government offices in all states are open from 8am to 4.15pm on weekdays and from 8am to 12.45pm on the sixth day.

What to wear

Light clothing all year round. For more formal occasions: jacket and tie/long sleeve batik for men and dresses for women.

> **Trafficking in illegal drugs carries the death penalty.**

TASKS

13 Look at the information that you have. On the basis of it begin to plan your few days in the city.

Write your plan in the form of a proposed itinerary.

14 If you had the chance to visit any city in the world, where would you choose to go?

Write about your choice of city, explaining why visiting it would be so special for you.

The Monument

(2 hours)

Throughout history people have built great monuments to celebrate victories, to remember very special people or even simply to say 'we're better than everyone else'.

Printed below is an account of the building of the Arc de Triomphe in Paris.

Napoléon's Sacred Gate

It is the largest monument of its kind ever constructed. In its 156-year life millions have admired it, walked under it, climbed to its lofty platform to view the city. It is as much a symbol of Paris as the Eiffel Tower, which it predates by half a century. What is the reason for this pile of ornamental stones in the heart of the French capital?

The significance of triumphal arches is generally thought to stem from a religious ceremony of Roman warfare: at the end of campaigns the returning legionnaires were marched under a sacred gate, a symbol of the harmony between the gods and the emperor, to rid themselves of the destructive energies with which they were still charged and which would otherwise prove disruptive in peacetime domestic life. This rite of passage, if it was effective in its day, would have provided a

psychotherapeutic 'decompression' lacked by many modern societies faced with battle-hardened men returning to civvy street.

The sacred gates were erected at the entrance either to the town or the forum. Originally only simple, temporary, wooden affairs dismantled after the 'demob' ceremony, in due course they were succeeded by more-enduring structures. Restrained in form, still built with superstitious belief in mind, these quickly developed into monuments of deification, and commemorations of imperial victories – such was the Porta Triumphalis at Rome. The single gateway of the earliest designs progressed into double, triple and then quadruple arches, allowing thereby separate portals for pedestrians and for traffic entering and leaving the city.

But another type also evolved, with no

practical application, being built not as part of a protective wall but usually to span a road, often seemingly in the middle of nowhere and usually dedicated to an individual emperor, god or heroic figure. A number of these have survived from the Roman Empire throughout Italy and the Mediterranean provinces.

As a style that appealed to victorious empire builders the triumphal arch found favour again after the Renaissance. Modern examples can be found all across Europe: London's Marble Arch, Berlin's Brandenburg Gate, Madrid's Puerta de Toledo and, in Paris, the 17th-century Porte St-Denis and Porte St-Martin. But nothing comes near the grandeur of Napoléon's Arc de Triomphe de l'Étoile. To equal it in height, the Arch of Constantine in Rome would have to be placed on top of the Porte St-Denis. And the impressive structure is made much more glorious by its position at the crown of a hill and the hub of 12 broad avenues.

In the 18th century the site of l'Étoile was already an important crossroads, although it stood well outside Paris, in open country. A huge avenue leading from the centre of the Tuileries Palace crossed the square, and many leading figures had suggested erecting some kind of memorial here. The most fanciful project envisaged an elephant surmounted by the royal statue, inside which stairs would lead to reception rooms, ballrooms etc.

But it was Napoléon I who, inspired by Roman imperial culture, issued a decree on 18 February, 1806, ordering the construction of a triumphal arch in honour of *la gloire des victoires des Grandes Armées de la France*. The foundation stone was laid the same year, on 15 August – the emperor's birthday.

Progress was slow, due to difficulties in laying suitable foundations. The first grand ceremony took place on 2 April 1810, following the marriage between Napoléon and Marie-Louise, on the occasion of the official entry of the imperial couple into Paris. But all was not as it seemed on the day – for the arch they passed through was a prop, made from painted canvas stretched over a wooden scaffolding, hastily constructed by 500 workmen over the previous 3 weeks. The real work had scarcely begun.

And time was running out for Corsica's little corporal. The fall of Paris in 1814 saw work on the arch stop for several years. It even came close to being demolished. But in 1823 the restored Bourbon monarch, Louis XVIII, decided to recommence construction. Despite his death the following year, and the flight of the Bourbons in 1830, the arch continued towards its completion – though its significance changed subtly. Louis-Philippe, the citizen king, saw it as an appeasement to a nation eager for glory after so many years of instability and disappointment. Unable to offer his country new territorial conquests, what better than to reawaken pride in past victories? The Count of Montalivet, founder of the Commission of Historic Monuments, summed it up as follows:

'Louis XIV had spurned the memory of François I and of Henri IV; Napoléon, that of Louis XIV; the Restoration, the great feats of Napoléon. For the first time a sovereign had enough depth of feeling for his country to mingle in his heart all the greatness that that country had achieved.'

Hence, far from rebutting the memory of Napoléon I, Louis-Philippe exalted the imperial achievements. Thirty years in the building, the Arc de Triomphe was officially inaugurated on 29 July 1836, and thus this bold statement in stone, in honour of the Grande Armée, finally took its place on the city's skyline. Four years later, on an imperial hearse drawn by 16 caparisoned horses, the repatriated remains of the emperor at last passed through his great arch on the way to his final resting place at Les Invalides.

In 1885 the monument witnessed the massive homage of the nation to another great son, when a million French came to render their last respects to the body of Victor Hugo as it lay in state overnight under the arch before being carried, on a pauper's hearse, to the Panthéon.

In 1919, after the Great War, the Arc was the focus for great celebrations and, a year later, on 10 November, 1920 the remains of an unidentified soldier were buried there to symbolise a nation's debt to those who died on the field of battle. This event marked a change for the Arc – not in its outward appearance, but in what it came to be seen to stand for – not so much a statue to triumphant conquest but a panegyric to peace.

Over the decades since the onset of the internal combustion engine, despite what must be the most impressive central 'bollard' in the world, l'Étoile (or Place Charles-de-Gaulle as it is now officially known) has become just a glorified roundabout. At busy times it is the motorist's equivalent of a hornet's nest, where normal driving skills are hardly sufficient to cope with vehicles attacking from every angle – and beneath which even the subsoil is intersected by the tunnels of the Métro.

The effect of traffic and other eroding elements has taken a toll on the arch and the attentions of conservationists are now needed to protect and preserve the sculpted façades which laud the departing, victorious and returning French armies.

But as much as one might abhor war and all the misery that aggressive military might has wreaked throughout history on so many populations, it would be hard to imagine that wonderful broad avenue, running from the Louvre to the much more recent arch of La Défense, if it were not crowned by Napoléon's sacred gate.

TASKS

15 Answer the following questions.

    a Explain briefly the history of triumphal arches.

    b How long did it take to build the Arc de Triomphe and what caused the delays?

    c What are some of the modern-day problems for the Arc de Triomphe and why have they occurred?

16 Let us suppose that you have the chance to build a great monument in the place where you live.

    ■ What would you want to celebrate?
    ■ Where would you put your monument?
    ■ What would your monument look like?

Write the speech which you would make at the unveiling of your great monument.

YOUNG AND OLD

The Man by the Fountain

(45 minutes)

You have already studied the story *The Man by the Fountain* in class. You will find it reprinted below. First of all read the story again.

The Man by the Fountain

As always, John Deweck sat by the fountain.

The spring sun loomed up out of the seething foam. The children honoured the memories of heroic admirals. Their galleons and cutters backed to and fro across the wide pond. Nursemaids and grandmothers glanced anxiously at frocks and trousers. Over the wide world the fountain sang, thrusting a quivering plume of water at the scudding clouds. Liquid pattered noisily into bowls of marble.

John Deweck sat on his usual bench, speaking to no one. There were a few rules he stubbornly clung to. People spoke so much ill of each other. He no longer listened to their chatter. He had eyes now only for students and soldiers, for young girls and children. Young people fascinated his old carcass. He knew a great deal and had forgotten even more. He craved for youth and approached death's kingdom with reluctant steps.

One by one the frequenters of the fountain left the park. It was time for lunch. John smiled without quite knowing why. Now that he was alone it seemed to him that he was the head park keeper. It was Thursday. The day on which his wife always used to serve his veal-steak with a delicious sour sauce and potatoes as round as marbles. She had been able to work miracles with a potato. Since her death he had fallen into irregular eating habits. Three slices of bread and jam in the morning. At midday, often not even a bite. Round about five, some lumpy porridge with rusks and some fruit. Usually a sour apple. Sour apples, he believed, kept the mental juices clean and preserved the understanding.

He sat now alone with the violence of the fountain.

Perhaps some little boy would turn up? He longed for a serious conversation. Eyes that were still keen swept the avenue that led to the outskirts of the town. Far off in the distance, as in a dream, the little boy came into view. The youngster came tearing up to him, flopped down on the bench and gazed spellbound at the rippling surface of the pond and at the dragons letting the water flow over their green breasts.

'Hello, young man,' said John Deweck solemnly.

The child stared at him but said nothing.

'Isn't it your dinner time?'

'I'm not hungry,' said the boy. 'I eat once a day. Raw buffalo-meat, as I roam the prairie on my bronco.'

'Well, now,' said John Deweck, 'Well now... who might you be then?'

The boy looked up at him full of pride.

'I am the last of the Mohicans. I lost my friend – the paleface. He was caught in an ambush. But I scented danger. Now I wander alone through the wood and valley...'

'Where are your feathers?' asked old John sternly.

The child gazed at him with lively interest. Tiny flames flickered in the golden eyes. He flushed with excitement.

'I don't wear feathers in enemy country,' he said in a whisper. 'But still, I'm on the warpath. I've no warpaint on but I've dug up the hatchet. I am the last of my tribe. Are you my friend or foe?'

'What a thing to ask! My name is John. I have always been the foe of the buffaloes and the friend of the Indians. I made a block-pact with Winnetou. Now I am too old for the hunt. Against whom have you dug up the hatchet?'

'Against the tribe of grown-ups,' answered the boy. 'They threaten my hunting-grounds and my freedom. They don't understand a thing. How can an Indian live in stuffy school-buildings?'

'Of course he can't,' said John. 'Though a paleface myself, I'm all for freedom, too. But still, I think school is necessary....'

The youngster threw him a piercing look.

'Perhaps you're a spy,' he said thoughtfully. 'The enemy is cunning.'

John Deweck gave a high-pitched laugh.

'Nonsense. Take a look around. We're quite alone here. No, I'm not a member of the tribe of grown-ups.'

'How strange. So old, yet still a good Indian.'

The old man gave a loud sniff. He held his hand out to the young brave.

'Peace,' he said, 'and many scalps.'

'I'll tell you my adventure,' said the boy, 'provided you can keep a secret.'

'Even if I was bound to the torture-post I wouldn't breathe a word.'

'This morning I had to hunt for buffalo. As you know, the time has come. Besides, I'm looking for a squaw for my new wigwam. I was creeping out of the kitchen when Dad caught me by the hair. He walloped me for not being ready for school. I didn't make a sound. Only cunning could save me. Meekly I let myself be led to Hook Nose.'

'Who is Hook Nose?'

'The school chief,' replied the boy. 'He's not strong but he's terribly cunning. He laughed like a wild horse and spoke of giving me lines. At ten o'clock, during break, I sneaked out at the gate. I ran as fast as I could.... I don't want to go home again. My homeland is the prairie. Tonight I'm looking for a boat and tomorrow I'll be sailing across the seas.'

John Deweck looked at the fountain. Impetuously as life itself it leapt up towards the light of the boundless sky. Cherubs spattered with water, blew on their conches as if to warn of impending danger.

A wrinkle creased the aged forehead.

'It's not going to be an easy plan,' sighed John Deweck.

'I *must* get a boat,' said the boy stubbornly. 'You've got to help me.'

Heavy clouds drifted towards the spring sun. The birds were silent in the pruned trees.

'First come and eat in my wigwam,' faltered John Deweck.

'I'm not hungry.'

'You can't refuse bread and salt....'

The boy thought this over.

'Your mouth speaks the truth,' he said. 'I must set out on my long journey free from hunger. But I shan't eat meat.'

'Bread and salt, O Warrior....'

The boy trotted at the old man's side, looking neither left nor right. He thought of the wild scents of the prairie. He had met an old buffalo hunter who gave him invaluable tips.

They stepped into the police station. The door closed behind them with a bang. The boy looked about him and understood.

He sat down on a bench and freely volunteered information to a fat man with a ruddy complexion. His head sank on his chest. He did not even glance at John Deweck.

The car arrived shortly afterwards. The father stepped out and thanked the old man. The boy took his place in the car. Suddenly, he turned to the buffalo hunter.

'You belong to the tribe of grown-ups,' he said. 'You have betrayed my confidence. I will pay for it at the torture-post. I despise you.'

He spat on the ground.

'What did he say?' asked the father.

'That you ought to make him happy,' said John Deweck.

Father and son vanished in a cloud of dust.

'The youth of today,' grunted the inspector.

Slowly the old man paced through the streets of the little town.

He was never seen again at the fountain.

GEORGE HEBBELINCK

TASK

1 In one of the classbook tasks you were asked to place yourself in the position of the old man and to write about his feelings at the end of the day.

Now imagine that you are the boy at the end of the story. Write about your thoughts and feelings.

Badger on the Barge
(1 hour 45 minutes + reading time)

You have studied the story *The Man by the Fountain* which is about an old man and a little boy. Here now is part of a story about an old woman and a little girl. Read it and then answer the questions which follow.

Badger on the Barge

The barge was moored by the towpath. Although she quite often came by the canal on her way home from school, she had never seen it there before. Or perhaps it was just that she had not come by the canal for a long time. Frowning, she tried to remember.

The boat was long and low, and brightly painted. The hull was black, with green rubbing strakes and a red gunnel. The panels on the cabin sides were painted with roses – four flowers making a diamond shape. A striped green and red pole stuck out of the end. From a distance it looked like a picture in a book, but close to, Helen saw that some of the paint was peeling, and there was a heap of dirty straw on the small semi-circular poop-deck.

A plank led from their towpath to the deck, but Helen was not sure what to do. She could see the little cabin door with roses painted on it, but she was not sure she should go aboard. Crouching, she tried to see in through the windows, but the curtains were drawn.

Everything was quiet on the black water of the canal. The sun hung like a red balloon in the branches of horse-chestnut tree. Only a swan came sailing, leaving a wake of ripples, from under the bridge. It was white on the water, all alone.

'Here, Cobbler! Here, cob, cob, cob.... Here, Cobbler!' called a voice from the barge. 'There's a good fellow. There's a grand lad.' It was an old voice. The barge rocked gently as someone moved inside.

Helen stepped back. A thin yellow arm and hand appeared through a window on the far side of the boat. The swan arched its neck. A few scraps of bread floated towards him and he clicked at them with his yellow beak. Wagging his white tail feathers, he glided out of sight behind the barge.

The hand reappeared, poking through the window, and tossed some more bread. 'There's a grand old lad who can't sing for his supper. There's my old faithful Cobbler...' said the voice.

Helen wished she had some bread to throw for the swan, but her basket contained only the box of apples and oranges. Nothing that swans liked, she thought. Anyway, at least she had a reason to go on board. She walked up the gang-plank. 'Hello?'

No one answered. Then the barge lurched. The cabin doors were pushed open a crack.

'Who is it? What do you want?' The voice did not sound friendly.

'I'm Helen Fisher, from Heighton School. I've brought you a basket from our harvest festival,' said Helen, for the seventh time today.

'Beg your pardon?' said the old voice. The cabin door opened a bit wider, and an eye looked at her from the dark crack.

'I'm Helen Fisher. This is for you, from our harvest festival.' She took the box of fruit from her basket.

The swan slid away nervously. Autumn leaves rippled against the canal bank.

'Is it now? Then I expect you'll have to come in. Quickly, girl!' The door was pushed open. Helen climbed down the three steps of the companionway and found herself standing before Miss Brady.

The old woman's hair was grey and white in streaks, tied back in a bun. Her face was as thin and brown as cardboard, with deep lines round her nose and mouth. One leg was stretched stiffly in a bandage, her heel resting on a coil of rope. She was wearing a long brown skirt and a tweed jacket with leather patches on the elbows. She still held a slice of bread in her hand.

'Well, close the door.'

Helen pulled it shut with a bang.

'Shhh!' hissed Miss Brady. 'Now, talk quietly.'

Mrs Philips had told Helen to speak up when she called on old age pensioners, but she did not dare disobey the fierce old woman.

'I'm Helen Fisher,' she whispered.

'Yes, yes, I heard,' snapped Miss Brady. 'Now what's this?'

Inside, the barge was long and thin and low, but surprisingly roomy. There were shelves, a small sink and cooker, bare boards, a black stove, and pieces of rope tied in incredible knots hanging on the cabin walls. A cushion lay on the floor, with a hole torn in it and all its stuffing falling out.

'From our harvest festival,' Helen whispered. She looked at the old woman who was watching her suspiciously. There was a strange smell in the boat, strong and sour. On the floor were two saucers. One was full of milk and the other was full of... Helen looked again. It was full of raw liver and worms. Some of the worms wriggled.

'This is for me, is it? Well, well,' said the old woman. 'A booby prize for hurting my leg, I suppose.' She glanced at the box of fruit, but she did not seem pleased. 'Wonder which nosey do-gooder told them about me? Put it on the sink, out of harm's way.'

Surprised, Helen did as she was asked. All the other old people had been delighted – or at least that's what they said. The sink and draining-board were quite small, like toys. Through a sliding door she could see a big heap of hay and leaves under a bunk. The cushion which made the seat of the bunk looked as if it had been slashed with a knife, and all the foam was bursting out. The smell was stronger, almost a stink.

Tree shadows flickered through the cabin, reflected up from the water.

'Might as well make yourself useful, girl, seeing as you're here. Put the kettle on will you. There's matches on the shelf.'

Helen frowned. The old woman did not say please or thank you. She just gave orders like a blooming soldier!

'Here, Cobbler. Come on you old devil.' Miss Brady threw some more bread through the window. When she talked to the swan her voice was gentler than when she talked to Helen.

'Is that his name, then?' Helen asked, as she lit the gas and put the kettle on. She was trying to be friendly. She liked being in the boat, but she was not at all sure about Miss Brady.

'What?'

'Cobbler, Is that his name?'

'Lord, no!' said Miss Brady, with a sharp unfriendly laugh. 'Swans don't have names! They're not like dogs, you know. It's just a noise he comes to. I only call cobbler because it's like cob. Cobs are male swans, you see?'

'Oh,' said Helen. She felt a bit flustered, as if she had asked a stupid question in class.

'And you're Helen eh?' Miss Brady gave her a long look.

'Pleased to meet you, I suppose.' She held out her hand.

'How do you do,' Helen said politely, shaking hands. She had never shaken hands with a woman before. It seemed odd.

'Could be better. Oh Lord!' Miss Brady exclaimed, staring at the floor by Helen's feet. 'Put that worm back on the saucer, will you.'

'Yack!' Helen stepped away from it. It was a big purple worm slithering by her shoe.

'It won't bite you, girl!'

'I don't like worms,' Helen said, pulling a face.

'Well, pick it up with that bit of newspaper then.' Miss Brady glared at her and shook her head. Her look made Helen feel silly.

Quickly, she snatched up the worm and dropped it back on the saucer with the rest. Some of them were swimming in the blood from the raw liver. It made her feel a bit sick.

'You see,' crowed the old woman. 'It didn't bite.'

'It felt horrible and slimy though.' Helen wiped her fingers down her jeans. 'What do you want with worms?'

But Miss Brady only gave her a quick smile and said, 'Kettle's boiling. Teapot's on the shelf. Take two spoons. Then you'd better be off.'

Helen decided she did not like this old woman one little bit. She was bossy, and, somehow, she made Helen feel misjudged. Just because she had not wanted to pick up the worm, Miss Brady had decided she was soft and silly – which wasn't fair.

Miss Brady's face looked hard as a table leg,

except for her cheek-bones which stuck out a little and were pale. Sometimes she caught her breath when she moved, as if her ankle hurt badly.

She could open tins with that blooming sharp nose! thought Helen crossly as she spooned the tea into the pot.

'Milk's in the cupboard. Mug's on the draining-board.'

There was only one mug. Obviously, she was not going to invite Helen to stay for a cup. Helen felt annoyed. After all, she had brought her a present from school. 'Thank you,' said Miss Brady, for the first time, as Helen handed her the mug. 'Ah, that's the stuff.' She sipped the tea.

'I suppose I'd better be going them,' said Helen, still half expecting to be offered some tea or coffee.

'Right-ho!'

Helen scrambled back out onto the deck, stopped, and looked back at the old woman, puzzled. She'd never met anyone like her. 'Is there anything you want me to do, like? I mean with you having a gammy leg?'

Miss Brady peered at her over her mug of tea. 'Well now. There is one thing, come to think of it.'

Oh no, thought Helen. She did not really want to go shopping or fetching library books for a bossy old bag. She wished she hadn't opened her mouth. She had only asked out of politeness. 'Yes?'

'Worms,' said Miss Brady. 'You could fetch me a bucket full of worms and soil.'

'Worms?' Helen stared at her.

'Worms,' said the old woman. 'You know, those horrible slimy things you don't like?'

'Oh. I suppose so. I'll try and bring some tomorrow.'

'Promise, Helen Fisher?' Suddenly, Miss Brady's face looked much thinner and older.

'Alright. I promise,' said Helen. 'Tarra.'

'Au-revoir!' called Miss Brady.

'God our maker does provide

For our wants to be supplied....' Helen sang as she ran down the towpath towards home. Worms! She thought. Perhaps she eats them! and she swung her empty basket high into the air.

JANNI HOWKER

TASKS

2 Miss Brady is the seventh person Helen has visited. She didn't enjoy the other visits. Look at the extract again.

   a Make a list of the things which Helen finds unusual or strange about the visit.

   b Describe the signs which suggest to begin with that this visit might not turn out well.

3 Write the next part of the story, dealing with Helen's second visit to the barge.

A task which you might like to tackle.

4 This is the first story in a collection called 'Badger on the Barge and other stories' by Janni Howker. Your school or library may have a copy. Why not read the rest of this or another story? When you have read further write a letter to a friend telling her or him about this author.

Agnes Grey

(1 hour + research time)

Below you will find printed again the extract from *Agnes Grey* by Anne
Brontë which you have already studied in class.

Agnes Grey

The useful pony phaeton was sold, together with the stout well-fed pony – the old favourite that we had fully determined should end its days in peace, and never pass from our hands; the little coach-house and stable were let; the servant boy and the more efficient (being the more expensive) of the two maid-servants were dismissed. Our clothes were mended, turned, and darned to the utmost verge of decency; our food, always plain, was not simplified to an unprecedented degree – except my father's favourite dishes; our coals and candles were painfully economised – the pair of candles reduced to one, and that most sparingly used; the coals carefully husbanded in the half-empty grate: especially when my father was out on his parish duties, or confined to bed through illness – then we sat with our feet on the fender, scraping the perishing embers together from time to time, and occasionally adding a slight scattering of the dust and fragments of coal, just to keep them alive. As for our carpets, they in time were worn threadbare, and patched and darned even to a greater extent than our garments. To save the expense of a gardener, Mary and I undertook to keep the garden in order; and all the cooking and household work that could not easily be managed by one servant girl was done by my mother and sister, with a little occasional help from me: only a little, because, though a woman in my own estimation, I was still a child in theirs; and my mother, like most active, managing women, was not gifted with very active daughters: for this reason – that being so clever and diligent herself, she was never tempted to trust her affairs to a deputy, but on the contrary, was willing to act and think for others as well as for number one; and whatever was the business in hand, she was apt to think that no one could do it so well as herself: so that whenever I offered to assist her, I received such an answer as – 'No, love, you cannot indeed – there's nothing here you can do. Go and help your sister, or get her to take a walk with you – tell her she must not sit so much, and stay so constantly in the house as she does – she may well look thin and dejected.'

'Mary, mamma says I'm to help you; or get you to take a walk with me: she says you may well look thin and dejected, if you sit so constantly in the house.'

'Help me you cannot, Agnes; and I cannot go out with you – I have far too much to do.'

'Then let me help you.'

'You cannot, indeed, dear child. Go and practise your music, or play with the kitten.'

There was always plenty of sewing on hand; but I had not been taught to cut out a single garment, and, except plain hemming and seaming, there was little I could do even in that line; for they both asserted that it was far easier to do the work themselves than to prepare it for me: and, besides, they liked better to see me prosecuting my studies, or amusing myself – it was time enough for me to sit bending over my work, like a grave matron, when my favourite little pussy was become a steady old cat. Under such circumstances, although I was not many degrees more useful than the kitten, my idleness was not entirely without excuse.

Through all our troubles, I never but once heard my mother complain of our want of money. As summer was coming on, she observed to Mary and me, 'What a desirable thing it would be for your papa to spend a few weeks at a watering-place. I am convinced the sea-air and the change of scene would be of incalculable service to him. But then, you see, there's no money,' she added, with a sigh. We both wished exceedingly that the thing might be done, and lamented greatly that it could not.

'Well, well!' said she, 'it's no use complaining. Possibly something might be done to further the project after all. Mary, you are a beautiful drawer. What do you say to doing a few more pictures in your best style, and getting them framed, with the water-coloured drawings you have already done, and trying to dispose of them to some liberal picture-dealer, who has the sense to discern their merits?'

'Mamma, I should be delighted if you think they could be sold; and for anything worth while.'

'It's worth while trying, however, my dear: do you procure the drawings, and I'll endeavour to find a purchaser.'

'I wish I could do something,' said I.

'You, Agnes! well, who knows? You draw pretty well, too: if you choose some simple piece for your subject, I dare say you will be able to produce something we shall all be proud to exhibit.'

'But I have another scheme in my head,

mamma, and have had long, only I did not like to mention it.'

'Indeed! pray tell us what it is.'

'I should like to be a governess.'

My mother uttered an exclamation of surprise, and laughed. My sister dropped her work in astonishment, explaining, 'You a governess, Agnes! What can you be dreaming of!'

'Well! I don't see anything so very extraordinary in it. I do not pretend to be able to instruct great girls; but surely I could teach little ones: and I should like it so much: I am fond of children. Do let me, mamma!'

'But, my love, you have not learned to take care of yourself yet: and young children require more judgement and experience to manage than elder ones.'

'But, mamma, I am above eighteen, and quite able to take care of myself, and others too. You do not know half the wisdom and prudence I possess, because I have never been tried.'

ANNE BRONTË

TASK

5 Under the title, 'Children – then and now', write an account of childhood one hundred years ago and today.

To do this task well you will need to do some research. What information will you need? Where will you find it? How will you make a record of it?

Wider Reading

(as long as you like)

TASK

6 Reading for pleasure and for study is an important part of the way you could use your time. Here are some suggestions on the theme of this chapter, 'Young and Old'. They deal with characters of different ages and the relationship between parents and children.

You may already have heard of some of them; you may have read some; there are, however, probably at least some which can provide you with a new challenge.

A Kestrel for a Knave	Barry Hines
Roll of Thunder, Hear My Cry	Mildred Taylor
To Kill a Mockingbird	Harper Lee
David Copperfield	Charles Dickens
The Red Pony	John Steinbeck
A Mislaid Magic	Joyce Windsor
The Rector's Wife	Joanna Trollope
A Little Love, a Little Learning	Nina Bawden

So how do you get started? At times, starting to read a whole novel may seem too difficult. Here are some tips to set you off on reading a full novel.

- Set aside a particular time to get started.
- Read several chapters or 50 or so pages to start with.
- Agree with your family that reading counts as work.
- Arrange with your English teacher to tell others about your first impressions of the novel.
- As you get on with the book, jot down thoughts and impressions about the plot, characters and the ideas involved.

The outcome of all this may be that you want to write about the book you have read in some way. Arrange this with your teacher. It could become part of your GCSE English or English Literature coursework!

No Game for the Playground
(1 hour 30 minutes)

The article which is printed below is one which provides a great deal of food for thought. It is about a problem which is considered to be very serious and has received a great deal of publicity. The article was first printed in *The Sunday Times*.

People often think about growing up and the way that they change. One of the things which seems to happen as we get older is that parents and their children don't agree; there can be resentment and bad feeling on both sides.

No Game for the Playground

In the week that a BBC survey showed that children as young as seven are experimenting with drugs, Helen, a 38-year-old antiques dealer, tells of her own experience with her 16-year-old son, Jack. The names have been changed....

Five weeks ago I made a terrible mistake as a mother. I found some cannabis tucked into my 16-year-old son's bedroom drawer as I was putting away clean clothes. Then, further down, in among a secret stack of page three pictures, there was a tiny, very tiny, packet of white powder: cocaine.

My heart was pounding as I stood clutching the drugs, staring around my child's room. At times like this you notice the oddest things; his favourite childhood story, Erik The Viking by Terry Jones, on the bookshelves and the giant furry panda my husband bought six years ago, before he died.

Over the past 18 months Jack had become so arrogant and difficult he was almost unbearable. He was moody, frequently exhausted yet couldn't sleep. Often I would hear him moving about the house at night. I had asked him, as tactfully as I could, if he was taking drugs, and was dismissed with outbursts of anger. Over the summer I even discreetly examined his tanned arms for needle marks, feeling faintly ludicrous.

My terrible mistake was that I rang the police; just to frighten him, you see. As a single parent you sometimes feel so lonely in a crisis that you take too strong measures because there's nobody around to suggest an alternative. I just wanted someone to help me stop him, to give him a shock, frighten him into understanding the danger.

They came when Jack was back from school and they

were wonderful to me, but, foolishly, I hadn't realised how frightened, ashamed and angry Jack would be. He was ashen when they took him away and locked him in a police cell overnight to teach him a lesson. There were no charges, as they had promised, just a stiff talking to.

That evening my two other children, a boy of ten and a girl of eight, talked to me about drugs with a matter-of-fact knowledge that was startling. In their London junior school, they said there was a small group who regularly smoked hash, which they got from their elder brothers and sisters. And some do 'trips'. 'Oh you know, Mummy, it's speed or Ecstasy.' They were vague about the source of these drugs, but explained that everybody in the playground knew who had them, and you could buy what you wanted with your pocket money. Most of their friends don't, they said, because it's too scary if the teachers or your parents find out. But they told me that some of their playmates regularly sniffed Tipp-Ex, butane lighter gas, even aerosols could be effective.

Had they ever tried them? Both admitted they had tried sniffing at school, but only once. They knew it was bad, and I believe them and I also believe they knew nothing of Jack's habits. He hid it so well.

That night, I stayed awake thinking of my son. The next day he came home, refused to talk to me, packed his bags and left to stay with friends. And for the next three weeks,

he stayed away, going to school and talking to me on the telephone in angry monosyllables. 'I'll never trust you again,' he said. 'And now, I hope you realise I'm at school because I choose to be, not because it's the law, and if what you've done with the police means the headmaster finds out and I'm expelled, I won't forgive you, ever.'

A trained counsellor friend advised me to stay calm and let time pass. She said the concern he showed for his schooling was a plus factor. And I did stay calm for love of my son, who has missed his father so terribly, and whose grief, I now feel, has caused him to suffer such low self-esteem, that the drugs seemed a solution.

Two weeks ago, Jack came home, and slowly, slowly we are beginning to talk. This is what he says.

'In my school, Mum, about 80% of the pupils are taking or have taken some sort of drug. It's hard not to. You can buy speed, hash and "trips" from other boys. People smoke speed, they don't inject things because that's considered a bit serious. You always buy from people you know, otherwise you get skanked (conned) and find you've spent, say, £50 on half an ounce of hash and they've given you less. Half an ounce can keep you going for a month, so you but it to sell again and make extra money to go to the movies or a club or something. If people buy for themselves, they usually buy one-eighth of an ounce.'

Jack says he started smoke cannabis when he was nine,

and once tried sniffing my hairspray, but thought it was disgusting. 'When I was little we were always red in the face with terror because we thought it would be the end of the world if we got found out. As you get older, you realise you just get ticked off, or maybe a detention. Teachers don't really want to know, they don't want to take too much action and get the school a bad name.'

Cocaine you can't get from school so much. People go to Brixton to get it, but most people smoke it; they don't snort because your nose gets screwed up. These children have evolved a complicated set of snobberies and rules. Solvent abuse is for the youngsters. Sixteen-year-olds generally consider themselves too sophisticated to indulge. It's an unspoken law that you cover for someone regardless of whether you like them. *If someone is tripping at school, acting giggly, jumping about and making silly comments, the others play up to confuse the teacher.* It's also considered juvenile to take drugs between lessons, because others have to come to the rescue. And if you have taken something and feel 'screwed up' you don't go home until you have recovered, so the parents won't find out.

In city schools you can buy what you like, Jack says. In country schools it's only a little harder, and in country boarding schools the pupils bring their tuck box of supplies back with them after the holidays to last them through the term.

I've let my son talk, and he has listened to me, says he

understands my fear for him and won't do it again. And maybe he won't, especially after last weekend. He went to a party at a friend's house, a nice house with pleasant parents we have known since he was little. One of his schoolfriends, a boy I know and like, took cocaine, speed and drank vodka and by 11.30pm this 16-year-old was apparently sitting outside on the pavement surrounded by friends, virtually comatose. My son felt his friend's pulse and it was down to 50, then 45 and he said to the 16-year-old hostess (her parents were away) that they must call an ambulance. But they didn't because they were afraid their friend would get into trouble. Fortunately, he recovered.

At least Jack is now taking me into his confidence, although the incident with the police has, I think, dented his trust. It was a mistake. He says if I'd asked him, it would have been better, and I think he's right.

However, along with every other parent I am appalled by the drug culture that has our schools in its grip. Children are experimenting from the age of seven, and by the time they are in their teens they are very experienced indeed. How can teenage children resist such pressures and temptations? And how can we protect them and still give them the freedom they need?

TASKS

7 Jack is asked to take part in a radio programme which is a follow-up to the survey conducted by the BBC. He will lead off the programme by talking about his own experiences and his relief that he has given up drugs.

Imagine you are Jack and prepare your notes for the talk you will give. You will probably find that you want to draft your notes more than once.

8 It is some months later. Imagine you are Jack's mother and he has asked if he can have a party for his friends while you are away overnight.

Write your thoughts as you try to reach a decision about whether or not to allow the party to take place.

Rising Five

(30 minutes)

You have read this poem in your classbook.

> ## *Rising Five*
> ●
>
> *'I'm rising five,' he said.*
> *'Not four,' and little coils of hair*
> *Unclicked themselves upon his head.*
> *His spectacles, brimful of eyes to stare*
> *at me and the meadow, reflected cones of light*
> *Above his toffee-buckled cheeks. He'd been alive*
> *Fifty-six months or perhaps a week more:*
> *not four,*

But rising five.

Around him in the field the cells of spring
Bubbled and doubled; buds unbuttoned; shoot
And stem shook out the creases from their frills,
And every tree was swilled with green.
It was the season after blossoming,
Before the forming of the fruit:
not May,

But rising June.

                                        And in the sky
The dust dissected in the tangential light:
not day,
But rising night;

                                        not now,
But rising soon.

The new buds pushed the old leaves from the bough.
We drop our youth behind us like a boy
Throwing away his toffee wrappers. We never see the flower,
But only the fruit in the flower; never the fruit,
But only the rot in the fruit. We look for the marriage bed
In the baby's cradle, we look for the grave in the bed:

                                        not living,
But rising dead.

NORMAN NICHOLSON

TASK

9 This is a poem about a very young child viewed through the eyes of an adult. Write in detail about your reactions to the poem – are you amused, cross, or do you feel you have learnt something?

Letter Writing

(1 hour)

You have already completed one piece of work based on the article which is printed below.

My Daughter, My Friend

At the age of six my daughter Julie wrote a letter to the tooth fairy and put it under her pillow with her tooth. I wrote back, telling her to be a good girl and always brush her teeth carefully. I didn't know we were starting a tradition.

By the time Julie was nine years old, she had discovered that handwritten notes could do more than welcome the tooth fairy. Once, after a heated discussion we'd had about why she couldn't buy a pair of clogs, Julie wrote the following:

Dear Mum,
Here are the reasons I want clogs:
1 You wanted boots for a long time and you
*   finally got them.*
2 If clogs hurt my feet that's my problem.
3 When Granny gave us money for Christmas
*   she said we could get whatever we wanted*
*   with it.*
Love, Julie

I gave in – and Julie learned the power of the written word.

Over the next few years, Julie and I exchanged notes about boys, homework, phone calls and housework. Some notes were apologies after shouting matches. Others were just happy thoughts spilling on to paper. When Julie was 13, she responded to a love-note of mine:

Dear Mum,
Your letters make me feel great no matter
what kind of mood I'm in. Sometimes they even
make me cry because they touch me so deeply.
I'm really glad we have the kind of relationship
that we do, even though we have our arguments.
I suppose that's life with a teenager or with a
39-year-old!
I love you. Julie
PS Writing my feelings down to you is much
easier for me than trying to express them
verbally.

Julie's postscript explained why the note system worked so well for us. She was going through the traumas of adolescence, and I was having some problems of my own. Writing was the most effective way for us to communicate our feelings.

One summer Julie left her razor by the bath where her five-year-old brother might have cut himself. After I pointed out her carelessness, I asked Julie what she thought her punishment should be. She stomped off in a huff, but an hour later left a note on the kitchen counter.

Dear Mum,
I'm sorry for being so thoughtless. For my
punishment I will not:
1 Go to the shopping centre after school.
2 Watch television in the afternoon.
3 Snack before dinner.

She never left her razor by the bath again.

Two months later, on Julie's first day at a new school, we had a fight about whether it was appropriate for her to wear make-up.

That evening, I received a six-page, handwritten letter from her.

Dear Mum,
I'm sorry if I acted up this morning, but I
really got angry. You didn't even give me a
chance to say anything! If you would at least
discuss things with me maybe it would be a
little easier for us. Instead of telling me how
awful my eyes look, you could help to make
them look better.

Page three contained all the logic my tormented teen could muster.

1 I think I'm very responsible and can learn
*   to put make-up on in ways that both you*
*   and I would like.*
2 I don't 'cake it on' like some of my friends do
*   – I read the directions on the package and*
*   advice in magazine articles on how to apply it.*
3 I'm growing up; I want to add to my looks
*   and bring out my eyes.*
4 How about a three-week trial period to test
*   my ability to wear it?*

Needless to say, my daughter wore make-up – discreetly – from then on. Her whole face seemed to light up, not only from the touch of blusher, but from the sense of freedom she had prised out of her mother.

Not long after that my husband and I separated. The next few months were chaotic. Besides trying to provide stability for my four children, I had to budget our funds and work longer hours. As my raw emotions caused my mothering skills to dwindle, Julie came to the rescue with this note.

Dear Mum,
I know you're going through a hard time and
I wish I could make all your problems
disappear. Unfortunately, I can only tell you
how much I love you. We're all upset about
the divorce, but you're still a great, helpful
and loving mum.
Love, Jules

There were quite a few times that year when I took my frustrations out on the children. After one particularly nasty tirade, Julie dropped this message in my handbag for me to read at work:

Dear Mum,
I know things are difficult for you just now,
and we all understand. I think you should go
out more often to distract yourself. We are all
growing up and have our own interests and
friends. We'll always be your kids and you
won't lose us.
I love you! Jules

Just before her eighteenth birthday I asked Julie what she wanted. 'I'm working on it,' she said.

I should have known that Julie was writing me the letter of her life. Here's what some of it said:

Soon I will be living on my own at university.
I feel I have matured by following your rules
with very few exceptions.
For my eighteenth birthday I would like to be
treated and respected as a mature and
responsible person. I'd like:
1 A later curfew or none at all.
2 Permission to make and receive telephone
*   calls after 10pm.*
3 The freedom to make my own decisions.
4 To be thought of as a close friend.

Now it was my turn to respond. I sat writing late into the night.

Dearest Julie,
Adulthood isn't a sudden jolt of freedom to do
whatever you want. It is simply being
responsible. If you believe you can behave like
an adult, I will treat you as one.

I then answered her birthday proposition list, asking her to be considerate about curfews and phone calls. I agreed that she should make decisions and said I would offer advice only when requested.

I ended with this:

Julie, I wish you a happy life filled with love
and solid decisions based on solid values. I
hope you continue to develop the many talents
God has given you.
Happy birthday, my friend! Mum

My daughter left home for university a few years ago. I've missed her tremendously, but our tradition has pulled us through again – her letters have been wonderful!

PATRICIA LORENZ

TASK

10 In class you have written a letter to your parents trying to persuade them to your point of view.

Now put yourself in your parents' shoes and write their answer.

Write About Your Family

(1 hour 30 minutes)

You have already used some photographs of people in your classbook as the basis for some imaginative writing. Look through your family photographs and choose one which will form the basis of an interesting piece of biography. It might be a photo of someone you see every day; it might be the photo of a relative who lived some time ago and who you only know from stories your parents or grandparents have told you.

TASK

11 Start by sticking either the photograph or a photocopy of the photograph to your paper and continue the biography from there...

Poetry Stimulus

(3 hours)

Printed on the next pages are four poems, all of which reflect the views of teenagers about their parents.

Protest of a Sixth Former

Oh Father can cease to exist
If his nagging must persist.
Respect for parents may be,
But he just drives me crazy
With his craving for a perfect son,
Not this scruffy lout and bum.

Oh Mother can live elsewhere,
For me she has only one care:
That of my Sixth Form work
Just so I can be a clerk.
Why can't I go out at nights
Instead of having parental fights?

Oh Gran can go away,
She has nothing useful to say,
Just goes on about her youth
And telling me that I'm uncouth.
Why can't she shut up and draw her pension –
She knows I'm beyond her comprehension.   ROBERT HAYES

Mother and Son

At nine o'clock in the morning
My son said to me:
Mother, he said, from the wet streets
The clouds are removed and the sun walks
Without shoes on the warm pavements.
There are girls biddable at the corners
With teeth cleaner than your white plates;
The sharp clatter of your dishes
Is less pleasant to me than their laughter.
The day is building; before its bright walls
Fall in dust, let me go
Beyond the front garden without you
To find glasses unstained by tears,
To find mirrors that do not reproach
My smooth face; to hear above the town's
Din, life roaring in the veins.

R S THOMAS

The Young Ones

They slip on the bus, hair piled high.
New styles each month, it seems to me. I look,
Not wanting to be seen, casting my eye
Above the unread pages of a book.

They are fifteen or so. When I was thus,
I huddled into school coats, my satchel hung
Lop-sided on my shoulder. Without fuss
These enter adolescence; being young

Seems good to them, a state we cannot reach,
No talk of 'awkward ages' now. I see
How childish gazes staring out of each
Unfinished face prove me incredibly

Old-fashioned. Yet at least I have the chance
To size up several stages – young yet old,
Doing the twist, mocking an 'old-time' dance:
So many ways to be unsure or bold.

ELIZABETH JENNINGS

The Boys

Six of them climbed aboard,
None of them twenty yet,
At a station up the line:
Flannel shirts rimmed with sweat,
Boots bulled to outrageous shine,
Box-pleats stiff as a board.

Pinkly, smelling of Bass,
They lounged on the blue moquette
And rubbed their Blanco off.
One told of where to get
The best crumpet. A cough
From the corner. One wrote on the glass

A word in common use.
The others stirred and jeered.
'Reveille' was idled through
Till the next station appeared,
And the six of them all threw
Their Weights on the floor. Excuse

For a laugh on the platform. Then
We rattled, and moved away,
The boys only just through the door.
It was near the end of the day.
Two slept. One farted and swore,
And went on about his women.

Three hours we had watched this lot,
All of us family men,
Responsible, set in our ways.
I looked at my paper again:
Another H-test. There are days
You wonder whether you're not

Out of touch, old hat, gone stale.
I remembered my twenty-first.
In the NAAFI, laid out cold.
Then one of them blew and burst
A bag; and one of the old
Told them to stow it. The pale

Lights of the city came near.
We drew in and stopped. The six
Bundled their kit and ran.
'A good belting would sort out their tricks',
Said my neighbour, a well-spoken man.
'Yes, but...' But he didn't hear.

ANTHONY THWAITE

TASKS

12 Imagine you are a parent. Write a poem from the parent's point of view about difficulties with a teenager. You might try to imitate the rhythm of the first poem.

13 Take the title 'Advice on Becoming a Teenager'. Write to a younger person giving your dos and don'ts as he or she approaches 13.

14 Your school's parents' association wants to advise parents on coping with teenage children. Prepare a speech, or other form of presentation, in which you, as the teenage spokesperson, offer that advice.

15 Parents may grumble about how difficult it is sometimes to cope with teenagers. Devise a leaflet for young people of your own age from the other point of view. It could be called, 'Coping with Parents and Teachers'.

The Boilerman

(1 hour)

In your classbook we invited you to do some writing based on the play *David and Broccoli*. First re-read the scene.

The Boilerman

The school boiler-room

This small, warm shed is where David comes as a refuge to see his friend, the old gnome-like man who looks after the boiler and does odd jobs abut the school.

BOILERMAN:
(looking at the broken glider) I'll give it a touch of glue when I've got a moment.

DAVID
He did it on purpose.

BOILERMAN
Broccoli? (He puts the glider on a shelf.) Scares you, doesn't he? (David nods.) When's the next lesson?

DAVID
Thursday... I wish there wasn't a next Thursday.

BOILERMAN
Then it's... over the top? Like in the nineteen-fourteen. Over the top tomorrow, they said... and I thought, tomorrow is a day that won't ever be missed. Let's go to sleep and wake up next summer. Of course they offered you comforts, tots of rum, nice hymn, new pair of khaki mittens knitted by her old ladyship in some nice, safe dugout in Wimbledon. There was I, like you, boy, staring straight in the face of danger...

DAVID
What did you do?

BOILERMAN
Well, you had three alternatives. Go through with it, shoot yourself in the foot, or run away. Personally, I took my courage in both hands, and I runned away.

DAVID
That was brave...

BOILERMAN
Damned stupid. I runned in the wrong direction. Slap into the Jerry trenches. Saw a young chap there and I said, 'For God's sake give me a whiff of gas, just to put me under for the duration'. Of course, not being educated, he couldn't understand what I was saying. He shot me in the hand, just lovely. They put me on cook-house duties after that. They got some terrible meals. There was one Christmas dinner... Not fit for human consumption. We gave it to the officers....

DAVID
Does it hurt much? Being shot in the hand?

BOILERMAN
No... irritates a bit, that's all. Here. Don't you go and get ideas, now. Don't you go to the length of self-inflicted wounds... He's not so bad, old Broccoli. Well, just a bit horrible, perhaps. He can't help that. It's his living. He comes in here, with those magazines what he reads... and talks about the end of the world....

DAVID
The what?

BOILERMAN
He's got it fixed for the year three thousand. Says it's a mathematical certainty. Well, it's got to end some time, hasn't it? I mean, it just can't go on and on, stands to reason.

DAVID
No.

BOILERMAN
But he gives us till the year three thousand....

DAVID
That's a long time....

BOILERMAN
It'll see him out, anyway.

DAVID
I wish it was next Thursday!

BOILERMAN
What?

DAVID
The end of the world.

BOILERMAN
  Why… Oh, I see. To stop the lesson. (David nods.) You'd carry it to those lengths?
DAVID
  If I could put a stop to it….
BOILERMAN
  You've got a very brilliant brain, I don't doubt.
DAVID
  Quite clever….
BOILERMAN
  Which is where you'll finally be one up on Mr Smith.

DAVID
  (incredulous) I will?
BOILERMAN
  I don't doubt that, boy. But leave the rest of the universe alone, Will you? Do me a great favour? Leave the world turning until next Saturday week. I haven't got my peas planted, not yet….

JOHN MORTIMER

TASK

16 The world doesn't come to an end and the boxing lesson does take place the next week. After it David goes once again to visit the boilerman.

Write the scene which takes place in the school boiler-room on that occasion.

David will want to explain to the boilerman how he coped with Mr Smith (Broccoli). Perhaps he managed to outsmart Mr Smith, and if so how?

9

DEATH AND DESTRUCTION

Cider with Rosie

(1 hour 30 minutes)

In your classbook you have looked at a couple of extracts from *Cider with Rosie*. Printed below you will find another extract which tells the story of a death in the community.

Cider with Rosie

A few mornings later we were sitting round the kitchen, waiting for Fred Bates to deliver the milk. It must have been a Sunday because the breakfast was spoilt; and on weekdays that didn't matter. Everybody was grumbling; the porridge was burnt, and we hadn't yet had any tea. When Fred came at last he was an hour and a half late, and he had a milk-wet look in his eyes.

'Where were you, Fred Bates?' our sisters demanded; he'd never been late before. He was a thin, scrubby lad in his middle teens, with a head like a bottle-brush. But the cat didn't coil round his legs this morning, and he made no reply to the girls. He just ladled us out our usual jugful and kept sniffing and muttering 'God dammit'.

'What's up then, Fred?' asked Dorothy.

'Ain't nobody told you?' he asked. His voice was hollow, amazed, yet proud, and it made the girls sit up. They forced him to sit down a minute. Then they all gathered round him with gaping eyes, and I could see they had sniffed an occurrence.

At first Fred could only blow hard on his tea and mutter, '*Who'd* a thought it?' But slowly, insidiously, the girls worked on him, and in the end they got his story....

He'd been coming from milking; it was early, first light, and he was just passing Jones' pond. He'd stopped for a minute to chuck a stone at a rat – he got tuppence a tail when he caught one. Down by the lily-weeds he suddenly saw something floating. It was spread out white in the water. He'd thought at first it was a dead swan or something, or at least one of Jones's goats. But when he went he went down closer, he saw, staring at him, the white drowned face of Miss Flynn. Her long hair was loose –

which had made him think of a swan – and she wasn't wearing a stitch of clothes. Her eyes were wide open and she was staring up through the water like somebody gazing through a window. Well, he'd got such a shock he dropped one of his buckets, and the milk ran into the pond. He'd stood there a bit, thinking, 'That's Miss Flynn'; and there was no one but him around. Then he'd run back to the farm and told them about it, and they'd come and fished her out with a hay-rake. He'd not waited to see any more, not he; he'd got his milk to deliver.

Fred sat for a while, sucking his tea, and we gazed at him with wonder. We all knew Fred Bates, we knew him well, and our girls often said he was soppy; yet only two hours ago, and only just down the lane, he'd seen drowned Miss Flynn with no clothes on. Now he seemed to exude a sort of salty sharpness so that we all wished to touch and taste him; and the excited girls tried to hold him back and make him go through his story again. But he finished his tea, sniffed hard, and left us, saying he'd still got his milk-round to do.

The news soon spread around the village, and women began to gather at their gates.

'Have you heard?'

'No. What?'

'About poor Miss Flynn.... Been and drowned herself down in the pond.'

'You just can't mean it!'

'Yes Fred Bates found her.'

'Yes he's just been drinking tea in our kitchen.'

'I can't believe it. I only saw her last week.'

'I know: I saw her just yesterday. I said, 'Good morning, Miss Flynn'; and she said, 'Good morning, Mrs Ayres,' – you know, like she always did.'

'But she was down in the town, only Friday it was! I saw her in the House-and-Colonial.'

'Poor, sad creature – whatever made her do it?'

'Such a lovely face she had.'

'So good to our boys. She was kindness itself. To think of her lying there.'

'She had a bit of a handicap, so they say.'

'You mean about those fellows?'

'No, more'n that.'

'What was it?'

'Sssh!'

'Well, not everyone knows, of course....'

Miss Flynn was drowned. The women looked at me listening. I stole off and ran down the lane. I was dry with excitement and tight with dread; I just wanted to see the pond. A group of villagers, including my sisters, stood gaping down at the water. The pond was flat and green and empty, and a smudge of milk clung to the reeds. I hid in the rushes, hoping not to be seen, and stared at that seething stain. This was the pond that had choked Miss Flynn. Yet strangely, and not by accident. She had come to it naked, alone in the night, and had slipped into it like a bed; she lay down there, and drew the water over her, and drowned quietly away in the reeds. I gazed at the lily roots coiled deep down, at the spongy weeds around them. That's where she lay, a green foot under, still and all night by herself, looking up through the water as though through a window and waiting for Fred to come by. One of my knees began to quiver; it was easy to see her there, her hair floating out and her white eyes open, exactly as Fred Bates had found her. I saw her clearly, slightly magnified, and heard her vague dry voice: 'I've been bad, Mrs Er. It's my mother's spirit. She won't let me bide at night....'

The pond was empty. She'd been carried home on a hurdle, and the women had seen to her body. But for me, as long as I can remember, Miss Flynn remained drowned in that pond.

As for Fred Bates, he enjoyed for a day a welcome wherever he went. He repeated his story over and over again and drank cups of tea by the dozen. But his fame turned bad, very suddenly; for a more sinister sequel followed. The very next day, on a visit to Stroud, he saw a man crushed to death by a wagon.

'Twice in two days,' the villagers said. 'He'll see the Devil next.'

Fred Bates was avoided after that. We crossed roads when we saw him coming. No one would speak to him or look him in the eyes, and he wasn't allowed to deliver milk any more. He was sent off instead to work alone in a quarry, and it took him years to re-establish himself.

LAURIE LEE

TASK

1 Write a story of your own in which someone discovers a dead body.

Of Mice and Men

(1 hour)

Of Mice and Men is a popular book. It is easy to read but makes us think a lot and feel things deeply.

Overleaf is what a 16-year-old student wrote, trying to show her understanding of George.

Imagine you are George two months later. Describe your experiences and also your memories of the ranch.

I'm lonely now. It's been two months since Lennie got killed, and I really miss him. I left the ranch soon after that night. When we went back to the ranch after I'd shot Lennie, I talked with Slim for hours. He was a good bloke, Slim, the sort of person you could confide in, who'd understand you. And he was respected too. Even Curly had some respect for Slim. I remember after Lennie had done Curly's hand in, Slim said 'I think you got your hand caught in a machine' to Curley. He was good and kind, Slim, trying to protect Lennie like that.

I talked with Slim for a long time. He told me it was best, that it was like Candy's dog, except that I was brave enough to go through with it myself. I mean, Candy, he didn't shoot his dog himself, he hadn't got the guts to do it. Sometimes I wonder how I did it, then I start examining everything, trying to convince myself that it was the only thing to be done. That was what Slim kept telling me.

'Never you mind', he said, 'A guy got to sometimes.' Sometimes I want to shout and scream and hurl things about, but most times I try to forget. But, hell, it's useless. You can't forget somethin' like that.

That night I left, I couldn't stay 'till the morning. I couldn't face Curley or Carlson not even Candy after that. They wouldn't have understood. It wasn't their fault, they just weren't capable of understanding. Carlson killed Candy's dog, but it belonged to Candy. Lennie belonged to me, and I killed him. It's different, but nobody seems to understand, 'cept Slim.

I remember me 'n' Lennie had a little fantasy, about living 'offa the fatta the land'. It nearly came true. But that fantasy, it's been me 'n' Lennie, see. Without Lennie it wasn't important any more. It could've been me 'n' Candy, but it ended up with just me, 'nd I wouldn't care for nothing like that, not without Lennie.

I needed Lennie, you know. He meant a lot to me. More than you could imagine, I guess. Lennie was a part of me, he was my anchor. He kept me sane, and I was responsible for him. But I never really appreciated him not 'till now. I could go mad with loneliness.

When I left that night, I set off back to find Lennie's relatives. At first I planned to stop at places on the way, but I can't be bothered now. I didn't think I could stop bothering, but I have. I don't care what I look like, or what I say. I understand Candy now. He was lonely, he was lonely as hell. But Candy, I guess he kinda got used to it. I s'pose I will eventually. But right now it's too much. Sometimes I talk to him, even though I know he isn't there any more. I think I'm going mad, then I get kinda scared. I worry about that, the talkin' to myself.

I blame Curley. It's stupid blaming people, but I gotta do it. It makes me feel better somehow. And maybe it was Curley's fault too. From the moment he saw Lennie I knew there was gonna be trouble. I could tell he was against Lennie. But when I got talking to the man, I realised that it was just insecurity. Mind you, I wouldn't trust that wife of his. I start to think maybe it was her that was to blame, tryin' to seduce Lennie. I wonder why she did it, what she was lookin' for, or if maybe she was just tryin' to get at Curley. But you could tell that Lennie liked her the minute he saw her. But Lennie didn't like women because they were women, he treated them like mice or rats.

Sometimes I get to wishin' that I had killed her myself while I was at it, but I can't see the point anymore. Whether I'm alive or dead don't make no difference, all that matters is that Lennie isn't any more. I'm lonely, an' I killed him. But I've already said that.

It was funny how Lennie could get on with some people. He got on with Crooks okay. Nobody else would have bothered about Crooks, but really I guess he jus' didn't wanna get hurt. Lennie he managed to penetrate that barrier. Even though Crooks was hostile at first, Lennie just' didn't care. He was good like that, Lennie not caring 'bout what you should do. Don't s'pose he realised that he gave Crooks hope for a while, but I guess that it was good of him all the same.

But it was Lennie's strange way of carin' about people that killed him wasn't it? Sometimes I think maybe I'll get myself another friend, somebody like Lennie but then

I know that only time will make me better eventually.

It's grief that's my trouble. But this ain't no ordinary grief, not like when my pop died. No, cos I didn't kill my pop, did I?

Candy 'n' Crooks got friends. They got a-talking after I'd killed Lennie. Funny combination that. Candy's as lonely as anything, but then I s'pose Crooks was too. Both of 'em had got something up with them physically an' all. Crooks got a bad back, 'n' Candy, he only had one arm. S'pose I'm lucky really, I'm still in one piece. Lennie was like a limb to me I guess. But Candy, he recovered from using an arm so I s'pose I'll get over it soon. I know one thing though, it'll take a long time, probably more time than I got. So I guess I'll spend the rest of my life missing Lennie 'n' regrettin' decisions. But life's lonely as hell without someone....

TASK

2 Write a letter to the writer of the essay expressing your opinions about what she has written and the way in which she has made her points. Has she written in a way which makes you feel that you understand George?

Death of Thomas Becket

(2 hours)

Thomas Becket was Archbishop of Canterbury during the reign of King Henry II. In her novel, *Thomas*, Shelley Mydans describes his death in Canterbury Cathedral.

Thomas

The church was dark. Only the alter lights glowed in the choir, far away. Thomas, with Robert, crossed the transept and started up the steps. But then he heard the door close and the sound the bolt made sliding into place. He stopped.

'This is the house of God,' he called. 'Let all come in who will.' And he went back again. The clerks stood huddled in the darkness, barring his way. 'Out of the way, you cowards.' He pushed them aside. 'The church is not a fortress. Open the door.'

He wrenched the bolt back and the door swung in. Some of his followers who had come panting, late, pressed in the doorway and he pulled them through. Now he heard heavy running and he saw, as they came past the chapter-house, the glint of mail. Four heavy figures. Four armed men.

The clerks pressed around him, pushing, whispering. 'Hide in the darkness....' 'Come into the crypt....' 'Across the nave and out....'

He thrust them off him, saying, 'No! Where is my crozier?'

Grim stepped out.

'Then lead me to the alter, for we will serve God.'

Again he crossed the transept, had his foot upon the stair.

A shout: 'Where is the traitor!' Fitz Urse was through the door.

The clerks had fled. The monks had left their service and there was silence in the wavering dark.

'Where is the Archbishop?'

Now Thomas turned. 'Here am I. Not a traitor, but a priest of God. If you seek me, you find me here. What would you have?'

Morville called out in the darkness, 'Flee! You are a dead man!'

'No, I will not flee.' He came back down the steps towards them and facing them he put his back against the pillar and stood still. 'I do not fear you. If you bring death, then in the Lord's name do I welcome it!'

They closed in towards him, groping in the dark. Behind them, Ranulf swung round to the open door. Some monks peered in. One scuttled past him, fleeing from the scene. Ranulf brought down his hammer and the man groaned and fell. Ranulf turned from him. 'Guard all the doors!' he bellowed. 'Guard the doors!'

Morville took his sword in hand and crossed the nave towards the south transept to keep the people back.

The three came on and Thomas saw the bulk of shoulders in the dark, a glimmer on the mail, the pointed helmets and the blur of white – their faces, cloven by the nasal guards. Robert stood by him, and the stranger, Grim, holding the crozier out and crying, 'This is the house of God!'

They came on, crouching, arms held wide.

'This is your archbishop!'

'We know the man.'

And Fitz Urse, very close, said, 'Do not move. You are our prisoner.'

And Tracy: 'Come with us.'

'I will not go. You can do here what you have come to do.'

Fitz Urse sprang at him and clutched the pallium around his neck, and Tracy, crowding Grim, reached for his body to lift him off his feet. The monk cried once again, 'This is a church!' But Thomas stood against the pillar and fought back. They would not drag him like a villein where they liked. He would not run behind their horses. He would not kneel to them.

He swore at Fitz Urse. 'Take your hands off me! You are my vassal!' And he flung him back. He turned on Tracy, grappled, shook him with such force he fell back on the floor.

Fitz Urse came on again, not speaking, growling in his throat, and Thomas grated, 'Reginald, you pimp, don't touch me. Take your hands off me!'

Fitz Urse crouched back and drew his sword: 'Then have it! Strike!' he screamed. He swung his sword. It arched and whistled in the darkness, grazing Thomas's head, knocking his cap off, leaving the tonsure bare.

Tracy was up again, sword in both hands held high. 'Then strike!' he shouted, and he brought it down.

Grim held the crozier up to ward it off. It glanced along the shaft, sliced through his arm. Then, bloodstained, it descended on the tonsured head.

Thomas stood wounded, blood upon his face. He felt Grim drop beside him, felt him roll away. He heard the voice of Robert: 'Father.... Son....' And then no more.

This was his moment; he had chosen it. Not Henry. And he died for God. For God alone. No other way. He crossed his hands and bowed his wounded head. 'Now am I ready to die for Christ, and for the Blessed Virgin, and for the Church....

He saw the bloody sword come up again. Now was the time. 'Into thy hands, O Lord....'

Fitz Urse struck first and Tracy after. He faltered to his knees. Brito ran up and struck him, struck him as he fell, a blow so savage that the iron sword broke off against the stones. 'King's men!' he cried out. 'Take that for the King!'

The others stood back, panting. Now de Broc pushed through. He looked down at the body and nudged it with his foot. He put his heel upon the neck and thrust his sword-point into the broken skull and scooped the brains out.

'He will not rise again!'

He swaggered as he walked away. He was so sure.

But when the knights had gone away, when all the church was still, the people came in, crowding at the doors, and crept up to the fallen body and knelt down. They kissed the feet. They wept. And while they wept they reached their hands out and touched the body, dipping their fingers into the healing blood.

SHELLEY MYDANS

In his play, *Murder in the Cathedral*, T S Eliot deals with the same topic.

Murder in the Cathedral

PRIESTS:
Bar the door. Bar the door
The door is barred.
We are safe. We are safe.
They dare not break in.
They cannot break in. They have not the force.
We are safe. We are safe.

THOMAS:
Unbar the doors! Throw open the doors!
I will not have the house of prayer, the
church of Christ,
The sanctuary, turned into a fortress.
The Church shall protect her own, in her
own way, not
As oak and stone; stone and oak decay,
Give no stay, but the Church shall endure.
The Church shall be open, even to our
enemies. Open the door!

PRIESTS:
My Lord! these are not men, these come not
as men come, but
Like maddened beasts. They come not like
men, who
Respect the sanctuary, who kneel to the
Body of Christ,
But like beasts. You would bar the door
Against the lion, the leopard, the wolf
or the boar,
Why not more
Against beasts with the souls of damned
men, against men
Who would damn themselves to beasts. My
Lord! My Lord!

THOMAS:
You think me reckless, desperate and mad.
You argue by results, as this world does,
To settle if an act be good or bad.
You defer to the fact. For every life and
every act
Consequence of good and evil can be shown.
And as in time results of many deeds are
blended
So good and evil in the end become
confounded.
It is not in time that my death shall be known;
It is out of time that my decision is taken
If you call that decision

To which my whole being gives entire consent.
I give my life
To the Law of God above the Law of Man.
Unbar the door! Unbar the door!
We are not here to triumph by fighting, by
stratagem or by resistance,
Not to fight with beasts as men. We have
fought the beast
And have conquered. We have only to conquer
Now, by suffering. This is the easier victory.
Now is the triumph of the Cross, now
Open the door! I command it. OPEN THE
DOOR!
[*The door is opened. The* KNIGHTS *enter,
slightly tipsy*]

PRIESTS:
This way, my Lord! Quick. Up the stair. To
the roof.
To the crypt. Quick. Come. Force him.

KNIGHTS:
Where is Becket, the traitor to the King?
Where is Becket, the meddling priest?
Come down Daniel to the lions' den,
Come down Daniel for the mark of the beast.
Are you washed in the blood of the Lamb?
Are you marked with the mark of the Beast?
Come down Daniel to the lions' den,
Come down Daniel and join in the feast.
Where is Becket the Cheapside brat?
Where is Becket the faithless priest?
Come down Daniel to the lions' den,
Come down Daniel and join in the feast.

THOMAS:
It is the just man who
Like a bold lion, should be without fear.
I am here.
No traitor to the King. I am a priest,
A Christian, saved by the blood of Christ,
Ready to suffer with my blood.
This is the sign of the Church always,
The sign of blood. Blood for blood.
His blood given to buy my life,
My blood given to pay for His death,
My death for His death,

FIRST KNIGHT:
Absolve all those you have excommunicated.

SECOND KNIGHT
  Resign the powers you have arrogated.
THIRD KNIGHT
  Restore to the King the money you
    appropriated.
FIRST KNIGHT
  Renew the obedience you have violated.
THOMAS
  For my Lord I am now ready to die,
  That his Church may have peace and liberty.
  Do with me as you will, to your hurt and
    shame;
  But none of my people, in God's name,
  Whether layman or clerk, shall you touch.
  This I forbid.
KNIGHTS
  Traitor! traitor! traitor!

THOMAS
  You, Reginald, three times traitor you:
  Traitor to me as my temporal vassal,
  Traitor to me as your spiritual lord,
  Traitor to God in desecrating His Church.
FIRST KNIGHT
  No faith do I owe to a renegade,
  And what I owe shall now be paid.
THOMAS
  Now to Almighty God, to the Blessed Mary
    ever Virgin, to the blessed John the
    Baptist, the holy apostles Peter and Paul,
    to the blessed martyr Denys, and to all the
    Saints, I commend my cause and that of
    the Church.
  [*The Knights kill him*]
                                    T S ELIOT

TASKS

3 Compare these two ways of presenting Becket's death. What do they have in common?

4 How, do you think, does Shelley Mydans make us admire Becket?

5 T S Eliot's play needs careful presentation. How could this scene be staged to make Becket seem heroic?

6 Becket believed he was dying for a great cause. What causes do people think are worth dying for? Make your list and put an explanation or opinion by each one.

7 Choose one of the causes which you have listed above and, in detail, write your views on the subject.

King Charles I

(1 hour 30 minutes)

In the classbook chapter you studied an extract from Antonia Fraser's account of the execution of King Charles I.

You will find that we have reprinted the extract below for you to read again.

Cromwell: Our Chief of Men

So on the morning of Tuesday, 30 January, Charles Stuart walked with calm dignity and religious resignation from St James' Palace to the designated place of his death at Whitehall. Once arrived, he rested within Whitehall itself, and strengthened himself with a little red wine and a little bread. There was a slight delay, probably because the Commons was even then passing an urgent Act which forbade the proclamation of his successor after his death. They had suddenly taken into account Pride's words on the problems of cutting off the head of an hereditary King, when they had not yet officially abolished monarchy: they would simply find themselves with another sovereign on their hands. It was two o'clock in the afternoon when Charles stepped forth from the Banqueting House windows in front of the enormous, silent crowd. The weather was icy – Charles was secretly wearing two shirts so that he should not shiver and be accused of fear. With him came only his chaplain, Bishop Juxon, for his faithful servant Sir Thomas Herbert who had accompanied him on the mournful march from St James' Palace begged to be excused from the painful task of being a witness. There were the two Colonels, Hacker and Tomlinson, on the scaffold to supervise the execution, and serried troops below, lest even now the King should appeal to his people – or the people perhaps to their King.

To the spectators indeed their King seemed greatly aged, his beard grey and his hair silver. Now they could see that, but his words could only be heard by those very close to him, Bishop Juxon, the two Colonels, and the two masked executioners, for the ban on any form of public appeal remained absolute. To this tiny audience, but every word would be lovingly treasured by

his chaplain to reach the audience of the world, he regretted nothing: 'For the people truly I desire their liberty and freedom as much as anybody whatsoever; but I must tell you that their liberty and freedom consists in having government, those laws by which their lives and goods maybe most their own. It is not their having a share in the government; that is nothing appertaining to them; a subject and sovereign are clean different things....' So the sovereign went to his death at the hands of his subjects, proud and unrepentant on that interpretation of government whose inflexibility had brought about his downfall: those words alone did much to show why Charles died. Yet another of his sayings showed also why another section of his people would always regard him as King Charles the Martyr: 'I go from a corruptible crown to an incorruptible crown,' he told Juxon, 'where no disturbance can be, no disturbance in the world.' And it was Andrew Marvell, very likely present among the crowd, in an ode intended to celebrate Charles's mortal adversary Cromwell, who penned the words which later immortalised the King's courage in his last moments, as he bent his neck in silent submission on to the black-draped block:

Nor call'd the Gods with vulgar spite
To vindicate his helpless Right
But bow'd his comely Head
Down as upon a Bed.

A minute later the executioner (believed to be the common hangman named Brandon, but with his assistant he had insisted on the utmost precautions being taken to preserve his identity, including a false beard and wig) was holding up the severed head with the traditional cry: 'Behold the head of a traitor!' In less than a quarter of an hour, said the French Ambassador, this whole sad ceremony was over. But from the people watching went up not the raucous cries of the crowd at justice done, not the human response to blood lust of so many public executions; something so deeply shocking had been perpetrated that up from the people went a great deep groan, a groan, said an eye-witness, 'as I never heard before and desire I may never hear again', it was a lament that would be heard as long and as far as the problems of justice and injustice were caused for. For whatsoever could be said of the execution of King Charles I, that it was inevitable, even that it was necessary, it could never be said that it was right.

ANTONIA FRASER

TASK

8 Imagine that you are one of the crowd watching the execution.

Describe the scene and your feelings as you watch.

Murders

(1 hour)

The details which are printed below show the relationship between victims and murderers for England and Wales 1992.

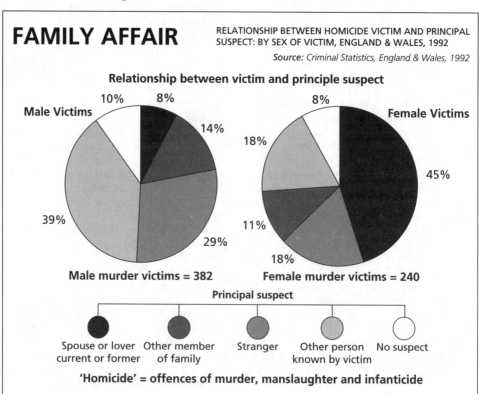

FAMILY AFFAIR

RELATIONSHIP BETWEEN HOMICIDE VICTIM AND PRINCIPAL SUSPECT: BY SEX OF VICTIM, ENGLAND & WALES, 1992

Source: Criminal Statistics, England & Wales, 1992

Relationship between victim and principle suspect

Male Victims
10% 8% 14% 39% 29%

Male murder victims = 382

Female Victims
8% 18% 45% 11% 18%

Female murder victims = 240

Principal suspect

Spouse or lover current or former | Other member of family | Stranger | Other person known by victim | No suspect

'Homicide' = offences of murder, manslaughter and infanticide

TASK

9 Study the figures carefully.

Write a report to cover the facts included in these statistics.

Auschwitz

(1 hour 30 minutes)

The article which follows tells you about a concentration camp at Auschwitz, 50 years after its liberation. Read the article carefully.

Auschwitz

In the 50 years since the liberation of Auschwitz, time has eroded much evidence but healed few wounds, and there is now bitter controversy over how the dead should be remembered

IT IS 50 years since the liberation of Auschwitz. It was on 27 January 1945 that the first Soviet soldiers entered the camp, abandoned by the Germans several days before. Now people from all over the world are arriving there to honour the anniversary, and as they arrive they make an unnerving discovery. Auschwitz has grown old. The place of death is itself dying.

Somehow, this is unexpected. Auschwitz is a symbol of many different things. But one of its best-understood meanings is about the contrast between life and machinery, between defence-less human bodies and the concrete and iron of the great industrial process put here to consume them. A million and a half people, more or less, were killed here. In comparison with their mortality, the steel of the barbed wire and the iron of the crematorium furnaces and the reinforced concrete of the gas chambers all seem invinc-

ible. But even these things, though infinitely more slowly, must perish too.

The Nazis did not build this camp to last. The only solid part is the original nucleus, the rows of two-storey brick blocks which were once an Austro-Hungarian barracks and which the Germans took over from the defeated Polish Army in 1939. This was opened as a concentration camp in 1940. But then came the construction of Birkenau (Auschwitz II), the gigantic wire enclosure a mile away which could hold 100,000 prisoners in wooden huts and which also contained the great industrial killing installation: a railway siding and unloading ramp, four purpose-built gas chambers, batteries of cremat-orium ovens with chimneys. Later still, and even further away, the SS used slave prisoners to erect the camp at Monowitz (Auschwitz III), to house the labour force for the Buna artificial rubber plant.

It was wartime. One could not get proper craftsmen, but had to rely on starving, half-trained prisoners to build the camps. The cement for the posts of the electrified fence was badly mixed and of sub-standard quality. The huts were dumped directly on the sandy soil, without waiting for brick or concrete underfloors. Anyway, the SS programme was to demolish completely all the camps concerned with the 'final solution of the Jewish question' – the genocide of European Jewry – when they had completed their work. In most cases this target was met. The sites of Treblinka, Sobibor and Belzec were cleared and planted with trees when they had served their purpose, as if nothing had ever happened there. The SS were not in the business of leaving evidence around.

At Auschwitz, they began the demolition process by blowing up the Birkenau gas chambers, but were interrupted by the Soviet advance before they could finish their work. That is why so much remains to be seen, even now. And it is that surviving Auschwitz which is now crumbling away.

The wire fences, stretching away in perspective to the misty horizon, are rusty and beginning to show gaps. The posts still carry their white insulators, but they are discoloured and starting to fragment. The surviving huts at Birkenau (most of them burnt down after the liberation, because they were crawling with typhus-infected lice) are rotting away. The steel rails which brought the cattle-wagons of doomed Jews up to the Birkenau ramp are still hard and clear, but the stones of the track-bed are vanishing beneath earth and weeds.

Time cannot be imprisoned. When I first visited Auschwitz, more than 30 years ago, I could pull up the turf anywhere in the open ground beyond the end of the railway track and find the earth white-ish: a paste of calcined human bone and ash. Now, the carbon cycle has quietly done its work over half a century, and the soil is brown again. At that time, the poplars planted by the SS to screen the gas chambers and the crematorium blocks from view were still scrawny saplings. Today they are vast, graceful trees, gently waving their tips against the clouds.

Since the war, Auschwitz has been a museum, funded and administered by the Polish state. But no museum in the world has to face such problems of choice. What is to be done with this place? It is, as I would say, the worst place in the world. But that does not tell posterity how, or even if, it should be conserved.

One argument is that Auschwitz should be left to fall apart in its own natural time. In this view, what took place at Auschwitz is so terrible that any human intervention, even an attempt to organise the site in order to teach visitors what happened in the camp, is impious. It is necessary, of course, to educate the world about the Final Solution and the nature of Himmler's empire, but not here. The great camp is primarily a place of death, a form of cemetery. Visitors should go to meditate or to grieve in silence. They should not throng in organised guide-parties down a 'Holocaust Heritage Trail' from Visitor Centre to Info-Point to Museum Shop.

The opposite extreme is to turn Auschwitz into a theme park. A theme with solemn intentions, admittedly – but the strategy would be to create an international visitor site in which surviving reality is deliberately adapted or even replaced in order to deliver a pre-planned experience. Everything would be rebuilt; or if not quite everything – for the Auschwitz complex at its peak of activity in 1944 was the size of a small conurbation – at least the 'representative core' of the place. The fences, wire, lights and guard-towers, together with some of the wooden bunk-houses, would be entirely restored and redecorated to their original appearance in a sample area of the camp. And one of the Birkenau gas chambers might be reconstructed so that visitors could enter it, look around at the 'shower' openings, and experience appropriate feelings.

Neither of these radical solutions appeals much to the Polish custodians. They have not had a great deal of time to brood on Western doctrines of 'museology'. Until 1989, the job of the Auschwitz Museum was to display what remained of the camp as an international 'monument to the crimes of Fascism', playing its part in the Communist bloc's campaign against alleged West German 'militarism'.

To fulfil this task, the museum authorities carried out a certain amount of restoration in the early post-war years. Right after liberation, there had been chaos on the Auschwitz site. An obscene gold rush took place. Poles with spades and sieves overran the camp to dig through its earth and to pan the nearby Sola river, in search of the gold coins and tooth fillings which they imagined the 'rich Jews' had left behind. Others with horses and carts loaded up anything they could find which might serve as building material or be sold for scrap. There was much destruction.

The museum, once established, rebuilt several huts at Birkenau, renewed stretches of barbed wire which had been stolen and – most controversially – restored the first gas chamber, a building in Auschwitz I which had been subsequently converted and rebuilt by the SS to use as an air raid shelter. This restoration was not made plain to visitors, who were encouraged to think that they were seeing the unretouched place of murder. Later, when the truth came out, the post-war building work was used by right-wing 'Holocaust denial' writers as evidence that no gas chambers had ever existed except as Communist propaganda fakes.

During the Communist period, there was no coherent policy for or against restoration; after the initial replacement work, the museum administration more or less restricted itself to maintaining the site in the semi-ruined condition in which it had found it. If something actually fell down, it was usually put back by Polish workmen in a simulation of how it had looked before. The 'message' delivered by the museum was also contradictory. The labelling of displays and relics, like the wording on the various memorial plaques, deliberately underplayed the fact that Auschwitz had played a central part in the Jewish Holocaust; instead, it was vaguely presented as a place where all nations had suffered under Hitlerite German oppression. Among the tablets honouring nations whose people had been murdered here, the name of Israel did not occur, while East Germany (which of course did not exist in 1945, any more than Israel) absurdly had a tablet of its own. At the same time, the museum staff would

usually treat this 'party line' with contempt and, in taking visitors round, would make clear the central significance of Auschwitz as the place of Jewish martyrdom.

In the later 1980s, everything changed. Again, it was a museum researcher, Franciszek Piper, who broke through the propaganda wall. To official consternation, he demonstrated that the Auschwitz victims had numbered between 1.1 and 1.4 million (not the traditional 4 million, a figure apparently plucked out of the air by Soviet propagandists in the late 1940s), and that 90 per cent of them had been Jews. At about the same time, a merciless and fanatical quarrel between American Jews and Polish Catholics broke out over the establishment of a Carmelite nunnery in an old SS store building adjacent to the camp. The most extreme Jewish group denounced the nunnery as an anti-Semitic provocation and demanded that Auschwitz should become an exclusively Jewish memorial.

This dispute blazed on for some years after the collapse of Polish Communism in 1989, but has now been precariously settled by a set of compromises. One of them, dating back to 1989, is the establishment of an 'International Auschwitz Council', which includes Jewish and Gypsy representatives as well as Polish officials, to advise the museum. This has already produced new and much more truthful exhibition material on the site. And in the new climate, the West has begun to participate in funding the

Auschwitz relics and museum, in years when state funding has been drastically cut back and the Polish budget can no longer afford even the maintenance costs, let alone new display or restoration projects. Ronald Lauder, once American ambassador to Austria, is using his personal foundation to raise a target of over $40 million for 'long-term preservation'.

None of this, though, removes the fundamental choices which have to be made about Auschwitz. It might seem that the option of just standing back, declaring Auschwitz a graveyard and letting it vanish under the grass, has been pre-empted by the recent changes. The Lauder money is committed to maintenance, while the International Council stands for an educational policy which will use the place as an organised teaching resource to inoculate the human race against genocide and dictatorial terror. And yet even the abandonment option is not entirely closed. One of the worst sights at Auschwitz is the room filled with human hair, shorn off corpses or off those who were about to become corpses a few minutes later. There are nearly two tons of it, plaits and braids, curls and tresses of every colour, found by the Russians ready-baled for delivery to German industry – a small fraction of the total. But the hair is beginning to disintegrate. The preservation methods invented and applied by the Poles over the years have not been enough, and indeed no museum in the world knows how to treat so large a quantity of hair against deterioration. At Auschwitz, in its glass-fronted display room in Block four, the hair is now beginning to turn to dust. Some people, including many camp survivors, insist that ways must be found to preserve it for future generations. But there are others whose respect for the irreversible fact of death makes them want to return dust to dust – to remove the decaying hair from the showcases and bury it at last.

THE TRUTH about Auschwitz is that there can never be consensus about the use of its ruins. It has too many symbolisms for too many different, and sometimes mutually suspicious, groups of people. Those who want to meditate about what was done here will always resent the organised crowds of visitors flowing through the site – chattering, taking snapshots, eating or smoking – and feel that they defile the commandment to remember. Those who want the place to teach something and to be visited by millions of pilgrims annually will always resent the 'mediators' for their refusal to exploit the potential of the site. Some survivors find it painful that anything whatever is allowed to remain; others find the camp's decay an offensive symbol of the world's indifference and would like radical restoration. Germans will feel that any further commer-

cialisation will get in the way of their own need to confront their national past. Poles will often suspect that Jews are 'using' the site to imply unfair slanders about Polish anti-Semitism; Jews will often regard the 'international' character of the museum displays as an attempt by Christian Europeans to conceal their complicity in the Holocaust.

But this inner discord, which can never fully be overcome, is what Auschwitz and its memory are about. What happened here was not just death, but abandonment. Behind this wire, people felt forsaken in a way so utter and final that their loneliness somehow survives their transformation into smoke and ash. Many Jews and Christians thought that their God had abandoned them. Others blamed earthly powers. Poles thought that it was Europe that had once again abandoned them to death, as so often in the past. All the prisoners, watching the Allied bombers passing far overhead, felt that the world had abandoned them, caring nothing for their fate. Where was the Vatican, the Red Cross, the League of Nations, President Roosevelt, the Royal Air Force? Those who survived, and those who took up the cause of the dead, inherited this sense of abandonment, and it has proved incurable. Those who profess to care now did not care then. Where were all these wealthy,

concerned universities and churches and governments when the trains were steaming up to the ramp, and the Sonderkommando was stoking the crematorium fires?

There is no answer to that. And there is no single answer to the way in which Auschwitz still makes people – even visitors – feel lonely, as if every other group or nationality were somehow concealing hostility and indifference. The consequence of that misery is that any agreement on the future of the Auschwitz site can only be a compromise, and that such a compromise will never be comfortable and always hurt some people.

The SS, tramping through the morning frost to their duties inside the wire, used to sing:

'Everything will be over, everything passes away;
After every December, there comes again May....'

The trees grow, the glittering barbed wire turns brown and then powders away, the cruel bricks are softened by moss – and it is 50 years since the last of over a million helpless human beings was murdered. The rest of the world was unable or unwilling to save them. But now the rest of the world – which has come to mean us – is able and willing to save the gallows and the furnace instead. The irony of that is foul. But we have earned it.

NEAL ASCHERSON

TASKS

10 Summarise what the article tells you about the camp
   a in the years before 1945,
   b at the present time.

11 The article raises the issue of how to preserve the camp.
Write a report in which you:
   a outline the problems of preserving the camp;
   b suggest a solution to these.

Let The Children Live
(1 hour 30 minutes + research time)

In the classbook chapter you studied the story of Peter Walters and wrote about his work.

There are many organisations which set out to relieve human suffering and to save lives. Find out about some of them. You may find the information in school; you may find it in your local library. You may want to write to some organisations such as the 'Save the Children Fund' or 'Oxfam'.

Then, using the information, write an article for publication in school or in your local community entitled 'Living is better than dying'.

Fire
(2 hours)

Printed below is an article which offers guidance on how to prevent fire in the home, plus advice on what to do if a fire does break out.

Fire – Ways To Save Your Family

Early on Christmas Day when fire raced through a terraced house in Bury, Lancashire, the horror made headlines. Five children and four adults died in the inferno. To one survivor that meant the loss of her two children, her mother, two sisters, grandfather, a nephew and a niece.

Such killer fires occur all too often. Each year an estimated 370,000 fires break out across the country, sweeping away 900 lives, more than 150 of them children. Many more victims are left with severe burns and serious injuries.

The blaze at Bury in 1984 spread from discarded wrapping-paper smouldering in an unguarded grate. Most of the fires that break out in people's homes can be traced back to the one factor we can all prevent: human error.

Every day, people stub out cigarettes in ashtrays, then empty the still-hot butts into paper-filled rubbish bins. Or they smoke in bed. We leave matches within children's reach and switch on electric blankets that are in need of servicing. Often, we turn our homes into fire-traps without realising it. We keep flammable paints, oily rags and piles of newspapers under the stairs, and fill lofts with combustible junk.

The list of fire hazards in the modern home is lengthy and the only way to avert disaster is for householders to take their own fire safety precautions.

Because smoke can disorient and panic you if you are unprepared, an escape plan and fire-drills are crucial. Know how to escape 'blind' from each room. Devise an alerting system, such as a bell or whistle by everyone's bed.

Everyone in the family should be involved in planning for an emergency; decide who will aid small children, invalids and the elderly. Hold regular firedrills, along the lines of a serious game. Pick a spot outside to assemble. The golden rule is: once out, stay out. No one goes back for pets and possessions – or to telephone for help. Call the fire brigade from a neighbour's house.

Warning devices can increase your chances of escape. Most fires begin with smoke and smoke detectors cost about £15 in the electrical departments of large stores or Do-It-Yourself shops. Place detectors close to where fires are most likely to start – in living-rooms and kitchens – but within earshot of sleeping quarters, since most fires occur between 11pm and 6am.

Says Eric Rutter, Senior Divisional Officer of the London Fire Brigade's Fire Prevention Department, 'In the average house it's a good idea to have a detector on the landing, linked to one in the living-room and another outside the kitchen – not inside, where cooking fumes may set it off.' Alarms and batteries should be checked regularly.

Domestic fire extinguishers used swiftly can cope with small, localised fires – in a waste-paper basket, say, or an ashtray. All extinguishers should carry a British Standards mark. Make sure every family member capable of operating them knows how to do so. In the kitchen, keep a fire blanket to extinguish blazing fat pans (failing this, use a damp tea-towel). Some 15,000 fat pans catch fire every year.

If you live in a block of flats or hostel, find out where the fire exits are. If fire-alarms and extinguishers are provided, make sure you know how to use them.

As a tenant you can improve the level of fire safety. Says Eric Rutter, 'Anyone who is worried about fire hazards in a block of flats or hostel should get advice from their local fire brigade.

If necessary, a fire prevention officer will visit the premises and make safety recommendations to the landlord or local housing authorities.' Equally, fire prevention officers will be pleased to help house-dwellers with advice about fire prevention and escape planning.

Often fire hazards can be eliminated before they show their potential. More than two in every five domestic fires are of electrical origin. Check flexes regularly and replace any that are frayed or split.

Avoid overloading power sockets – adapters can create a dangerously high flow of current. At night switch off and unplug all appliances except low current users like bedside light, clock or tea-maker, and fridge, freezer and video-recorder, which are designed to be left on in safety.

One in ten fires is caused by a faulty or carelessly used space-heating appliance. Keep radiant heaters at a distance from furniture. Never leave an open fire unguarded, especially if there are children or elderly people in the house.

Soot is potentially flammable and chimneys should be swept twice a year. Don't fill or carry about heaters fuelled by paraffin or liquefied petroleum gas cylinders, paraffin and other flammable liquids outside, away from the house, in purpose-made containers.

Fire safety involves a daily effort. It means taking care with smoke materials, cause of almost half the fatal fires in the home. Since 1983 upholstered furniture has been treated to resist ignition from a dropped cigarette, and flame-retardant mattresses are now available. But most chairs, sofas and mattresses in our homes are untreated; they ignite easily and blaze rapidly, particularly if filled with cellular foam, which brings the added hazard of poisonous fumes.

Fire safety means not leaving tea-towels to dry over the cooker, or cooking in billowing clothes. It means cleaning the stove so grease doesn't accumulate. It means checking each room for fire hazards last thing at night, then closing the door behind you; doors make good fire-breaks, taking on average ten minutes to burn through. It means making sure night-time escape routes are clear.

If, in spite of all your precautions, fire does break out, do your best not to panic. Part of the value of an escape plan is that some of the thinking for survival has already been done:

staying calm makes it work. Parents should forewarn children that panic is a natural response, but one that must be suppressed.

In the event of a fire, there are many things you can do to increase the chance of reaching safety.

1. If you wake to the smell of smoke, do not sit up but roll out of bed and drop to the floor: lethal smoke and gases rise. If you can, cover your mouth and nose with a heavy, preferably damp, cloth.

2. If the bedroom door feels cool at the top, brace your body against it. Open it a few inches but be ready to shut it if you feel pressure or a hot draught on your hand. Try to escape via the stairs, but beware of stairwells becoming a funnel for smoke, fire and toxic gases.

3. If you are going to exit through the window, make sure the door stays closed. Otherwise, the draught from opening the window or breaking the glass may suck the heat or flames into your room.

4. If you must break the glass, stand aside so that flying fragments don't injure your face.

Remove the jagged pieces from the frame with a chair leg or shoe. Place a thick cloth over the sill before escaping.

5. If you have to exit by an upper window, slide out backwards feet first and hang from the sill. Bend your knees, drop and roll when you land. If you are higher than the first floor, drop only as a last resort.

6. If you cannot leave your room, stop smoke and fumes from entering by stuffing the cracks between the door and door-frame with cloths.

7. If the room does fill with smoke, lean out of the window. If smoke and fire outside the window make that impossible, lie close to the floor and wait for help. Many people have survived fires by staying put.

Above all, remember that you can dramatically reduce the dangers of fire in your dwelling by the adoption of simple safety measures and family drills.

DEBORAH SAWYER

TASK

12 Analyse the advice which is given in the article.

Now use the article to help you write your own list of pieces of advice clearly and concisely, in a way which would fit on the two sides of a laminated postcard for people to keep a copy in each room of the house.

Death of a Teenager

(1 hour)

Death comes in all forms and sadly a common one is a road accident.

Read the article on the next page.

Death of a Teenager

Recently I went to a funeral which nobody present is ever likely to forget. It had been a dramatic, tragic death. But it did not hit the headlines. It was much too common.

The wooden box contained a boy, just 17, son of a friend and colleague. He was a healthy, happy, active youth, pupil at a sixth form college, founder-chairman of a local scooter club – the leader of the pack. A very safe, careful rider, everyone said.

One Sunday he set out on an errand in quiet, suburban north London and never came back. A week later, the police were still working out what happened.

Two cars and a concrete lamppost were involved. An ambulance came in record time. The doctors who spent several hours trying to put together the bits were weeping at the finish.

So were mourners at the cemetery. He must have been a popular lad. There were as many standing as sitting in the crematorium, with every age, class, race and hair-style represented.

The occasion was secular and not too sombre. After the orations, his girlfriend played tapes of his favourite pop songs. It seemed fitting. We were celebrating a good life: light-hearted, sensible, funny, generous, full of hope and love and promise.

There were many emotions as the blue curtains closed – shock, sympathy, anger at the pointless pity of it, even perhaps a frightful feeling that the Fates had been propitiated: *at least it wasn't my child*. But for the men in black top hats it was all part of the day's work. There's nothing unusual, after all, about the death of a teenager on two wheels.

Perhaps it is because road killings are so ordinary, when they happen to strangers, that we take them for granted. Big, comfortably remote mega-death disasters get the attention. But it is the mundane, domestic motor smash that takes the most lives, causing violent death on a scale only exceeded by the slaughter of war.

In 1985, a staggering 5,165 fatalities on the roads were recorded. Of these, 1,182 people were killed on motor or pedal bikes. In the 15–19 age group, road accidents accounted for more deaths than any other single cause.

Drink is the biggest killer. More than one in four road deaths are linked to this socially acceptable poison. Excessive speed, faulty brakes or steering, a split second's inattention, a signal not given, can also be deadly. And the victim's only offence is usually to have been, by bad luck, in the wrong place at the wrong time.

'He will be remembered,' it was said at the funeral. Yet what will never be known, or remembered, are the things which those that are lost might have said, or done, or been.

'If only' gives birth to a thousand regrets. Unpredictable and unmotivated, accidents shatter faith in an ordered world and destroy belief in reason and endeavour. Sickness has a cause. An accident is often sheer stupidity.

Yet which of us can say that we have never – behind a wheel – gambled with the lives of others?

Accidents provide no explanation, no comfort for the bereaved. If, however, a moment's reflection on their absurdity may lead a single driver to drink one glass less, or check the mirror before turning, a mother or brother or lover may be luckier than they will ever know – and a commonplace statistic will never have been in vain.

BEN PIMLOT

TASK

13 Put yourself in the position of the driver of one of the cars and write your story.

A Vicious Sport

(1 hour)

Many sports can be dangerous and very often they are justified by saying that the people who take part in them know what the risks are.

Below you will find a short article about boxing, a sport which has been banned in several countries.

A Vicious Sport

Doctors have become increasingly concerned with damage inflicted in the boxing ring. Recent studies have shown evidence of brain damage in more than half of the boxers examined; even relatively minor blows to the head can cause cumulative damage.

The individual boxer is inflicting injury in the ring which if inflicted anywhere else would result in conviction for assault. Fit young men lose their intellect and memory, become slurred in speech and lose co-ordination, eventually dying 20 years before their contemporaries.

To reduce the risks, headguards are used in Olympic boxing, but the guards actually increase the rotational forces, causing the brain to hit the sides of the skull harder.

As for younger boxers, it has been argued that they do not damage their opponents' brains because they lack punching power. The death of Joseph Stricklen after his second amateur fight two and a half years ago confirmed that studies showing brain damage to younger boxers were indeed valid, and increased concern that boys too young to appreciate the risks were being encouraged to box.

The British Medical Association's campaign to educate the public is now producing results where it matters most: among younger teenagers. In the past ten years boxing club enrolments have fallen significantly, and many clubs cannot field opponents at every weight. Barry McGuigan and the manager Frank Warren have both stated that they will advise their sons not to box.

I look forward to the day when this gladiatorial contest ceases worldwide.

JEFFREY CUNDY

TASK

14 The writer of the article has a clear point of view with which you may or may not agree.

Write the words of a talk in which you try to dissuade a group of young children who are keen to learn to box.

10

THE FUTURE

Star Tours

(1 hour)

Printed below is a photograph from the souvenir programme of EuroDisney.

It is a photograph of Star Tours, which is a ride you can take 'into the future'.

TASK

1 This first task in this homework chapter gives you the opportunity to use your imagination and to write a piece of narrative.

Imagine that you are sitting in the front seat of this spacecraft. Write about your journey.

The Day of the Triffids

(2 hours)

In your classbook you have already studied an extract from *The Day of the Triffids*, by John Wyndham. You will find the extract printed below to remind you.

The Day of the Triffids

'It will not be easy: old prejudices die hard. The simple rely on a bolstering mass of maxim and precept, so do the timid, so do the mentally lazy – and so do all of us, more than we imagine. Now that the organisation has gone, our ready-reckoners for conduct within it no longer give the right answers. We *must* have the moral courage to think and to plan for ourselves.'

He paused to survey his audience thoughtfully. Then he said:

'There is one thing to be made quite clear to you before you decide to join our community. It is that those of us who start on this task will all have our parts to play. The men must work – the women must have babies. Unless you can agree to that there can be no place for you in our community.'

After an interval of dead silence, he added:

'We can afford to support a limited number of women who cannot see, because they will have babies who can see. We cannot afford to support men who cannot see. In our new world, then, babies become very much more important then husbands.'

For some seconds after he stopped speaking silence continued, then isolated murmurs grew quickly into a general buzz.

I looked at Josella. To my astonishment she was grinning impishly.

'What do you find funny about this?' I asked, a trifle shortly.

'People's expressions mostly', she replied.

I had to admit it as a reason. I looked round the place, and then across at Michael. His eyes were moving from one section to another of the audience as he tried to sum up the reaction.

'Michael's looking a bit anxious,' I observed.

'He should worry,' said Josella. 'If Brigham Young could bring it off in the middle of the nineteenth century, this ought to be a pushover.'

'What a crude young woman you are at times,' I said. 'Were you in on this before?'

'Not exactly, but I'm not quite dumb, you know. Besides, while you were away someone drove in a bus with most of these blind girls on board. They all came from some institution. I said to myself, why collect them from there when you could gather up thousands in a few streets round here? The answer obviously was that (a) being blind before this happened they had been trained to do work of some kind, and (b) they were all girls. The deduction wasn't terribly difficult.'

'H'm,' I said. 'Depends on one's outlook, I suppose. I must say, it wouldn't have struck me. Do you- ?'

'Sh-sh,' she told me, as a quietness came over the hall.

A tall, dark, purposeful-looking, youngish woman had risen. While she waited, she appeared to have a mouth not made to open, but later it did.

'Are we to understand,' she inquired, using a kind of carbon-steel voice, 'are we to understand that the last speaker is advocating free love?' And she sat down, with spine-jarring decision.

Doctor Vorless smoothed back his hair as he regarded her.

'I think the questioner must be aware that I never mentioned love, free, bought, or bartered. Will she please make her question clearer?'

The woman stood up again.

'I think the speaker understood me. I am asking if he suggests the abolition of the marriage law?'

'The laws we knew have been abolished by circumstances. It now falls to us to make laws suitable to the conditions, and to enforce them if necessary.'

'There is still God's law, and the law of decency.'

'Madam. Solomon had three hundred – or was it five hundred? – wives, and God did not apparently hold that against him. A Mohammedan preserves rigid respectability with three wives. These are matters of local custom. Just what our laws in these matters, and in others, will be is for us all to decide later for the greatest benefit of the community.

'This committee, after discussion, has decided that if we are to build a new state of things and avoid a relapse into barbarism – which is an appreciable danger – we must have certain undertakings from those who wish to join us.

'Not one of us is going to recapture the conditions we have lost. What we offer is a busy life in the best conditions we can contrive, and the happiness which will come of achievement against odds. In return we ask willingness and fruitfulness. There is no compulsion. The choice is yours. Those to whom our offer does not appeal are at perfect liberty to go elsewhere, and start a separate community on such lines as they prefer.

'But I would ask you to consider very carefully whether or not you do hold a warrant from God to deprive any woman of the happiness of carrying out her natural functions.'

The discussion which followed was a rambling affair descending frequently to points of detail and hypothesis on which there could as yet be no answers. But there was no move to cut it short. The longer it went on, the less strangeness the idea would have.

Josella and I moved over to the table where Nurse Berr had set up her paraphernalia. We took several shots in our arms, and then sat down again to listen to the wrangling.

'How many of them will decide to come, do you think?' I asked her.

She glanced round.

'Nearly all of them – by the morning,' she said.

I felt doubtful. There was a lot of objecting and questioning going on. Josella said:

'If you were a woman who was going to spend an hour or two before you went to sleep tonight considering whether you would choose babies and an organisation to look after you, or adherence to a principle which might quite likely mean no babies and no one to look after you. You'd not really be very doubtful, you know. And after all, most women want babies, anyway – the husband's just what Doctor Vorless might call the local means to the end.'

'That's rather cynical of you.'

'If you really think that's cynical you must be a very sentimental character. I'm talking about real women, not those in the magazine-movie-make-believe world.'

'Oh,' I said.

She sat pensively awhile, and gradually acquired a frown. At last she said:

'The thing that worries me is how many will they expect? I like babies, all right, but there are limits.'

After the debate had gone on raggedly for an hour or so, it was wound up. Michael asked that the names of all those willing to join in his plan should be left in his office by ten o'clock the next morning. The Colonel requested all who could drive a lorry to report to him by 7.00 hours, and the meeting broke up.

Josella and I wandered out of doors. The evening was mild. The light on the tower was again stabbing hopefully into the sky. The moon had just risen clear of the Museum roof. We found a low wall, and sat on it, looking into the shadows of the Square garden, and listening to the faint sound of the wind in the branches of the trees there. We smoked a cigarette each almost in silence. When I reached the end of mine, I threw it away, and drew a breath.

'Josella,' I said.

'M'm?' she replied, scarcely emerging from her thoughts.

'Josella,' I said again. 'Er – those babies. I'd – er – I'd be sort of terribly proud and happy if they could be mine as well as yours.'

She sat quite still for a moment, saying nothing. Then she turned her head. The moonlight was glinting on her fair hair, but her face and eyes were in shadow. I waited, with a hammered, and slightly sick feeling inside me. She said, with surprising calm:

'Thank you, Bill, dear. I think I would, too.'

I sighed. The hammering did not ease up much, and I saw that my hand was trembling as it reached for hers. I didn't have any words,

for the moment. Josella, however, did. She said:
  'But it isn't quite as easy as that, now.'
I was jolted.
  'What do you mean?' I asked.
  She said, consideringly: 'I think that if I were those people in there' – she nodded in the direction of the tower – 'I think that I should make a rule. I should divide us up into lots. I should say every man who marries a sighted girl must take on two blind girls as well. I'm pretty sure that's what I should do.'
  I stared at her face in the shadow.
  'You don't mean that,' I protested.
  'I'm afraid I do, Bill.'

JOHN WYNDHAM

TASK

2 There is some discussion in this extract of the future of the family unit and it is clear that the characters have different views.

Quite a lot of publicity is given to the idea that marriage is becoming a thing of the past and the family unit is no longer the norm.

Think through your own ideas and plan, draft and write an essay entitled:

'The future of family life.'

Heating or Eating

(2 hours)

In the classbook chapter you studied two leaflets which were concerned with how some people might be given a future.

Here is another leaflet which, in another way, tackles the same issue.

Heating or Eating?

That's the choice Jack is forced to make.
  Please give £12 so that an elderly person won't go cold or hungry this winter.

Dear Friend,
  An elderly gentleman contacted Help the Aged recently. I'll call him Jack. He was desperately worried about his heating bills. This is what he said:
  'All I have is a gas fire and it costs me a fortune. I often have to sit in my overcoat and sleep downstairs in the chair, it's too cold upstairs.'
  Jack knows that when the winter really starts to bite, he won't only be forced to sleep in a chair at night to keep warm, he'll be faced with a stark choice: either to heat the one room he's living in or to eat a proper meal.

Like thousands, perhaps millions of other elderly people, Jack simply can't afford to do both.
  But a gift of just £12 could pay for heating for someone like Jack for three weeks.

The pensioners who are struggling against impossible odds to make ends meet
  We estimate that there are about 3.6 million pensioners in this country who aren't quite needy enough to qualify for means-tested benefits, yet who cannot afford the very basics: heat and food.
  The recent decision to impose VAT on fuel bills, even though it was accompanied by promises of help for elderly people, will still mean an increase in fuel bills – stretching already tight budgets to breaking point.
  I was talking to one elderly man recently who fell into this fuel poverty trap. He doesn't

want to be identified so let's call him Bert.

Convector heaters are the only source of heating in his flat. His landlord won't install a more efficient, cheaper kind of heating. Bert is frightened to switch them on. He has a key meter which is preset to collect £3 for every £10 he puts in to satisfy an existing fuel debt.

When the weather is very cold, Bert visits the library just so he can sit somewhere warm. He told me:

'They haven't asked me to leave yet, but it's getting embarrassing. I don't know how I'm going to cope with the extra VAT, it's hard enough already.'

My heart went out to Bert. But he didn't want my sympathy, that's why he insisted that his identity be kept secret. All he wants is enough money not to have to live with the nagging, wearing, desperate worry of not being able to pay his heating bills. All he wants it to be warm this winter.

The cold that can and does kill 30,000 elderly people every winter

Even in very mild winters, at least 30,000 susceptible elderly people die from cold-related illnesses every year. The fact is that if their homes were adequately heated and insulated, if they could afford to eat proper meals as well as heating their homes, their lives might well be saved.

I know that sounds dramatic, even incredible. I wish it didn't because the stark, simple truth is that elderly people in this country *are* dying of cold … and they needn't.

Because just £12 will heat one room in an elderly person's home for three weeks, and that could be enough to save their life.

Agnes dreads the winter

Agnes, like Bert, doesn't want her real name to used, but she agreed to let me tell her story.

Aged 84 and widowed, Agnes lives alone relying on electric fires for warmth. She knows only too well how expensive they are to run, but what choice has she got? She applied to the Local Authority for a grant to install a cheaper, more efficient form of heating but because she has some savings was told she would have to make a contribution towards the cost. In fact, all Agnes has is £600 and she's frightened to use it, as she says:

'There'd be nothing left to bury me with.'

So Agnes tries to keep warm by staying in bed as much as possible.

Why they suffer the misery of being cold

It seems inconceivable to me, as it probably will to you, that in this country elderly people are suffering so much, even dying, of the cold.

But happen it does and for two reasons. Firstly, the standard of housing most elderly people have falls far below the ideal. Poor insulation, expensive, inefficient forms of heating all contribute towards huge fuel bills. Secondly, many elderly people fall just short of having enough money to exist on. They cannot apply for benefits because according to the rules they are not needy enough, yet they can't manage.

As this elderly lady called us to say:

'I'm not on income support but I have angina and poor circulation, and my husband has rheumatoid arthritis, we need to be warm but we can't get help with our fuel bills now.'

Elderly people in this position either turn off the heating or cut down on food. Being constantly cold or hungry makes them more susceptible to illness. The more often they are ill, the weaker they get, and the less able to cope with cold and hunger. It's a vicious circle.

What you and I can do to break the vicious circle

Help the Aged raises funds to improve the lives of needy elderly people – people who have nowhere and no one else to turn to for help.

We are in desperate need of more supporters. Could you become one of them?

All we are asking for is a gift of £12. That relatively small amount of money will keep a gas fire burning in one room of an elderly person's home for three weeks.

If you could give more than that – say £50 – we could buy insulation materials to begin to provide permanent solutions to the problem of high fuel bills. We could also support more day centres which provide warmth, company and hot meals for thousands of elderly people and we could help ensure that more specialist transport is available to help take them there.

Whatever you decide to give, please send it quickly

If you've ever had to wait for a bus in winter, or have had to sit in an unheated room for even an hour, you'll know that the weather doesn't have to be icy for it to feel bitterly cold.

You'll know how miserable being cold can make you feel, how numb your hands and feet get. Imagine if you felt like that day in, day our for months on end.

Imagine if you decided to eat less so that you could be a little warmer. Soon the nagging ache of the cold would be replaced by the dull ache of hunger.

There are elderly people suffering like that right now. That's why the speed of your reply is almost as important as the amount of your gift.

£12 will heat one room in an elderly person's home for three weeks. It might seem meagre, but one warm room could be a life-saver.

Staying warm is just one of the many challenges facing elderly people in the UK – whatever you send will go straight towards helping them to cope.

Please send whatever you can now to ensure an elderly person like Jack, Bert or Agnes doesn't have to make the choice between heating or eating this winter. Your gift will be used to help those elderly people most in need. Thank you.

Yours sincerely,

Peter Gray

UK Housing & Care services

PS Unfortunately, it is impossible for us to check if you support Help the Aged in other ways. If so, we'd like to take this opportunity to apologise for writing to you and ask you to pass this letter on to a friend who might be interested in supporting Help the Aged too. Help the Aged badly needs new supporters who will make elderly people in need a priority.

Thank you.

TASKS

3 Write about a day in the life of Jack or Bert or Agnes.

4 Answer the following questions:
  a Explain the different ways in which money given to this organisation might be used.
  b Analyse the way in which this leaflet is set out and the language it uses.
  c Do you think it is an effective way of encouraging donations?

Invest in an Ostrich

(1 hour 30 minutes)

Printed on the following pages is an article from *The Independent* newspaper which puts forward one idea for a way to invest for the future.

On a Wing and a Prayer

Investing in an ostrich can bring a return of 785%. By Frances Howell.

Fed up with receiving apologetic notes from his stockbroker about the state of the market, the writer Duff Hart-Davis bought an ostrich. 'I paid £3,500 for an 18-month-old hen, which should start laying eggs next year, and for the next 30 years,' he explains. 'The returns should go up to 100 per cent a year and, as a seven or eight-year-old mature breeding hen, she should be worth about £10,000.'

Better than a punt on the Footsie?

Ostrich farming is increasingly common in the UK, with up to 200 farms now supporting up to 500 birds each. It is a rare opportunity for the private investor to dabble in farming. Nobody, for example, preaches the virtues of the humble cow as an investment vehicle.

The Ostrich Farming Corporation advertises annual returns of anything up to 785 per cent over a 10-year period, which may tempt even the most urban of investors. However, to the wary, these promises will appear as exotic as the bird.

You can buy ostrich hens at various stages of their 25- year commercial breeding cycle. Prices range from £6,000 for a two-to three-year-old hen in her first year of breeding to £14,000 for an eight-year-old in her fifth year. The return on investment comes mainly from the sale of the chicks, which the OFC will buy from you once they are 12 months old. If you do invest, the OFC offers a variety of five-year deals in which it will buy a fixed number of chicks each year for a guaranteed £500 each. After the five years it will still buy the chicks, but at market-determined prices.

In the case of a £6,000 bird, for example, the OFC deal promises to buy five chicks in breeding years one and two, nine chicks in year three and 12 chicks in years four and five. So in year two you get £2,500. You get another £2,500 in year three, £4,500 in year four and £6,000 in year five. Total return: £15,500 on a £6,000 investment over five years.

The OFC will also buy the 12 chicks produced in breeding year five, but not at the guaranteed price of £500. Any spare chicks disappear in livery charges. A mature eight-year-old breeding hen costs £14,000 and is guaranteed to produce 20 chicks in the first three years (£10,000 in years two, three and four) and 24 chicks in years four and five (£12,000 in year five). Total return £42,500.

The Ostrich Farming Corporation makes its money on eggs produced over and above the figures guaranteed for that age of bird. In exchange, it provides livery for free, and will immediately replace for free any hen whose perform-ance isn't up to the mark. However, ownership of the bird rests wholly with the purchaser. The payment of excess eggs to OFC forms part of separate livery agreement. So, there is money to be made – at the moment. However, the high profits made so far rely partly on the scarcity of the birds. With each hen producing an average of 10–12 young females a year, the industry view is that saturation point for breeder hens is about 5 years away.

And 5 years is the length of time for which the OFC guarantees to pay £500 for each 12-month-old chick. It claims that breeder hens will keep their value as they will supply a world-wide meat market. But there must be a real risk that their currently exaggerated value will slide. Indelicate as it may be, the bottom line of ostrich farming is the value of the carcass. At present a 12-year-old is worth up to £1,000. But as the market expands, this will halve.

The original ostrich farming boom of the nineteenth century relied on a high demand for ostrich feathers. However, the fashion changed, and the bottom fell out of the market. Is the current revival also riding a wave of fashion and fad? This time, ostrich hide is being turned into purses, briefcases, and even jeans. But the main market is seen as the future meat market.

Ostrich meat is a low cholesterol fat-free meat which apparently tastes like fillet steak, but currently costs about 30 per cent more. 'To supply 10 per cent of the existing beef market in the UK would require a minimum of 100,000 breeder hens,' says Brian Ketchell, managing director of the Ostrich Farming Corporation. 'Even a tiny percentage of the existing meat market would mean a huge market for ostrich.'

Despite its popularity in countries like Australia, ostrich is rarely on the menu in Europe, and to this extent, talk of a future meat market is speculative.

Before you buy an ostrich
Owning an ostrich is not covered by the 1986 Financial Services Act because of the legal structure of the owner-ship and livery agreements. If the market were to collapse and the company to go into liquidation, guaranteed returns could be worthless. Owning an ostrich as an investment is farming. Income depends on produce and the market price for it. Remember that guaran-teed returns are based on the current state of what is still a developing market for both breeder hens and for meat.

TASKS

5 Look carefully at the financial arguments which are put forward.

Summarise the positive points in favour of buying an ostrich as an investment for the future.

6 Explain what the dangers are of such an investment.

7 Imagine the scene round the breakfast table at home when you announce that you are going to buy an ostrich.

Write the scene in the form of a playscript.

The Environment

(2 hours)

Printed below and on page 166 is the main part of an examination paper. The theme of the paper is the future of the environment. Peter and Henry are trying to extend environmental research; whilst the politicians have a more hard-headed look at current environmental issues.

Your task is to treat this examination paper as a practice for the real thing.

Part 1

Read the following two passages carefully; then answer questions 1 and 2.

Even before they reached the 2,000 metre depth, the steadily decreasing sunlight had disappeared altogether, and outside the small portholes there was only total blackness.

The gauge for water temperature showed merely minor fluctuations in its inexorable drop towards near freezing. The pressure on the tiny submarine's hull would continue to build to a force sufficient to flatten the hulls of lesser vessels just like empty drinks cans.

The cramped and dimly lit interior was filled with instrumentation and controls, condemning the two men inside to limited movement. After a dive of several hours it would be almost unbearably confining.

Peter Wayne Williamson, PhD, geologist, was experiencing the same sensations as during his first dive: his pulse rate had risen, he knew that his blood pressure would have increased, and most markedly, he was aware of a heightened sense of alertness, as if an internal switch had been thrown the moment the water had risen above the portholes and the sky had disappeared.

'Three thousand metres,' Henry, his companion, said. 'Still not much to see yet, but we might as well have some light anyway.' He flipped on the external floodlights to illuminate the monochromatic world beyond the portholes.

They were 4,000 metres down and Pete suddenly saw the escarpment. He watched the dimly defined bulk of the submerged cliff come into view. They were descending into a massive canyon near the nineteenth parallel of the South Pacific, wide and deep enough to contain the Grand Canyon as a minor wrinkle, but still only a tiny part of the largest geological feature on earth – a submerged mountain range and rift system over 50,000 kilometres in length, extending into and through all the oceans of the world.

And of all that, Pete was thinking, people had actually seen only 70 kilometres or so, which was why he and Henry were making this dive, the seventh of the expedition's planned fifteen. It was all part of the continuing effort to unlock the secrets of the earth's origins and to understand the undersea behaviour of the oceans and ocean currents.

Pete stared at the canyon wall and at the same time brought into focus his memory of the way it had looked 19 months ago. There were changes, as he had anticipated. Almost 5,000 metres, and yes, there was the broad ledge Pete remembered, curving off into the murky distance beyond the range of the floodlights. He studied it carefully, searching for more tell-tale changes.

When they reached the bottom of the trench, Pete and Henry would busy themselves with the multitude of tasks assigned to this dive – sampling, measurement, observation, gathering. But Pete's interest right now was on the canyon walls that loomed closer on either side as the minisub descended into the gigantic V-shaped abyss.

Pete was silent, his eyes still fixed upon the canyon walls, measuring the fresh visual data against his memory of the dive 19 months before. He stored it in his mind for later consideration. But already the uneasiness had begun, based at last on more than purely statistical suspicion.

Adapted from the novel *Tsunami* by Richard Martin Stern

Environment: a tricky topic

For seasoned politicians, the topic of environment is a tricky one to pronounce views on. For ruling presidents and prime ministers it frequently proves to be even trickier, as was evident from the speech US President George Bush made at a conference on global warming.

Failing to gauge the depth of feeling of the concerned conference delegates, Bush proclaimed that environmental policies which ignore economic realities are destined to fail.

They may well be, but the experts who gathered in Washington to map out strategies to combat global warming and general pollution were alarmed by the President's lack of commitment.

Such sober reflections as expressed by the President on the need to strike a balance between clean environment and economic prosperity are generally expected from developing countries but not one that is already paying the wages of industrialisation.

Many of those present had also registered their reservations about the way the Americans used up conference time to hammer home their point which is that more research is needed before imposing a blanket ban on a range of gases and chemicals without which our lives would be that much harder to live.

While those monitoring global warming, and those who want to do anything they can to clear up the mess left by industrialisation, are horrified that the gentler and kinder nation is being anything but that on issues most close to their hearts, many Third World governments will be heartened by the President's lack of penchant.

After all, they will say, this is the line of argument they have been following every time an environment group has rounded on them for abandoning industrialisation while struggling to give a better life to their people.

Environment is a noble cause but poverty is a worse enemy to win against. The balance of Bush is what we need.

From *Gulf News*, 19 April, 1990

1 (a) Imagine that you are Pete. Summarise in detail your personal and professional feelings and concerns as the dive gets under way and continues. (10)

(b) You were a conference delegate, representing the country where you live, sitting listening to George Bush speaking. You increasingly found yourself disagreeing with him. Write a letter to him explaining your disagreement. You may justify your disagreement with reference to your own country. (10)

2 You are a member of an organisation which is determined to understand more about the world and to prevent those practices which spoil different aspects of the environment. You have been asked to make a speech about your beliefs. In about 250 words write your speech. (20)

There are points in both passages which you should use and develop, together with ideas of your own.

MEG 1992

TASK

8 Answer questions 1 and 2 as printed.

Debbie Pulls It Off

(1 hour)

Printed below is the article which you have already worked with during your classbook study.

Debbie Pulls It Off

*DEBBIE SIMMONS has seen the future and it is filthy, unless she and her 800 child delegates can get their hands on it. Later this month, they fly in from all over the world to a conference in Eastbourne. She will be chairing it. She is 13 years old. **Jessica Berens** reports.*

On 23 October, 800 children aged between 10 and 12 will travel from more than 50 countries to stay in hotels along the seafront at Eastbourne. They will assemble at the Devonshire Park Centre where why will present projects on the environ-ment and formulate a charter to take back to their respective governments.

Delegates include Dominique Godino from the Philippines who has seen the waterfalls of Hinulugang Taktak ruined by refuse and who is spearheading a campaign to rehabilitate the area; Sulmaan Khan, from Pakistan, illuminating the plight of endangered wildlife, in particular the houbbara bustard, the snow leopard and the Himalayan brown bear; and Ibrahim Alex Bangura, from Sierra Leone, who, through Peace Child International, has planted 10,000 trees in areas eroded by deforestation. Things have come a long way since recycling meant making models of Dougal out of old Fairy Liquid bottles, the days when a 'meeting' was an egg sandwich in a tent in the garden.

The International Children's Conference on the Environment – with its slogan LEAVE IT TO US – is the first of its kind, inspired by children, run for children and with the key decision-making remaining in the hands of children. Workshops, to be held in the afternoons, offer a sophisticated range. Subjects include the Internet ('discover the potential of global communication'), conference radio ('learn how to use the media to communicate your ideas'), and enviroscoping, DNA finger-printing and bio-diversity.

The driving force behind it all is Debbie Simmons, a 13-year-old British girl. Debbie, despite her wide, disarming smile and her dynamic plans for world improvement, is not the sinister dwarf of Hollywood lore. At home, she has a collection of carved owls, and is saving up to buy a flute. She is 'not good at PE'. She used to be quite shy. When she first joined the junior board of Drusillas Park – a private zoo near Eastbourne – at the age of eight, she 'found it difficult to speak out'. Now, as chairperson of the International Children's Conference on the Environment, she has found herself with responsibilities.

Meetings of the junior board are held at Drusillas Park on Saturday afternoons. Once in the boardroom, Debbie becomes a focused individual with a bulging A4 folder and a firm and articulate manner. Pavel, who is from Russia, is 12 and has run straight from school. Rebecca, 12, and Anna, 11, both have bobs and are business-like; Ben, 11, is quiet; Dermot, 12, is absent because he is at a Liverpool match. 'Dermot's favourite word is 'patronising'. Debbie tells me this before the meeting. 'He doesn't like children's presenters because they are patron-ising.'

Michael Ann and his wife, Kitty, both directors of the zoo, have always felt that, since children are their main customers, it is children who are likely to have the most pertinent ideas about the zoo. The junior board, launched in 1989, began by initiating schemes for the zoo – dustbins in the shape of animals, a play area for toddlers – but raised the idea of an international conference on the environment three years ago. A second group of children was then selected to organise the conference after letters were sent to local schools asking teachers to nominate candidates. Debbie, as a long-term member of the original junior board, was co-opted as chair-person. 'The children felt that there was so much more that they could be doing', says Kitty Ann, 'all they needed was a voice and some encouragement.'

The project has involved argument, compromise, patience, endless telephone calls, faxes and letters, long days for the Anns (who organised backing and sponsorship) and stalwart commitment from Debbie and her team who meet twice a month. Finance has been provided by British Airways (who, acting as sponsors, are giving free flights to delegates – 600 of whom are from overseas) as well as organisations such as East Sussex County Council, Eastbourne Borough Council, the English Tourist Board and the United Nations Environment Programme. Delegates will pay a fee of £94 and for their accommodation (at subsidised rates); most have been sponsored by their schools and local environmental organisations. A number of the children will present projects, chosen after hundreds of applications were examined by a conference sub-committee and the junior board, whose brief was to find inter-esting ideas from a wide geographical spread.

Thus the junior board has learned much of the specifics involved in the democratic process (the importance of voting, for instance) and Debbie can claim a working knowledge of how power works. The adults, meanwhile, may be credited with helping to realise what is, in essence, a child's fantasy.

'If you have one person saying "I think you should do this", no one is going to take any notice,' says Debbie. 'But if you have 800 children standing there saying "We think you should do this because you are ruining the world" then governments and the media might listen', She hopes that the event will 'make people aware that children know what is going on'.

Debbie is most reluctant to see herself as a heroine. Does she feel proud? 'Yes,' she says, 'in a way. You come up with a small idea and it grows … but it wasn't actually me, it was the whole board.' She is not precocious or bossy, feeling only 'a bit annoyed' when she sees someone dropping litter in the street. She would not dream of accosting the offender. 'Even if you did', she says, 'it wouldn't make any difference.'

Debbie was born in East-bourne. Her father, Anthony, is a solicitor and her mother, Joanne, an occupational therapist. The family live in a street full of gabled mock-Tudor houses. Debbie remembers a time when their garden stretched into fields in which there were sheep. Now there is a main road. The reduction of space is a tangible experience; a generation has grown up with a deterioration from which it has been impossible to escape. 'The world', she says simply, 'is turning into a tip.'

Debbie's mother had watched *Blue Peter* as a child and had saved milk bottle tops for Guide Dogs for the Blind, a task familiar to anyone who grew up with John Noakes and his nice dog, Shep. 'I don't throw things away' she says. 'I just never have. But it was from the children that we got the recycling. Boxes go to the school; tin cans go to Drusillas for the rainforest.' She had been a Girl Guide and, as a mother, took Debbie and her younger sister, Emma, on the pond-dipping expeditions that she had enjoyed when young. These helped to foster Debbie's love of animals and concern for their welfare, as did the school plays in which Debbie took part. The *Bumble Snouts* featured aliens who appeared on earth and were horrified by what they saw. In *Ocean World*, which addressed the endangerment of whales, she played the part of a coral reef, wearing a white catsuit decorated with fabric paints; and at ten, she appeared in *Save the Human*, in which society was run by animals and the humans faced extinction. These, she says, 'made us more aware'.

Joanne worries sometimes that Debbie will be agitated by the pressures of the limelight but thinks that, in general, she copes very well. 'She knows I am here, but it is her thing and I let her do it.'

The junior board settles down to address its business. An official conference song must be chosen, but songs sent in by hopeful contenders all sound like 'We Are The World'. Things liven up considerably, however, when the subject of lunch is broached. The board is particularly sensitive to the problems that may be encountered by visiting children unfamiliar with the English language and English food. Kitty Ann wonders how 800 people are going to eat at once. The talk is of buffets and roasts and cards you can fill in, like the ones you get in hospitals. Kitty Ann delivers the disheartening news that there will probably only be packed lunch.

'What kind of sandwiches do you have in Russia, Pavel?' she asks. He shrugs. 'Fish.'

'Ugh,' says Rebecca, 'I hate fish.' 'Egg mayonnaise?' suggests Ben, speaking for the first time. 'I like tuna salad sandwiches as long as they don't have mayonnaise,' says Anna. Marmite attracts a unanimous verdict: 'Really gross.' The subject flows swiftly on to crisps and soft drinks before suddenly arriving at Frank Bruno. Some people wish that he could come to the conference. Frank Bruno, you see, is not gross. And he is not patronising.

TASK

9 In one of the classbook tasks you were asked to take on the role of a delegate at the conference.

Take on that role again.

This time it is your job to prepare a presentation. There is a particular scheme for which you want to gain support; it might be the preservation of an area near your home; it might be that you want to oppose plans for a development in your area.

Prepare your presentation.

Science Fiction

(2 hours)

In chapter 2 of this homework book we looked at some science fiction. Now, once again, we turn our attention to this genre.

TASKS

10 Do some personal research and write your own definition of 'science fiction'.

11 Visit the library and investigate science fiction authors and their stories. Bring one science fiction story to class and be prepared to read an extract from it and to explain the story.

Your presentation in class might be assessed for the Speaking and Listening element of your GCSE.

Robot AL-76 Goes Astray

(2 hours)

In this homework you are invited to consider science fiction further. What is printed on the following pages is an extract from a story by Isaac Asimov called *Robot AL-76 Goes Astray*.

Robot AL-76 Goes Astray

Jonathan Quell's eyes crinkled worriedly behind their rimless glasses as he charged through the door labelled 'General Manager'.

He slapped the folded paper in his hands upon the desk and panted, 'Look at that, boss!'

Sam Tobe juggled the cigar in his mouth from one cheek to the other, and looked. His hand went to his unshaven jaw and rasped along it. 'Hell!' he exploded. 'What are they talking about?'

'They say we sent out five AL robots,' Quell explained, quite unnecessarily.

'We sent six,' said Tobe.

'Sure, six! But they only got five at the other end. They sent out the serial numbers and AL-76 is missing.'

Tobe's chair went over backward as he heaved his thick bulk upright and went through the door as if he were on greased wheels. It was five hours after that – with the plant pulled apart from assembly rooms to vacuum chambers; with every one of the plant's 200 employees put through the third-degree mill – that a sweating, dishevelled Tobe sent an emergency message to the central plant at Schenectady.

And at the central plant, a sudden explosion of near panic took place. For the first time in the history of the United States Robot and Mechanical Men Corporation, a robot had escaped to the outer world. It wasn't so much that the law forbade the presence of any robot on Earth outside a licensed factory of the corporation. Laws could always be squared. What was much more to the point was the statement made by one of the research mathematicians.

He said: 'That robot was created to run a Disinto on the moon. Its positronic brain was equipped for a lunar environment, and *only* a lunar environment. On Earth it's going to receive seventy-five umptillion sense impressions for which it was never prepared. There's no telling *what* its reactions will be. No telling!' And he wiped a forehead that had suddenly gone wet, with the back of his hand.

Within the hour a stratoplane had left for the Virginia plant. The instructions were simple.

'Get that robot, and get it fast!'

* * *

AL-76 was confused! In fact, confusion was the only impression his delicate positronic brain retained. It had started when he had found himself in these strange surroundings. How it had come about, he no longer knew. Everything was mixed up.

There was green under foot, and brown shafts rose all about him with more green on top. And the sky was blue where it should have been black. The sun was all right, round and yellow and hot – but where was the powdery pumice rock underfoot; where were the huge clifflike crater rings?

There was only the green below and the blue above. The sounds that surrounded him were all strange. He had passed through running water that had reached his waist. It was blue and cold and wet. And when he passed people, as he did, occasionally, they were without the space suits they should have been wearing. When they saw him, they shouted and ran.

One man had levelled a gun at him and the bullet had whistled past his head – and then that man had run too.

He had no idea of how long he had been wandering before he finally stumbled upon Randolph Payne's shack two miles out in the woods from the town of Hannaford. Randolph Payne himself – a screwdriver in one hand, a pipe in the other, and a battered ruin of a vacuum cleaner between his knees – squatted outside the doorway.

Payne was humming at the time, for he was a naturally happy-go-lucky soul – when at his shack. He had a more respectable dwelling place in Hannaford, but *that* dwelling place was pretty largely occupied by his wife, a fact which he silently but sincerely regretted. Perhaps, then, there was a sense of relief and freedom at such times as he found himself able to retire to his 'special deluxe doghouse' where he could smoke in peace and attend to his hobby of reservicing household appliances.

It wasn't much of a hobby, but sometimes someone would bring out a radio or an alarm clock and the money he would get paid for juggling its insides was the only money he ever got that didn't pass in driblets through his spouse's niggardly hands.

This vacuum cleaner, for instance, would bring in an easy six bits.

At the thought he broke into song, raised his eyes, and broke into a sweat. The song choked off, the eyes popped, and the sweat became more intense. He tried to stand up – as a preliminary to running like hell – but he couldn't get his legs to cooperate.

And then AL-76 had squatted down next to him and said, 'Say, why did all the rest of them run?'

Payne knew quite well why they ran, but the gurgle that issued from his diaphragm didn't show it. He tried to inch away from the robot.

AL-76 continued in an aggrieved tone, 'One of them even took a shot at me. An inch lower and he would have scratched my shoulder plate.'

'M-must have b-been a nut,' stammered Payne.

'That's possible.' The robot's voice grew more confidential. 'Listen, what's wrong with everything?'

Payne looked hurriedly about. It had struck him that the robot spoke in a remarkably mild tone for one so heavily and brutally metallic in appearance. It also struck him that he had heard somewhere that robots were mentally incapable of harming human beings. He relaxed a bit.

'There's nothing wrong with anything.'

'Isn't there?' AL-76 eyed him accusingly. '*You're* all wrong. Where's your space suit?'

'I haven't got any.'

'Then why aren't you dead?'

That stopped Payne, 'Well – I don't know.'

'See!' said the robot triumphantly, 'there's something wrong with everything. Where's Mount Copernicus? Where's Lunar Station 17? And Where's Lunar Station 17? And where's my Disinto? I want to go to work, I do.' He seemed perturbed, and his voice shook as he continued. 'I've been going about for hours trying to get someone to tell me where my Disinto is, but they all run away. By now I'm probably 'way behind schedule and the Sectional Executive will be as sore as blazes. This is a fine situation.'

Slowly Payne unscrambled the stew in which his brain found itself and said, 'Listen, what do they call you?'

'My serial number is AL-76.'

'All right, Al is good enough for me. Now, Al, if you're looking for Lunar Station 17, that's on the moon, yes?'

AL-76 nodded his head ponderously. 'Sure, But I've been looking for it –'

'But it's on the moon. This isn't the moon.'

It was the robot's turn to become confused. He watched Payne for a speculative moment and then said slowly, 'What do you mean this isn't the moon? Of course it's the moon. Because if it isn't the moon, what is it, huh? Answer me that.'

Payne made a funny sound in his throat and breathed hard. He pointed a finger at the robot and shook it. 'Look,' he said – and then the brilliant idea of the century struck him, and he finished with a strangled 'Wow!'

AL-76 eyed him censoriously. 'That isn't an answer. I think I have a right to a civil answer if I ask a civil question.'

Payne wasn't listening. He was still marvelling at himself. Why, it was as plain as day. This robot was one built for the moon that had somehow got loose on Earth. Naturally it would be all mixed up, because its positronic brain had been geared exclusively for a lunar environment, making its earthly surroundings entirely meaningless.

And now if he could only keep the robot here – until he could get in touch with men at the factory in Petersboro. Why, robots were worth money. The cheapest cost $50,000, he had once heard, and some of them ran into millions. Think of the reward!

Man, oh man, *think of the reward*! And every cent for himself. Not as much as a quarter of a snifter of a plugged nickel for Mirandy. Jumpin' tootin' blazes, *no*!

He rose to his feet at last. 'Al,' he said, 'you and I are buddies! Pals! I love you like a brother.' He thrust out a hand. 'Shake!'

The robot swallowed up the offered hand in a metal paw and squeezed it gently. He didn't quite understand. 'Does that mean you'll tell me how to get to Lunar Station 17?'

Payne was a trifle disconcerted. 'N-no, not exactly. As a matter of fact, I like you so much, I want you to stay here with me awhile.'

ISAAC ASIMOV

TASKS

12 Explain the differences between the humans and the robot in this extract. You might argue that the robot is the 'better' character.

13 Continue the story for a few pages. Make sure that you continue in the same style of writing.

Science-Fiction Cradlesong

(1 hour 30 minutes)

People have often believed that something simply cannot happen only to find, that as we progress into the future, suddenly it does.

Printed below is a poem by C S Lewis, *Science-Fiction Cradlesong*.

Science-Fiction Cradlesong

By and by Man will try
To get out into the sky,
Sailing far beyond the air
From Down and Here to Up and There.
Stars and sky, sky and stars
Make us feel the prison bars.

Suppose it done. Now we ride
Closed in steel, up there, outside;
Through our port-holes see the vast
Heaven-scape go rushing past.
Shall we? All that meets the eye
Is sky and stars, stars and sky.

Points of light with black between
Hang like a painted scene
Motionless, no nearer there
Than on Earth, everywhere
Equidistant from our ship.
Heaven has given us the slip.

Hush, be still. Outer space
Is a concept, not a place.
Try no more. Where we are
Never can be sky or star.
From prison, in a prison, we fly;
There's no way into the sky.

C S Lewis

TASK

14 Write your own appreciation of this poem. You should consider:

■ the form of the poem;
■ the content;
■ the vocabulary and language of the poem;
■ your own thoughts and opinions.

GLOSSARY

There are a number of technical terms about language which are helpful in both reading and writing. In responses to reading – comprehensions, appreciations of literature, etc you may need to use some of the terms, and they may also help you with your own writing. This list includes the basic **parts of speech**.

You will also be aware that you are marked in some sections of your exams for **knowledge about language**. This sometimes involves the use of technical terms to identify and describe features of language. The terms are listed alphabetically here:

Accent: regional manner of pronunciation.

Acronym: an abbreviation, often instantly recognisable, usually formed from a combination of the first letters of a group of words. Sometimes acronyms are pronounced by their letters (AA, GCSE, RE, The UN, The USA, etc), sometimes by a word that becomes formed by the first letters of the sequence of words (NATO), and sometimes by a combination of letters (OXFAM).

Adjective: a word used to describe or qualify a noun. Adjectives can express various features, eg quality (*big, small, rough, smooth*), quantity (*many, six*), distinguishing features (a *terraced* house, as opposed to a *detached* house).

Adverb: a word used to describe or qualify a verb. Adverbs often end in the letters *ly*. (He ran *quickly*, she walked *briskly*) – but there are many exceptions (He moved *sideways*, she ran *forward*, they were *often* late). Adverbs also serve the purpose of qualifying adjectives (He was *definitely* late, she was *beautifully* tanned), and other adverbs (She ran *extremely* quickly, he walked *very* slowly).

Alliteration: repetition of consonants, commonly used in poetry, to create an effect associated with meaning (*He spoke; the spirits from the sails descend* – 'The Rape of the Lock', by Alexander Pope, l.137).

Ambiguity: double meanings – often writers deliberately want to suggest or imply more than one meaning in a phrase or word (*see also* irony).

Analogy: a comparison which does not use imagery – writers often describe a situation or event which is comparable to another one, the effect being that we can then understand the second situation more clearly (eg a story about tragic young love might be *analogous* to the story of *Romeo and Juliet*).

Argument essay: writing which presents points of view or opinion, usually backed up by facts and evidence.

Glossary

Assonance: a combination of vowel sounds, commonly used in poetry, in order to add to the meaning (*The morning-dream that hover'd o'er her head* – 'The Rape of the Lock', by Alexander Pope, l. 22).

Attitude: the outlook or point of view held by a writer.

Audience: now a commonly used term to mean reader – writers with a clear sense of audience are able to ask the key questions: who am I writing for and for what purpose? – they will then be able to use the most appropriate style, tone or register. The term is particularly useful if you are writing for a clear group of readers, eg a story for young children, a set of rules for school, a letter to the newspaper to complain about an issue. But it is not always a useful term – sometimes we just write for ourselves, or for a very general purpose, with no particular audience in mind.

B

Ballad: a poem that tells a story. Ballads often rhyme, and are frequently associated with traditional stories, sometimes based on legend, often derived from old folk tales with romantic, supernatural or other atmospheric settings.

Blank verse: unrhymed poetry.

C

Characterisation: how a writer will use language to build up and reveal characters (eg through speech, description of appearance, actions, etc).

Clause: a distinct part of a sentence – as opposed to *phrases*, which are often just a few words. Clauses form units of meaning, like a sentence within a sentence, always with one main verb.

Cliché: a tired, habitually overworked phrase.

Colloquialisms: words or phrases which are informal, familiar, part of everyday speech, rather than appropriate in formal styles of writing – try to avoid colloquialisms in more formal writing, but you can use them to good effect, providing they fit the style, in more imaginative pieces.

Conjunction: a joining or linking word in a sentence (*and, or, but, because, if, though*, etc).

Connotation: a word which carries with it a suggested or implied meaning – names of animals often hold connotations (pig, fish, snake, etc) – that is, the words have come to hold associations for us other than just as animals.

D

Derivation: the origins of words.

Description: language used to create a picture of places, people, objects, moods, etc – some might say that all parts of literature are, by their nature, descriptive, but some passages are brought more vividly to life by a writer's careful use of detail.

Dialect: local variation of standard English.

Dialogue: two or more characters speaking with each other. Such speech is very important in literature to create characters.

Diction: the choice of words to give a particular slant to meanings – consider, for example, the differences suggested by these words: pupil/student; spectator/fan; storm/tempest.

Direct speech: speech reported in writing.

Drafting: the process of writing – early stages, through to refining ideas, then final copy, including proof-reading and editing.

E

Empathy: the ability of a writer to relate to an experience outside their own – to get into somebody else's mind or experiences; this is a skill commonly required in your writing at GCSE – frequently you are asked to take on the role of a particular character.

Evocation (evoke/evocative): the capacity of a writer to bring to life certain memories, feelings, associations – sometimes to call up a certain mood or atmosphere, or a sense of place.

F

Figurative language: non-literal use of language, often in the form of imagery, but sometimes as figures of speech, eg in sayings or proverbs (*a bird in the hand is worth two in the bush … out of the frying pan, into the fire*).

Formal and **informal registers:** a formal register of language will be marked out by complete sentences, precise vocabulary, complex grammar, and an informal register might use colloquialisms, slang, shortened sentences, in writing which will seem more like conversation.

G

Genre: a type or collection of writing, eg romantic, realistic novel, gothic, fable, ballad, satire – the key thing is that to belong to a genre, a work will contain certain distinguishing features marking it out as a particular type of writing.

Grammar: the construction of language.

H

Hero: the principal character in a novel or play; usually to be a hero we expect the main character to be a decent sort of character, one who can be admired or held in high esteem.

Hyperbole: exaggeration – to coin a modern phrase, this is when writers 'go over the top' with their use of language, suggesting that something is the strongest, the best, the greatest, which of course distorts the truth, (Here is another example from 'The Rape of the Lock': *Belinda smiled, and all the world was gay.*).

I

Idiom: a phrase or expression in current use – often like colloquialisms, these will be familiar, or conversational, or even figurative (*Nice weather for the ducks … She gave me a piece of her mind*).

Imagery: a non-literal contrast. There are three common types of images used: (examples are again taken from 'The Rape of the Lock'):

> **Similes:**   *her eyes*
> *like the sun, shine on all alike*

(a simile makes a comparison by stating that one thing is like another).

> **Metaphors:** in another part of the poem, the writer refers to a pair of scissors:
> *The little engine on his fingers ends …*

(a metaphor allows the object simply to become what it is being compared with, so in this case the scissors become the little engine, and there is no need for the writer to state that they are like the engine – in this way a metaphor is a more direct comparison).

> **Personification:** this involves turning an object – either inanimate or from nature, into a human or animal form, with human or animal actions and feelings. Pope is here writing about the River Thames:
> *Thames with pride surveys his rising towers.*

It is essential to understand what is meant by *non-literal* language: eyes cannot literally be the sun; a pair of scissors cannot literally be an engine; a river cannot literally survey towers with pride!

Irony: irony is saying, or writing, one thing, and meaning another; think of it as a form of sarcasm – sometimes people are 'put down', for example we might say 'well done' to somebody who trips over some steps. Irony in literature is much the same, and is quite often intended to make fun of characters, reveal their weaknesses, or to mock them – so to find ironic language, look for hidden or double meanings.

J **Jargon:** a sort of vocabulary. Known mostly to particular groups, eg of workers – 'buzzwords' or an 'in-language', may be used exclusively.

M **Mood:** often used nowadays to mean tone or atmosphere – you may be asked to describe the mood of some writing: is it sad, tragic, positive, optimistic, romantic, or what? Often you can see how mood has been created by analysing the use of adjectives and adverbs.

N **Narrator:** the teller of a story; we often talk of 'the narrator's voice' – who is telling the story?; does the teller of the story play a part in it?; is it written in the **first person**, or the **third person**, by the **omniscient narrator**? All of this makes up **narrative technique** – the ways in which a story is written.

Noun: that part of speech which is object (*knife*), thing (*gas*), place (*city*), abstraction (*happiness*), state (*death*), event (*game*), person (*mother*). **Proper nouns** are names or titles (*The Cup Final, John, London*, etc).

O **Onomatopoeia:** a word used to suggest its meaning by its sound – such as *crash* or *scream*, although clearly, in poetry, the effect will be less obvious, as in this, another example from 'The Rape of the Lock':

> *Now lap-dogs give themselves the rousing shake.* (l.15)

P **Plot:** the plan of events in a story or play – effectively the plot is what happens, as opposed to the subject or themes.

Pronoun: words such as *I, you, he, she, we, they, which, whose* – all words which replace nouns (or more accurately, which replace noun phrases).

Prose: the best way to define prose is to think of it as that writing which is *not* poetry; it is most commonly the writing in stories and novels, and will be characterised by the use of continuous sentences and paragraphs, but it is difficult to give a precise definition.

Pun: a play on words, involving double meanings, sometimes using homophones – words that sound the same, but with different meanings and perhaps different spellings. Shakespeare used a lot of these sorts of puns. *Julius Caesar* begins with a famous one: A citizen of Rome is asked what his job is, and he, a cobbler, jokingly replies that he is a 'mender of bad *soles*' – can you see the pun, or double meaning, suggested by the sound of the word?

A lot of modern newspaper headlines are full of puns, often where there is an association of meanings between words: FAMOUS CRICKETER GIVEN BAIL … POLICEMAN JOINS BEAT GROUP …VICAR IS PREY OF LOCAL THUGS … think of your own!

R

Realism: writing which shows life as it really is – frequently writing which captures a sense of the truth, almost like a photograph or descriptive painting. The effect is often created by mention of down to earth objects, recognisable features, or dialogue which can almost be heard as if spoken aloud.

Register: an increasingly common term, used to mean the type of language being used in any particular situation; perhaps the best way to define register is by the word *variety* – possible different registers are: literary, poetic, formal, informal, lecture, discussion, informative, persuasive … but really the list is endless.

Rhetoric: nowadays we tend to use this term to mean persuasive, frequently elegant language, used in speeches and argument. Sometimes it is used as a way of criticising a speaker by implying that he has used words powerfully and convincingly, but without much substance in the argument. In the past, rhetoric more accurately meant 'the art of speech-making'.

Rhyme: words placed in a relationship in poetry, frequently at the ends of lines, due to their sounding the same, eg

> Behold, four kings in majesty *revered*,
> With hoary whiskers and a forky *beard*. 'The Rape of the Lock', l. 37-8.

Rhythm: the metre, or the beat of lines in poetry.

S

Satire: mockery in literature, intended to poke fun at characters, in order to expose their weaknesses, their foolishness, or their immorality; the best way to think of satire is to think of the popular television programme, *Spitting Image*.

Slang: alternative words used by groups of people, often all from the same area.

Standard English: the form of written and spoken English generally agreed as most appropriate for work, formal communications, business, education, journalism, etc.

Soliloquy: a speech in a play spoken by one character to the audience only – really a character thinking aloud; a technique used a great deal by Shakespeare.

Style: that part of literature which is to do with the expression, as opposed to the content, ideas, themes or subject matter – style is always associated with *how* literature is written rather than *what* it is about.

Symbol: the use of one thing to represent or suggest something else, in literature. We talk about objects or events being symbolic of a mood, feeling or idea, even if, at first glance they do not appear related.

Syntax: the way that sentences are constructed.

T

Themes: connected ideas which arise in literature, often revealed through the actions of more than one character, a number of events, or with features of the language which are expressed more than once – we might discover themes of love, fate, power, despair, innocence, evil, all to be interpreted from different parts of a work of literature. Some of the main themes in Shakespeare's plays would be: 'Romeo and Juliet': *impatience*; 'A Midsummer Night's Dream': *mischief*; 'Julius Caesar': *honour*.

Tone: the overall mood or feeling of writing, for example the tone could be humorous, tragic, persuasive, mocking, serious, etc.

V

Verb: many young children are taught that verbs are doing words, but this definition is now rejected as inadequate; more strictly, a verb is a happening or occurring word – the word(s) needed for something to take place in a sentence. Sentences cannot be formed without verbs, they would end up making no sense, as would be the case in the following example:

> The athlete *won* the race.

> Remove the verb, and see what you are left with:

> The athlete the race.

Vocabulary: the variety and selection of words; it is an important skill to extend your vocabulary, and the best way to do this is by using a thesaurus.

Voice: now a common term used to mean the writer's sense of presence in a piece of writing – you have probably been told by your teachers to put something of yourself into your writing. This is achieved by being interested in what you have to say, so that there is evidence that you as a writer are genuinely expressing yourself.